The Asbury Theological Seminary Series in Christian Revitalization Studies

This volume is published in collaboration with the Center for the Study of World Christian Revitalization Movements, a cooperative initiative of Asbury Theological Seminary faculty. Building on the work of the previous Wesleyan/Holiness Studies Center at the Seminary, the Center provides a focus for research in the Wesleyan Holiness and other related Christian renewal movements, including Pietism and Pentecostal movements, which have had a world impact. The research seeks to develop analytical models of these movements, including their biblical and theological assessment. Using an interdisciplinary approach, the Center bridges relevant discourses in several areas in order to gain insights for effective Christian mission globally. It recognizes the need for conducting research that combines insights from the history of evangelical renewal and revival movements with anthropological and religious studies literature on revitalization movements. It also networks with similar or related research and study centers around the world, in addition to sponsoring its own research projects.

In this study, Johnson demonstrates continuity in the Christologies of Irenaeus, Tertullian, and Origen, with reference to their hermeneutical appropriation of the apostolic Rule of Faith, and in light of the New Testament. He also argues that this continuity suggests that their Christologies are developed from the intention of bringing about revitalization in early Christianity, in the wake of the heretical challenges which their interpretations of Christ address. This reading of their Christologies may also offer insight for contemporary movements of revitalization and church renewal, and for that reason is offered as an appropriate contribution to this Series devoted to research in movements of Christian revitalization.

J. Steven O'Malley
General Editor
The Asbury Theological Seminary Studies in World Christian Revitalization

Meesaeng Lee Choi, Ph.D.
Editor for the Sub-series on Early and Patristic Christian Studies

Jesus Christ and the Rule of Faith

The Confessional Christology of the Early Fathers

David L. Johnson

*The Asbury Theological Seminary Series in
World Christian Revitalization Movements in Early Christianity*

EMETH PRESS
www.emethpress.com

Jesus Christ and the Rule of Faith:
The Confessional Christology of the Early Fathers

Copyright © 2016 David Johnson

Printed in the United States of America on acid-free paper

All rights reserved. No part of this book may be reproduced, or stored in a retrieval system or transmitted in any form or by any means, electronic, mechanical, photocopying, recording, scanning or otherwise, except as permitted by the 1976 United States Copyright Act, or with the prior written permission of Emeth Press. Requests for permission should be addressed to: Emeth Press, P. O. Box 23961, Lexington, KY 40523-3961.

http://www.emethpress.com.

Library of Congress Cataloging-in-Publication Data

Names: Johnson, David, 1971- author.
Title: Jesus Christ and the rule of faith : the confessional Christology of the early fathers / David Johnson.
Description: Lexington, KY : Emeth Press, [2016] | Series: The Asbury theological seminary series in world Christian revitalization movements in early Christianity
Identifiers: LCCN 2016042138 | ISBN 9781609471057 (alk. paper)
Subjects: LCSH: Rule of faith--History of doctrines--Early church, ca. 30-600. | Jesus Christ--History of doctrines--Early church, ca. 30-600. | Bible. New Testament--Theology.
Classification: LCC BT88.5 .J64 2016 | DDC 232.09/015--dc23
LC record available at https://lccn.loc.gov/2016042138

To Perry Johnson

My first and best
instructor in theology

Contents

Abbreviations	ix
Preface	xi

Part One:
The New Testament and the *Regula Fidei*

Chapter 1. New Testament Christology — 3
  The Unique Divine Identity
  Worship Through Jesus
  Worship of Jesus
  Beyond the New Testament

Chapter 2. The *Regula Fidei* — 19
  The New Testament and the *Regula*
  The Christological Core
  The *Regula* as Composition in Performance

Part Two:
Irenaeus' Functional Theology

Chapter 3. A Theology Confined By The *Regula* — 33
  The Christological Core in the *Regula*
  Irenaeus' Variations in the *Regula*
  The *Regula* and Irenaeus' Hermeneutic

Chapter 4. A Functional Theology — 49
  The *Oikonomia*
  The *Logos* and the Son of God
  Creation
  Incarnation and Recapitulation
  The Eschaton
  The *Regula* and Economic Language

Part Three:
Tertullian's Transitional Theology

Chapter 5. Theological Elaboration Upon the *Regula* — 65
  The Christological Core in the *Regula*
  Tertullian's Variations in the *Regula*
  The *Regula* and Tertullian's Hermeneutic

Chapter 6. A Transitional Theology   79
    Logos Endiathetos and *Prophorikos*
    The *Monarchia* and *Personae*
    The Two-Natures Christology
    The *Regula* and the Transition to Ontological Language

Part Four:
Origen's Ontological Theology

Chapter 7. Theological Research Beyond the *Regula*   93
    The Christological Core in the *Regula*
    Origen's Variations in the *Regula*
    The *Regula* and Origen's Hermeneutic

Chapter 8. An Ontological Theology   109
    The Eternal Generation of the *Logos*
    The *Epinoiai*
    Incarnation
    Atonement
    Eschatology
    The *Regula*, Ontological Language, and Speculation

Part Five

Conclusion   127

Appendix: The Texts of the *Regula Fidei*   133
Bibliography   141
Scripture Index   153
Subject Index   155

Abbreviations

ACW	Ancient Christian Writers
Adv. haer.	*Adversus haereses* (*Against Heresies*)
Adv. Herm.	*Adversus Hermogenes* (*Against Hermogenes*)
Adv. Marc.	*Adversus Marcionem* (*Against Marcion*)
Adv. Prax.	*Adversus Praxean* (*Against Praxeas*)
ANF	Ante-Nicene Fathers
Apol.	*Apologeticum* (*Apology*)
CCSL	Corpus Christianorum Series Latina
Com. on John	*Commentary on John*
Com. on Matt.	*Commentary on Matthew*
Com. on Rom.	*Commentary on Romans*
Con. Cels.	*Contra Celsum* (*Against Celsus*)
Dem.	*Demonstration of the Apostolic Preaching*
De praes. haer.	*De praescriptione haereticorum* (*Prescription Against Heretics*)
De princ.	*De principiis* (*On First Principles*)
De virg. vel.	*De virginibus velandis* (*On the Veiling of Virgins*)
FOTC	Fathers of the Church
LCC	Library of Christian Classics
SC	Sources Chrétiennes

Preface

For some time the idea has circulated among some scholars that Jesus considered himself a teacher or prophet and nothing more, and further, that the early church never intended for Jesus to be worshiped as divine. Responsibility for seeing Jesus as divine has instead been attributed to Gentiles who gradually incorporated pagan culture in their practice of Christianity. Eventually the church as a whole embraced this conclusion at the Council of Nicaea in 325 and *made* Jesus divine. This historical interpretation has received growing scrutiny, resulting in a significant body of scholarly work that points instead to an early attribution of deity to Jesus in the New Testament period.

Understandably most of the literature pointing to this early recognition of Jesus as divine focuses on the New Testament and first century Christian belief. Naturally, this early recognition of Jesus' deity has implications for the intervening period leading up to Nicaea. And concomitant with those implications is the fact that a clearer understanding of the developing Christology and hermeneutical practices in the early church broadens the context for identifying the christological continuity between the New Testament and the Council of Chalcedon. Richard Bauckham's *Crucified God*, while addressing the New Testament primarily, provoked such thought for me as a doctoral student. The result was my dissertation on the Christology of the Rule of Faith in the early fathers, in many ways an extrapolation of Bauckham's analysis into the period following the New Testament.

But after graduation, the responsibilities of church ministry, teaching, and family life preempted research begun in graduate studies. Before long the dissertation was relegated to the dustbin of a UMI database somewhere in the distant reaches of the internet. Thus my surprise when Meesaeng Lee Choi, Professor of Church History and Historical Theology at Asbury Theological Seminary, contacted me about the work a decade after its writing.

The general content and conclusions of the initial study remain unchanged, but the related conversation about the New Testament Church's understanding of Jesus has developed considerably. I did not account initially for Larry Hurtado's significant contribution in *Lord Jesus Christ* due to its publication just prior to submitting my dissertation. In addition, Hurtado, Bauckham, and James Dunn have maintained a dialogue in publications and reviews over the past decade that warrants attention. Enough others have also contributed to the conversation that some have described the recognition of an early high Christology, as advocated by Bauckham and Hurtado, as an emerging consensus. This revision of the work, therefore, includes an additional chapter accounting for their discussion with appropriate revisions through the remainder of the work updating references and content.

The first chapter briefly introduces the work of the aforementioned New Testament scholars and assesses the applicability of their work to the present study. Chapter two is an introduction to the substance and perpetuation of the *regula fidei*, the rule of faith. In the subsequent parts the *regulae* and theology of Irenaeus, Tertullian, and Origen are each evaluated in two chapters respectively. The analysis of each father's *regulae* in the first chapter of each part begins with a demonstration of the continuity of the *regula*'s christological core. At the core of each theologian's *regulae* are two essential christological beliefs, that Christ is included in the unique divine identity and that "Christ died for our sins, according to the Scriptures." An evaluation of variations within the *regulae* further develops one's understanding of this continuity and helps identify the theologian's general hermeneutic and particular use of the *regula*. The *regula*'s flexibility in form means that it will pick up characteristics of each father's theology, allowing one to anticipate significant themes from variations in the *regula*. One will also find clues indicating the nature of his hermeneutical application of the *regula* to Scripture.

Once the place of the *regula* in each theologian's work is evaluated, the second chapter of each part provides an overview of each father's theology, explaining his unique contributions and demonstrating the continuity between his overall Christology and the church's. These chapters also explain the consequences of different hermeneutical approaches to foundational theological principles held in common. Each father maintains belief in the same christological core but articulates and expands upon this core using different categories. These different categories, often hinted at in the *regula*, are the basis for the subsections within the three respective chapters. For example, Irenaeus, Tertullian, and Origen all address the *Logos*, but they do so from varying perspectives. The outcome of successively evaluating the *regulae* and theologies presented in the works of Irenaeus, Tertullian, and Origen is a historical perspective affirming the early church's continuity in its beliefs about Jesus Christ.

I would like to thank Dr. Choi, Dr. O'Malley, and others associated with the Center for the Study of World Christian Revitalization Movements for their gracious assessment of a seemingly forgotten work. The work would never have started had it not been for the persistence of Norm Ellyson, my first mentor in ministry. Though now deceased, I can still hear him asking when I would continue my education. The similarly persistent encouragement and generous collegiality of Clint Ashley, former director of the Pacific Northwest Campus of Golden Gate Seminary, and my pastor, Tim Crownover, contributed to the completion of this work. Robert Bernard, associate professor seemingly of all things pre-Reformation at Southwestern Seminary, opened our eyes to the church fathers in a way that suggested personal encounter rather than study. Although we were saddened at his recent passing, Origen and Augustine have likely gained a humble partner in dialogue. And while many poured into me, my advisor David Kirkpatrick coaxed better work from me while teaching patience, persistence, and humility. Their critiques and suggestions have only improved the final product, while any shortcomings remain my own. Lastly, my wife Kristen and daughters Lily and Isabella remind me in subtle ways each day that Jesus is no academic abstraction, but the very source and sustainer of life.

Part One

The New Testament and the *Regula Fidei*

Chapter 1

New Testament Christology

"Who do you say that I am?" People have been answering this question since Jesus first asked it of his disciples two thousand years ago. As many answers as there were in his day—prophet, insurrectionist, Messiah—the answers have continued to multiply, though invariably these answers are only variations on longstanding themes. Those themes were well established within the first century or two after Jesus. Some claiming he was a prophet or rabbi, recognized him as an extraordinary human being, perhaps one specially chosen by God, but human nonetheless. Others considered him so unusual that he could only be explained as the appearance of a heavenly or divine being in the form of a man.

Those closest to him testified to hearing, seeing, and touching him as one would any other human person. But they also spoke of him as one sent by God to do what they believed only God can do, and seeing him alive and well days after a horrific execution they worshiped him. This response to Jesus' question has since persisted continuously in the life and teaching of the church. Attempts to explain the apparent incongruities between the belief in his full humanity and early followers' eagerness to worship him as God resulted in what we know as the orthodoxy defined in the first four ecumenical councils of the church.

The conciliar elaboration upon this answer concerning Jesus' identity became well established and, for all practical purposes, remained the dominant view of Jesus until the period of the Enlightenment. In the midst of the Enlightenment, with post-Kantian epistemologies at work, significant variations on the old themes began to develop. A sharp distinction was made between the historical person in first century Palestine known as Jesus and the ideal person that the church has held up as the image of religious truth. The result has been an increasing tendency in the West to discard the church's teaching for a Jesus who was a prophet, rabbi, or some other exemplary human given to us to emulate. Others have suggested that his historical existence is nearly irrelevant and that the *idea* of Jesus as a divine agent (the New Testament's *kerygma*) is enough for God to communicate his love and redemption to humanity. Even many who adhere to the traditional conciliar teaching about Jesus have entertained these Enlightenment categories and replaced the historic stance of *faith seeking understanding* with a fideist admonition to trust and believe.

These Enlightenment epistemologies have provoked similar assessments of the patristic elaboration upon the early Christians' view of Jesus. The church's teaching about Jesus certainly developed during the first few centuries, but this development can be characterized various ways depending on one's presuppositions. One perspective on this development sees the Trinitarian and christological concepts in the New Testament as primitive in comparison to fourth and fifth century theology. Where the New Testament generally portrays an economic Jesus who *functions as* God for man, the councils describe an ontological Christ who *is* God in nature and essence.

This modern distinction fails to recognize the unity of Christ's person and behavior and disregards essential aspects of the New Testament's testimony. At its worst, christological development becomes an increasing attribution of divinity to the historical Jesus, questioning the New Testament justification for worshiping him. But even at its best, when this theological development entails only the gradual recognition of Jesus Christ's ever present divinity, the interpreter finds it difficult to explain the spectacular rise of the church and the countless believers who gave everything for a man they were only beginning to recognize in some way as divine.

A better view of development within the early church recognizes the continuity of foundational beliefs and teachings within a changing or developing framework. The content of the church's message does not change between the New Testament and the ecumenical councils. What changes is the form in which this abiding message is articulated. The so-called ontological Christology of the fourth and fifth centuries, therefore, rather than being a higher view of Christ, is a New Testament Christology translated into the metaphysical language of the day.

For our present purposes, ontological means those things pertaining to the innate existence of beings, that which cannot be perceived but constitutes the real nature of a thing. Ontological vocabulary stands in contrast to functional or economic vocabulary, which refers to appearances or actions that can be perceived. The conciliar descriptions of Jesus Christ as *homoousios* with the Father and as one person existing in two natures use ontological terms; whereas, Jesus Christ who was born, lived, died, and rose again is described using functional or economic vocabulary. Both descriptions are true, but they see him from different perspectives using different language. In fact, understood rightly this transition in language and vocabulary itself becomes a tool for tracing the continuity of the apostolic message transmitted by the fathers.

Describing Irenaeus' theology as functional and Origen's theology as ontological, then, is a relative comparison of the manner in which they express similar content using different language and categories. Irenaeus would adamantly maintain the ontological deity of Christ, but he finds explication of the Son's nature in ontological or metaphysical terms to be superfluous to the essential gospel. Origen, on the other hand, vigorously defends Christ's functional characteristics and actions as indications of his innate ontological nature. A similar comparison could be made between Origen and the christological councils with the likely conclusion that the councils use even more intentionally metaphysical language than does Origen. In these comparisons, therefore, the differences are in the emphases of language which become increasingly metaphysical as time passes in the early church. The differences are not in christological content, which remains constant throughout early Christianity.

One avenue for demonstrating the continuity of the early church's Christology from the New Testament through key developmental stages in the ante-Nicene period is an examination of the *regula fidei*, the "rule of faith." Irenaeus, Tertullian, and Origen all produce versions of the *regula* with significant commonalities and notable differences. Utilizing a distillation of the New Testament's Christology as a common standard, the christological content of these *regulae* can be evaluated in order to identify what continuity may exist in their beliefs about Jesus. There are countless assessments of the early Christians' view of Jesus, but among those who take the New Testament seriously while accounting for Jesus' first century Jewish context are proposals by Richard Bauckham, James Dunn, and Larry Hurtado.[1]

The Unique Divine Identity

While scholars are once again recognizing that "it can be demonstrated with some ease that [Christianity] stands or falls by historical continuity" with the New Testament, a functional-ontological dichotomy persists in theological circles, especially in reference to Jesus Christ.[2] Christologies are often characterized as functional and dynamic or ontic and ontological. Unfortunately, this practice tends to dissect the individual and contrast what one *is* with what one *does* when personhood requires a unity of existence and action. We know who someone is by what he does, and reciprocally, individuals act on the basis of their nature. Jesus Christ is no different.

The New Testament is the most significant arena for the application of this dichotomy. It is often characterized as Jewish, and therefore "dynamic, dramatic, and functional." In this interpretation "Jesus is thought of much more in terms of what he does than in terms of what he is," and worse, supposedly "little or no attempt is made to relate his being to the being of God." To justify this position, passages like Phil. 2, Col. 1, and Heb. 1 are seen as "comparatively

---

[1] Other assessments of early Christian views of Jesus, especially in light of Jewish monotheism, include William Horbury, *Jewish Messianism and the Cult of Christ* (London: SCM Press, 1998) and James F. McGrath, *The Only True God: Early Christian Monotheism in Its Jewish Context* (Champaign, IL: University of Illinois Press, 2009). In the first of a promised four volumes, Crispin Fletcher-Louis surveys and assesses Bauckham, Dunn, Hurtado, Horbury, and others before offering the beginnings of his own proposal, which he calls "Jesus monotheism." Crispin Fletcher-Louis, *Jesus Monotheism, Vol. 1, Christological Origins: The Emerging Consensus and Beyond* (Eugene, OR: Cascade Books, 2015).

[2] R. P. C. Hanson, *The Continuity of Christian Doctrine* (New York: Seabury Press, 1981), 18.

rare" and their ontological concepts may be dismissed as "only a preliminary to a description of what Christ did."³ Furthermore, the entire book of John is passed off as no more than an "authoritative interpretation of the significance of Jesus," if it is considered at all.⁴

This modern distinction between function and ontology, a distinction completely foreign to first century Judaism and Christianity, has "seriously distorted our understanding of New Testament Christology." Reorienting our thought within a Jewish framework reveals "that the so-called divine functions which Jesus exercises are intrinsic to who God is."⁵ One christological perspective that recognizes this relationship between Jesus' being and his functional activity comes from Richard Bauckham and focuses upon what he calls the "unique divine identity."

Recognition of the "unique divine identity" rests upon the inviolable monotheism of Second Temple Judaism and early Christianity that distinguishes emphatically between God and everything else whether of heavenly or earthly origin. In terms of the former, however exalted a heavenly being may be, he is not enthroned with God, nor does he do what God alone does in creating and ruling over creation. Instead, he stands in service before God and refuses worship appropriate for God alone. Likewise, the idea of an earthly being, an exalted patriarch or prophet, exercising divine prerogatives is even less tolerable in a Jewish monotheistic framework.⁶ Thus, it is in divine activities like creating that we see God uniquely distinguished from all other things; and it is in narrowly defined worship that we see recognition of this distinction.

The personification of divine aspects or attributes, especially God's Word and Wisdom, is in a different class. While these personifications participate in divine activities, they do so not as agents distinguishable from God, but as expressions of the divine will. "They are not created beings, but nor are they semi-divine entities occupying some ambiguous status between the one God and the rest of reality. They belong to the unique divine identity."⁷ Consequently, God's Word and Wisdom neither impinge upon a consistent monotheism, nor do they question the radical distinction between creator and creation.

The New Testament writers maintain the same priorities in their teachings about Jesus Christ. While affirming the absolute distinction between God and his creation, they "develop a kind of christological monotheism which is fully continuous with early Jewish monotheism but distinctive in the way it sees Jesus Christ himself as intrinsic to the identity of the unique God."⁸ In this christological monotheism Jesus Christ is included in the unique divine identity by means of four identifiers. First, Jesus is included in the divine sovereignty over all

---

³ Ibid., 37-39.
⁴ Ibid., 45.
⁵ Richard Bauckham, *God Crucified: Monotheism & Christology in the New Testament* (Grand Rapids, MI: Eerdmans, 1999), viii.
⁶ Ibid., 17-19.
⁷ Ibid., 21.
⁸ Ibid., 26-7.

things, especially in the New Testament use of Ps. 110:1, the Old Testament passage most quoted and alluded to in the New Testament. In as many as twenty-one passages Jesus is exalted to the right hand of God, the place of incomparable sovereignty and authority.[9] While the text in the psalm is open to other interpretations, the New Testament contexts in which it is quoted indicate a unique application in the person of Christ that emphasizes his eschatological divine authority. Furthermore, "nowhere in early Judaism is it [Ps. 110:1] applied to one of the exalted heavenly figures" or to the Messiah "who is only to be a ruler on earth."[10] Essentially, the New Testament claim is unheard of since "He who is at the 'right hand of God' or whom God supports 'at his right hand,' is the one that is elected by God in a unique fashion and who is closely allied with God."[11]

In addition to the use of Ps. 110:1, the New Testament writers consistently refer to Christ's authority over all things. "All things have been committed" by the Father to Jesus (Matt. 11:27; Luke 10:22); the Father "has placed everything in his hands" (John 3:35); "the Father had put all things under his power" (John 13:3); everything but God himself is placed under Christ (1 Cor. 15:27-28); he brings "everything under his control" (Phil. 3:21); and "God left nothing that is not subject to him" (Heb. 2:8).[12] Jesus is also exalted above "all rule and authority" (Eph. 1:21-22) and above all angelic beings (Heb. 1:4-14).

The second means for identifying Christ's inclusion in the unique divine identity is his protological participation in the creation of all things, an activity reserved for God alone. Paul identifies this inclusion in 1 Cor. 8:6 by reworking the *Shema* to incorporate Jesus within the Jewish monotheistic conception of God while delineating his participation in creation.[13] In the first and third phrases, "there is but one God, the Father [*eis theos ho patēr*]" and "there is but one Lord, Jesus Christ [*eis kurios hiēsous christos*]," Paul is reproducing all the words of the *Shema* concerning YHWH and is effectively "redefining monotheism as christological monotheism."[14] The second and fourth phrases, "from [*ex*] whom all things came and for [*eis*] whom we live" and "through [*di*] whom all things came and through [*di*] whom we live," likely quotations of another Jewish formulation, further incorporate Jesus within the divine identity. The only distinction between God the Father and the Lord Jesus Christ in these phrases is

---

[9] Martin Hengel, *Studies in Early Christology* (Edinburgh: T & T Clark, 1995), 133. The passages are Matt. 22:44; 26:64; Mark 12:36; 14:62; 16:19; Luke 20:42-43; 22:69; Acts 2:34-35; Rom. 8:34; 1 Cor. 15:25; Eph. 1:20; Col. 3:1; Heb. 1:3, 13; 8:1; 10:12-14, and possibly Acts 2:33; 5:31; 7:55-56; Heb. 12:2; and 1 Pet. 3:22. Hengel provides an extensive analysis of the subject in the chapter "Sit at My Right Hand!," 119-225.

[10] Bauckham, *God Crucified*, 31.

[11] Hengel, 136.

[12] Bauckham, *God Crucified*, 32. See also John 16:15; Acts 10:36; Eph. 1:10, 22, 23; 4:10; Col. 1:20; and Heb. 1:2.

[13] Bauckham, *God Crucified*, 37-40.

[14] Ibid., 38; Barbara Aland and others, eds. *UBS Greek New Testament*, 4th rev. ed. (Stuttgart, Germany: Biblia-Druck, 1993). All Greek New Testament quotations are taken from the UBS, 4th rev. ed. unless otherwise stated.

the creative role attributed to each. The Father is the efficient and final cause and Christ is the instrumental cause.[15]

Col. 1:15-17 also identifies the Son as the agent of creation and designates him as final cause, an attribution given to God the Father in the 1 Corinthians passage. Heb. 1:2-3 likewise states the Son's role as instrumental cause and develops the statement with the idea that he sustains "all things by his powerful word." Finally, there are the powerful Johannine statements identifying the Word with God and calling Christ "the ruler of God's creation" (John 1:1-5; Rev. 3:14).

The giving of the divine name to Jesus is the third identifier of his inclusion in the unique divine identity. Phil. 2:9, where God "gave him the name that is above every name" at which "every knee should bow," and Heb. 1:4, in which "the name he has inherited is superior" to those of the angels, likely refer to the attribution of the divine name. Furthermore, the Old Testament phrase, "to call on the name of the Lord," meaning the invocation of YHWH, is used in the New Testament to call on "Jesus as the divine Lord who exercises the divine sovereignty and bears the divine name."[16]

The final identifier, the worship of Jesus as God, is present in the New Testament in both contemporaneous and eschatological settings. In Matt. 28:17 and John 20:28 the disciples see Jesus and worship him. The blind man given sight worships Jesus in John 9:38, and Heb. 1:6 commands the angels to worship him. In John 5:21-23 Jesus himself appropriates worship when he asserts the authority given to him by the Father "that all may honor [*pantes timōsi*] the Son just as they honor the Father [*kathōs timōsi ton patera*]." Phil. 2:9-11 and Revelation 5 depict the universal worship due only to the one who exercises absolute sovereignty over creation.[17]

In light of Jesus' unparalleled participation in divine activity and its acknowledgement in identification and worship, Bauckham concludes "that the highest possible Christology, the inclusion of Jesus in the unique divine identity, was central to the faith of the early church even before any of the New Testament writings were written, since it occurs in all of them."[18] Bauckham's proposal has the merits of intentionally incorporating first century Jewish categories for God, and it seems to account for much of the New Testament data. Nevertheless, it has not been without critique. James Dunn identifies some points of concern and suggests instead that the early Christians did not worship Jesus, but rather worshipped God *in* and *through* Jesus.

---

[15] Bauckham, *God Crucified*, 39.
[16] Ibid., 34.
[17] Ibid., 35.
[18] Ibid., 27.

Worship Through Jesus

Since Wilhelm Bousset's articulation of the perspective in *Kyrios Christos* a century ago, a number of scholars have advanced the view that a high Christology developed slowly over the course of the first century or more after Jesus. James Dunn, a scholar engaged in regular dialogue with Bauckham, sees this change taking place within the New Testament itself. According to Dunn, while the beginnings of this christological development can be seen in the Wisdom passages of Paul's letters, "only in the Fourth Gospel can we speak of a doctrine of the incarnation."[19] Essentially the New Testament itself is evidence of a transformation in the way Christians of the late first century viewed Jesus compared with how the earliest followers of Christ understood him.

Dunn addresses the question quite pointedly in *Did the First Christians Worship Jesus?* and concludes that they "did not think of Jesus as to be worshipped in and for himself. He was not to be worshipped as wholly God, or fully identified with God, far less as a god." Instead, any inclusion of Jesus in worship should be "worship offered to God in and through him, worship of Jesus-in-God and God-in-Jesus."[20] He derives this conclusion from an examination of several key factors in the New Testament, including worship language, worship practices, precedents within Second Temple Judaism, and important Scripture passages.

An analysis of New Testament worship language, especially *proskynein*, *latreuein*, and their cognates, seems to complicate the issue rather than answer Dunn's question. The most compelling affirmation of early Christian worship of Jesus in this analysis is that early Christians "call on the name of the Lord" with the understanding that Jesus is Lord. This is clearly an appropriation of the Old Testament practice of calling on God that is applied to praying to Christ. Nevertheless, the overall analysis suggests that early Christians saw Christ "as on both sides of the worship relationship—as in at least some degree the object of worship, but also as the enabler or medium of effective worship."[21]

Consideration of New Testament worship practices points to even more ambiguity for Dunn. While Second Temple Judaism had a well-defined location, time, and method for the appropriate worship of God, these change and become less clearly demarcated for the early Christians. The Temple location, though utilized early on by Christians seemingly as a matter of habit or convenience, is readily exchanged for worship in community and, in a spiritual sense, worship in Christ. The understanding of the body of Christ as the gathered community is central to this component. Similarly, the Sabbath is replaced with Sunday for the time of worship, and the Passover celebration is relinquished for Easter. The

---

[19] James D. G. Dunn, *Christology in the Making*, 2nd ed. (London: SCM Press, 1989), 259.

[20] James D. G. Dunn, *Did the First Christians Worship Jesus? The New Testament Evidence* (Louisville: Westminster John Knox Press, 2010), 146.

[21] Ibid., 28.

idea of Christ's body replacing the Temple as the sacred location and newly established sacred times pointing to Jesus' passion and resurrection can fit the view of Jesus in an instrumental role for the worship of God, but they are not convincing, even for Dunn. The Eucharist seems to affirm the worship of Jesus more directly, but Dunn also points to the preponderance of hymns *to* God and *about* Christ as an indication of Jesus' role as a mediator rather than as an object of worship.

The evaluation of precedents for the worship of a principal agent within Second Temple Judaism is a point of agreement between Bauckham and Dunn. Neither sees any evidence pointing to the worship of a heavenly being or exalted human as a representative of God or as a god himself within Judaism prior to Jesus Christ's appearance. Dunn does qualify this conclusion by suggesting that the gap between God as creator and the creation had diminished. Nevertheless, he notes that nothing prior to Christianity "provides sufficient explanation of the origin of the doctrine of the incarnation, no way of speaking about God, the gods, or intermediary beings which so far as we can tell would have given birth to this doctrine apart from Christianity."[22]

The most significant substantiation for Dunn's proposal comes in his interpretation of some critical New Testament passages. Interpreting Phil. 2:5-11, Dunn notes the highly monotheistic context for the Old Testament allusion in Isaiah 45, emphasizes that the eschatological worship of Jesus is intended for "the glory of the Father," and hesitates to say that Jesus, "God's plenipotentiary, is equally due the worship that should be offered only to God."[23] 1 Cor. 8:6 seems more straightforward in the juxtaposition of prepositions that make "a distinction between origin and agency." Jesus' role as the means or agent for God's self-revelation "is equivalent to the way Wisdom and Word were conceived of as sharing divine identity." The passage, therefore, highlights Jesus as a mediator of worship rather than its proper recipient.[24] Finally, 1 Cor. 15:24-28 stands as a clear statement of Jesus Christ's subordinate relationship with God. As authoritative and final as Jesus' rule is over all of creation, "there is a more ultimate kingship, that of God the Father."[25] Despite the fact that Jesus Christ "embodies the divine agency by which God accomplishes his creative and redemptive purposes," "the worship due to God the 'all in all' should always be beyond the submission and devotion given to the Lord Christ."[26] Consequently, while we should revere Christ, true worship is due God alone, at least according to Dunn's interpretation of these passages.

As thorough and sometimes convincing as Dunn's evaluation of the New Testament data can be, it raises some questions. For example, highlighting the absence of worship directed to Jesus elsewhere in the gospels, he observes that

---

[22] Dunn, *Christology in the Making*, 253. See also Dunn, *Did the First Christians Worship Jesus?*, 89.

[23] Dunn, *Did the First Christians Worship Jesus?*, 107.

[24] Ibid., 110.

[25] Ibid., 111.

[26] Ibid., 112.

the clearest example of worshiping Christ is after the resurrection.[27] Yet one would hardly expect otherwise considering the clear indication in the gospels that the disciples did not understand Jesus' significance until after the resurrection. Similarly, he notes that the *latreuein* word group, best suited for reference to "cultic worship," is never used to refer to Jesus.[28] Then in the following chapter he describes in elaborate detail the significant shifts among Christians away from Temple worship involving priests and sacrifice to a community centered worship in which all are priests and sacrifices are of a spiritual nature. This shift away from cultic worship seems to affirm Hurtado's proposal addressed below rather than dispute it as Dunn implies.

A practical observation about singing and worship might also be made before considering Dunn's exegesis of critical passages. He observes that the New Testament hymns overwhelmingly are *about* Jesus rather than *to* him. Admittedly, praise *for* the exaltation of Jesus Christ "would logically and naturally entail that praise be offered also *to* [him]."[29] So without explicit evidence that praise was offered directly to Jesus in the New Testament, Dunn argues from silence and suggests that this is another indicator of Jesus' place as mediator rather than as an object of worship. Yet it would seem that centuries of song writing that often speaks *about* Jesus and God without raising question of the appropriate object of worship would temper the weight of this conclusion.

The interpretation of Phil. 2:6-11 is another place at which Dunn departs from the norm. He argues that an Adam Christology is the dominant framework for interpreting christological texts at this point in the first century. Consequently, even though there are no explicit connections between Philippians 2 and the presumably prevalent Adam Christology of the period, Dunn sees enough parallels to assume that it is the underlying basis for the passage. This hypothesis leads him to conclude that the hymn neither assumes Christ's preexistence nor exalts him to divine status. Instead, Jesus is the second Adam who is unwilling to grasp for equality with God, lives obediently to the point of dying on the cross, and eventually receives the place God had intended for the original Adam, all to the glory of the Father. Considering the interpretation in individual steps, the rationale is not unreasonable, but it argues from silence, becomes highly improbable as the pieces are assembled, and has been widely criticized.[30] Dunn's more recent study on the worship of Jesus does not directly reference this previous interpretation, but it appears to be assumed.

Dunn's exposition of 1 Cor. 8:6 and 15:24-28 reveals even more of his fundamental differences with Bauckham and Hurtado. In 1 Cor. 8:6 Dunn sees Jesus purely as the agent of God, much like the Word and Wisdom are seen as

---

[27] Ibid., 12.
[28] Ibid., 15.
[29] Ibid., 42.
[30] Dunn, *Christology in the Making*, 114-120. Douglas McCready, *He Came Down from Heaven: The Preexistence of Christ and the Christian Faith* (Downers Grove: InterVarsity Press, 2005), 275-280. McCready reviews several of Dunn's critics, including some who personally deny Christ's preexistence.

extensions of God. He thereby maintains a strict monotheism by subordinating Jesus as a mere agent. Jesus' identification in this passage as the agent presumably would be a means for distinguishing Jesus Christ from the Father, thereby avoiding the modalism that concerns Dunn. In contrast, Bauckham sees this passage identifying Jesus with the Lord and God of the Shema.

The interpretation of 1 Cor. 15:24-28 comes to a similar outcome. An uncompromising subordination of Jesus Christ to the Father is Dunn's solution for maintaining monotheism, which is ironic considering his prior use of the Adam motif in Philippians 2 where it is unwarranted. Here he seems to minimize, if not overlook, Paul's explicit use of the Adam Christology, which would suggest that Christ's subordination to the Father is in his role as the second Adam. The quote from Psalm 8, a psalm establishing humanity's place in the created order, further emphasizes Jesus' solidarity with humanity. Where Adam could not rule over creation on account of his disobedience, Jesus Christ, the second Adam, will restore creation to its intended order and submit it to God at the end of humanity's designated stewardship. Consequently, rather than explaining an ontological reality within the Godhead, the subordination that Paul describes is humanity's rule over creation and subsequent submission to God in the representative man, Jesus Christ.[31]

Dunn's interpretation of these passages hints at his larger concerns, modalism and what he calls "Jesus-olatry." The former concern, modalism, appears both implicitly and explicitly. It appears to be the cause of an underlying uneasiness as when, in addressing John's Logos theology, he reminds us "that John too endeavoured to maintain a balance between the thought of Jesus both *as* God and *as not* God the Father."[32] He also expresses apprehension that Bauckham's use of "identity" could lead to modalism if it is not sufficient for identifying "the diverse roles attributed to Jesus that are distinguished from God's."[33] Dunn's concern is reminiscent of the apprehension expressed by Eusebius of Caesarea and others in the fourth century over the term *homoousios* when they often heard modalism in the expression. While there may be a better term, the concern seems premature within the context of the developing conversation.

The second concern, "Jesus-olatry," is not simply worship of Jesus, but "a worship that falls short of the worship due to the one God and Father of our Lord Jesus Christ."[34] This apprehension seems similarly overstated when Bauckham's intent (and that of others) is clearly not to replace worship of the Father with worship of Jesus. Instead Bauckham works to highlight their intimacy as so impenetrable that it retains Jewish monotheism while maintaining their

---

[31] Frank J. Matera, *New Testament Christology* (Louisville: Westminster John Knox Press, 1999), 98; Cf. Wolfhart Pannenberg, *Jesus, God and Man*, trans. Lewis L. Wilkins and Duane A. Priebe (Philadelphia: The Westminster Press, 1968), 369.

[32] Dunn, *Did the First Christians Worship Jesus?*, 123.

[33] Ibid., 143.

[34] Ibid., 147. Dunn raises a similar concern about a nascent ditheism within John's Gospel in which Jesus is "self-consciously distinct from his Father." Dunn, *Christology in the Making*, 264.

persisting and distinguishing characteristics in contrast to modalism. Overall Dunn appears to prefer a newly stated but essentially preconciliar christological synthesis that radically subordinates Jesus Christ to the Father, raising anew the question of Jesus' ability to reveal God fully and to provide for humanity's redemption.

Worship of Jesus

The most comprehensive attempt at present to ascertain Christians' earliest views of Jesus comes from Larry Hurtado in a number of articles and books, especially his *Lord Jesus Christ: Devotion to Jesus in Earliest Christianity*. Essentially he contends (1) that devotion to Jesus Christ emerged very early, perhaps within the first few years following his crucifixion; (2) that this Christ-devotion occurred with unparalleled intensity and diversity of expression; (3) and that this devotion arose among Jews of the Second Temple period committed to an exclusive monotheism.[35]

Hurtado assesses a great deal of data and engages most of the scholars in the field, but his position can be summarized fairly concisely with an examination of the Apostle Paul. Paul's New Testament writings are the earliest, he has experience with both Jewish and Gentile Christians, and this experience incorporates the conflict over the inclusion of Gentiles within the church. Additionally, Paul himself received "powerful religious experiences that struck the recipients (and other participants in these circles as well) as having revelatory validity and force sufficient to demand such a significant reconfiguring of monotheistic practice."[36] These sorts of religious experiences are integral to Hurtado's understanding of New Testament Christ-devotion.

Paul likely became a follower of Jesus within a few years of Jesus' crucifixion, a period during which he persecuted Christians. Paul does not say explicitly why he persecuted Jesus' followers, but Christian claims of Jesus' exalted status are the most reasonable. Other offshoots of Judaism and their leaders had made claims against the Temple, altered observances, and otherwise questioned the practices of Second Temple Judaism, but the responses of the authorities were relatively muted in comparison to the persecution in which Paul participated. His "zeal," since it was encouraged by the Temple leadership, probably fit within the Phinehas-zeal tradition, which would have justified the stoning of Stephen and other actions against Jewish Christians for offenses like idolatry, perjury, sorcery, and false prophecy.[37] Consequently, Christian practices were already perceived as threats to Judaism's worship of the one God.

Despite the possible perception of Christianity as a threat to monotheism, Paul's experience indicates a monotheistic belief within the early church that is

---

[35] Larry W. Hurtado, *Lord Jesus Christ: Devotion to Jesus in Earliest Christianity* (Grand Rapids, MI: Eerdmans, 2003), 2-3.
[36] Ibid., 65.
[37] Ibid., 94.

derived directly from Judaism. Paul's monotheistic framework also appears to be unaltered in his conversion experience. Furthermore, his desire to follow Jesus comes with a willingness to endure the persecution that he himself previously inflicted upon others. In seemingly no time Paul went from persecuting to being persecuted, and the best explanation for this transformation is his deeply religious experience with the risen Christ. Between an encounter with Jesus that arouses immediate devotion and an encounter that instigates a reassessment of his theological presuppositions and worldview, the latter is insufficient to explain his rapid reversal from persecutor to persecuted.[38] And while the other early Christians were not engaged in persecuting others prior to their experiences of the risen Christ, their willingness to endure such persecution is no less apparent and appears to have been acquired suddenly. Paul's conversion is strong evidence for an early Christ-devotion that assumes a monotheistic foundation. It also clearly speaks to an unparalleled intensity of devotion.

We see similar evidence within Paul's early writings, especially those passages discussed above. Phil. 2:6-11 is not only in one of Paul's earliest letters, but it is widely recognized as a hymn that Paul incorporates from elsewhere. In fact, the way that he uses it suggests that "Paul expected his readers to recognize and affirm either the passage or at least what the passage expresses *as reflective of what they already knew and affirmed about Jesus* [italics Hurtado's]."[39] So this passage is evidence that the early church already held a high view of Jesus in the brief time between Jesus' death and some time prior to this early letter.

The passage clearly has two sections. In the first verses Christ humbles himself and is the acting subject. In verses 9-11 God is the acting subject and Jesus Christ is the object. Discussion usually focuses on the beginning of the hymn where there is debate over the meaning of "form of God," *kenosis*, and related factors. Since clear passages should elucidate less clear passages, and since God is the main player from whom all others in the context derive their meaning, Hurtado begins with verses 9-11 where the hymn unmistakably incorporates Isaiah 45:23.

Isaiah 45 is one of the most explicitly monotheistic passages in the Old Testament. Its use in the Philippians hymn certainly alludes to this context, but its inclusion may be even more intentional and pointed. Hurtado agrees with Takeshi Nagata's analysis of its use in Phil. 2:10 as a creative interpretation drawn from the Septuagint. The ancient Greek translator of Isaiah 45:23, intentionally or not, effectively distinguishes between two objects, one in the first person and the other in the third person, that refer solely to God in the Hebrew. The early hymnist quoted by Paul may be taking the phrase "To me [*emoi*] every knee will bow and every tongue shall confess to God [*tōi theōi*]" to indicate two

---

[38] Larry W. Hurtado, *How on Earth Did Jesus Become a God? Historical Questions about Earliest Devotion to Jesus* (Grand Rapids, MI: Eerdmans, 2005), 34-35. Hurtado also points to a growing body of research that supports the view "that revelatory religious experiences can directly contribute to religious innovations." Hurtado, *Lord Jesus Christ*, 64-70.

[39] Hurtado, *How on Earth Did Jesus Become a God?* 87.

objects of monotheistic worship. The theory is that "the curious variation between the first-person pronoun ('to me') and the noun 'God' (i.e., a third-person referent) may have provided a textual opening for some early Christian to discover in the passage two figures who are to be given reverence: Jesus, the 'Lord' who speaks in first-person mode, and God."[40] This grammatical variation may have provided early Christians with an interpretive foothold for reading the Isaiah passage from a primitive "binitarian" perspective. Whether or not this accurately explains the genesis of the appropriation from Isaiah, the second half of the hymn explicitly connects an unequivocally monotheistic Old Testament passage with the worship of Christ Jesus by all of creation while still distinguishing between God the Father and Jesus Christ. In addition, the giving of "the name above every name" to Jesus and his identification as "Lord" are both likely references to the divine name, further substantiating a high view of Jesus in the clearer half of the hymn.

Returning to verses 6-8, the interpretation of "in the form of God [*en morphē theou*]," a highly disputed matter, raises among other things the issue of Christ's preexistence. Some argue that "form" and "image [*eikōn*]" are synonymous, and therefore "form of God" is equivalent to "image of God," making Jesus' initial position in verse 6 equivalent to Adam's state at creation. Connecting Philippians 2 with the creation account in this way results in a Jesus who is merely a human being willing to submit himself in obedience to God. The problem is that this stylistic link to Adam "would be a singular case without any analogy or precedent." Furthermore, such an allusion would be particularly inept since "one must use or adapt something from what one is alluding to that is sufficiently identifiable that the allusion can be noticed," and in this case there are no such connections between Philippians 2 and the beginning of Genesis.[41] If this criticism is accurate and "form of God" is not a reference to the "image of God" in humanity, the alternative is Christ's preexistence in some exalted position. Hurtado's analysis leads him to conclude that Paul's quotation of this hymn "may preserve for us one remarkable instance of earliest Christians discovering Jesus in the sacred scriptures of Second Temple Judaism under the impact of powerful religious experiences of revelation and inspiration."[42]

Additional Scripture passages and factors in the early church contribute to Hurtado's extensively developed proposal of an early and high Christology corresponding closely with Bauckham's proposal. Where he differs from Bauckham is in the impetus for such a novel and unprecedented development within Judaism. Bauckham's primary intent has been to identify the means by which early Christians were able to conceive of Jesus as included in the divine identity

---

[40] Ibid., 92; Takeshi Nagata, "Philippians 2:5-11: A Case Study in the Shaping of Early Christology," Ph.D. thesis, Princeton Theological Seminary, 1981, UMI Dissertation Services, 279-293.

[41] Hurtado, *How on Earth Did Jesus Become a God?* 99.

[42] Ibid., 107.

with early devotional expressions and practices as a secondary concern.[43] In contrast, Hurtado sees theological reflection, insight, and belief arising out of the desire to explain and vindicate the devotion and worship incited by early Christians' experiences of the risen Christ.[44] Jesus' followers were singing and praying to him, and baptizing, exorcising, prophesying, and celebrating the Lord's Supper in his name even as they tried to understand the meaning of their worship of him within an exclusive monotheism.

Beyond the New Testament

However complementary Bauckham and Hurtado's proposals are, Hurtado's emphasis upon experience as the stimulus for theological contemplation provides a broader explanation of early Christian beliefs and practices, especially considering the context of Second Temple Judaism and what we know of the apostles' experiences. Hurtado also better accounts for the sudden transformation in the earliest believers. Hurtado and Bauckham agree that early Christians were worshiping Jesus within a very short time while still considering themselves faithful Jews. Considering the time necessary for serious theological reflection, especially within a corporate faith environment, it is hard to imagine an early community of believers coming to theological conclusions that direct worship to Jesus so quickly. Recognizing the worship of Jesus as merited while reconciling that worship with his genuine humanity and a monotheism derived from Judaism was the most difficult of the early church's potential responses to Jesus. Adoptionism, docetism, and other answers that minimize or eliminate one or more of these factors were all relatively facile responses to the dilemma, and yet their adherents appear to take even longer to coalesce into recognizable communities.[45] Theological justification for the worship of Jesus that takes into account these theological tensions and then incites such worship, therefore, seems unlikely within the short timeframe posed by both Bauckham and Hurtado. Consequently, early Christian experiences of the risen Jesus that motivated devotion and worship, and which subsequently led to theological reflection seems most plausible for explaining early Christian beliefs and practices.

Despite the advantages of Hurtado's proposal for explaining New Testament Christians' devotion to Jesus, Bauckham's concept of the unique divine identity

---

[43] Ibid., 23; "While Hurtado has pursued this latter emphasis [Christ-devotion], my own continuing contributions to understanding early Christology have focused more on the way early Christians were able conceptually to include Jesus in the Jewish understanding of the identity of the one God, but I would certainly not wish to distance this from devotional practice." Richard Bauckham, "Devotion to Jesus Christ in Earliest Christianity: An Appraisal and Discussion of the Work of Larry Hurtado," in *Mark, Manuscripts, and Monotheism: Essays in Honor of Larry W. Hurtado*, ed. Chris Keith and Dieter T. Roth (London: Bloomsbury, 2014), 177.

[44] Hurtado, *Lord Jesus Christ*, 3-4.

[45] Hurtado, *How on Earth Did Jesus Become a God?* 54.

remains critical for assessing the early Christian understanding of Jesus. Furthermore, it is invaluable for correlating key christological ideas within the New Testament with the theological reflection of the second and third century church fathers. The early church fathers were handed the difficulty of explaining Jesus' inimitable and enduring significance in light of the early Christians' experience of him. "The doctrinal problem they worked on was not of their making. It was forced upon them by the earnest convictions and devotional practice of believers from the earliest observable years of the Christian movement."[46] What had begun in encounters with the risen Jesus now required explanation. Yet even as they passed their doctrinal dilemma to the church fathers, the New Testament Christians also provided initial answers to the dilemma in their experience of Jesus as creator, sovereign ruler, and Lord. Bauckham's concept of the unique divine identity distills these convictions into a cogent whole that can be traced through the New Testament and correlated with the christological teachings of the early church fathers.

In addition, Bauckham's assessment of the New Testament readily engages the contexts and methods of the second and third century fathers. Their own faith experiences, seldom described in detail, are not the dramatic encounters of the risen Christ experienced by the apostles. Instead, they come to the worship of Christ and the adoption of faith largely through instruction and theological reflection. Their different ministry contexts also demand catechetical, polemical, and apologetic writing rather than the evangelistic, epistolary, and pastoral works of the New Testament. Works like *Against Heresies*, *Against Praxeas*, and *On First Principles* demonstrate serious theological deliberation rather than the sudden transformation of religious experience.

So while the earliest Christians in the New Testament demonstrate a high Christology through their Christ-devotion, the early fathers articulate a correlative Christology in their doctrinal statements and writings. This experiential shift is relatively sudden compared to the gradual changes in language that develop over the first centuries of the church's christological ruminations and debates. Where the conciliar debates of the fourth and fifth centuries use predominantly ontological language to describe Jesus Christ, the initial theological reflection of the New Testament attributes to Jesus functions and accolades indicating his inclusion in the unique divine identity. Already in the New Testament his status as the uniquely divine Son of God is present in his divine sovereignty, his participation in creation, and the divine name and worship given to him.

Jesus Christ's participation in the unique divine identity qualifies him to be the sole arbiter of humanity's salvation, a role encapsulated in Paul's assertion "that Christ died for our sins according to the Scriptures" (1 Cor. 15:3). First, this statement embodies the continuity of God's message in the Old Testament with the message of the new covenant in Jesus Christ. An especially important point later in the church's battle with Marcion and the Gnostics, God's salvation plan is consistent throughout history from the beginning in the Pentateuch through the eschaton in Revelation. The same God lays out the plan of salvation

---

[46] Hurtado, *Lord Jesus Christ*, 651.

in the Old Testament and sends Jesus Christ to fulfill it. The old and new covenants form a unified whole rather than diametrically opposed positions as many heretics would later assert.

Second, "that Christ died for our sins according to the Scriptures" reaffirms the "correspondence of the Law and the Prophets (especially *Isaiah*) with that part of the 'covenant' made effective in the death of Christ."[47] This correspondence ties together the promises of salvation for all nations and peoples found in the Old Testament with the efficacious work of Christ and its preaching in the New Testament Church.[48] The conclusions of the Jerusalem Council and the fact that Paul was simply passing on what he had received from others confirm this as an agreed upon tenet within the early church. Christ died for all; the "our" in 1 Cor. 15:3 includes Jews and Gentiles, all who are willing to receive it.

Finally, 1 Cor. 15:3 contains the means for salvation, "that Christ died for our sins." Christ's atoning death on the cross is the center and focus of God's plan of salvation. The Scriptures portend his death, and in the significance of the cross is implied the resurrection that followed. Throughout the New Testament and the works of the early church fathers Christ's physical death, burial, and resurrection are stated explicitly. Faith in Jesus Christ, unlike any other system of belief, rises and falls on the historical continuity of the church and the believer with the atoning death and resurrection of Jesus Christ himself. If Christ has not died and "has not been raised, our preaching is useless and so is your faith" (1 Cor. 15:14).

These two issues, Jesus Christ's inclusion in the unique divine identity and his atoning death according to the Scriptures, are the essentials of a New Testament Christology. His claim to divine sovereignty, especially eschatologically, his participation in creation, the christological attribution of the divine name, and the worship of Christ all figure into the *regula*. This christological monotheism and the soteriological statement of 1 Cor. 15:3 constitute the basic New Testament concepts that form the christological core in the *regula*.

---

[47] William R. Farmer, "Galatians and the Second Century Development of the Regula Fidei," *The Second Century* 4 (1984): 167.

[48] See especially Isa. 11:10-12; 45:20-23; 49:6; 51:4-5; 52:10; 55:4-5; 56:3-8; 66:18-21.

Chapter 2

The *Regula Fidei*

The *regula fidei*, the rule of faith, provides an effective indicator for demonstrating the continuity of the early fathers' theological formulations with the New Testament's christological content.[1] The *regula fidei* was an essential tool for the survival and promulgation of correct doctrine in the church's battles with heresy during the first three centuries of its existence. It concisely and consistently presents the essential content of the gospel on an explicitly monotheistic foundation while remaining flexible enough to address the theological environment of the day. The *regula* uniformly states Jesus Christ's involvement in creation, his incarnation, his birth of a virgin, his passion, and his resurrection from the dead. Furthermore, this early statement of belief asserts the unity of the Old and New Testaments and the singular identity of the Creator God and the Father of Jesus Christ.

Irenaeus, Tertullian, and Origen, three of the most prominent church fathers of the period, place the *regula* prominently in their works as a control on their own theologies and to combat heretical interpretations of Scripture.[2] These three

---

[1] Comparisons of *regulae* have identified changes in its form with no "notable difference" in the content of the *regula* between 1 Clement and Origen. Farmer, 15. Cf. Prosper S. Grech, "The Regula Fidei as a Hermeneutical Principle in Patristic Exegesis," in *The Interpretation of the Bible*, ed. Joze Krasovec (Sheffield: Sheffield Academic Press, 1998), 593; R. P. C. Hanson, "The Church and Tradition in the Pre-Nicene Fathers," *Scottish Journal of Theology* 12 (March 1959): 27; Joseph F. Mitros, "The Norm of Faith in the Patristic Age," *Theological Studies* 29 (September 1968): 453.

[2] The *regula* bears authority as the rule "received from the apostles and their disciples" and protects true believers from those who "by their pernicious doctrines ... change [this truth into error]." Irenaeus, *Against Heresies* in *The Ante-Nicene Fathers*, vol. 1, *The Apostolic Fathers, Justin Martyr, Irenaeus*, ed. James Donaldson and Alexander Roberts (United States: Christian Literature Pub. Co., 1897; reprint, Peabody, MA: Hendrickson, 1994), 1.10.1, 1.22.1. Irenaeus, *Against the Heresies, Book I*, trans. Dominic J. Unger, Ancient Christian Writers, no. 55 (New York: Paulist Press, 1992). Irenaeus, *Contre les hérésies, Livre 1*, ed. and trans. Adelin Rousseau and Lewis Doutreleau, 2 vols., Sources chrétiennes, nos. 263, 264 (Paris: Éditions du Cerf, 1979). All quotations from the Latin version or Greek fragments, when available, are taken from SC and all English quotations are taken from ANF unless otherwise noted.

fathers delineate the *regula* more distinctly than others in the ante-Nicene period. In addition, their extant works are the most extensive and theologically significant for the period, providing a clear and reliable portrait of the early church's theology and the *regula*'s place in that theology. Their chronology also offers a running exposition of terminological development within early Christian theology.

Irenaeus, Tertullian, and Origen all defend a high view of Jesus Christ, using both Scripture and the *regula fidei* as the authorities for the same foundational christological assertions. They begin with monotheism as the basic theological principle and, following the New Testament, incorporate Christ in what has been called the unique divine identity. On account of their common belief in the historical events recounted in the New Testament and the *regula*, Christ's virginal conception, death, resurrection, and ascension, they articulate a christological monotheism proclaiming the deity of Jesus Christ. This foundation for their theologies remains unchanged, but each father's theology varies depending on his hermeneutic and the role of the *regula* in that hermeneutic. Therefore, despite differences in their theologies often attributable to linguistic and hermeneutical issues, Irenaeus, Tertullian, and Origen maintain the New Testament's inclusion of Jesus in the unique divine identity and preserve the core christological theme of the regula, that "Christ died for our sins, according to the Scriptures."[3]

Historical development in theological vocabulary and different hermeneutical uses of the *regula* help to explain differences in the three fathers' theologies. Irenaeus, Tertullian, and Origen all follow the *regula* as an authoritative guide to Scripture and theology, but the manner in which it restricts, guides, or expands theological inquiry differs with each theologian. Irenaeus stays very close to the biblical text, restricts theological language to that used in Scripture, and uses the *regula* to limit inquiry to those issues specifically addressed in Scripture and the tradition. Tertullian follows the same pattern but broadens the path to include those things which complement Scripture and the *regula* or at least are compatible with these authorities. Origen, on the other hand, views the *regula* as a starting point, a foundation which cannot be undermined by subsequent theological inquiry. The three fathers, therefore, all agree on substantially the same *regula* but apply it differently, which results in sometimes divergent theological conclusions.

These theological conclusions are generally characterized by functional or economic language when the *regula* is applied more strictly. As the *regula* is applied to interpretation less stringently the conclusions are delineated using more metaphysical language. The increasing availability of theological language and vocabulary in the early church also contributes to this trend. So while the hermeneutical application of the *regula* may not directly affect every theological construction, the use of the *regula* is indicative of the theologians' general theological methods. How each father uses the *regula* is at least a clue, if not a detailed description, of how he approaches theological interpretation as a whole.

---

[3] 1 Cor. 15:3 NIV. Unless otherwise noted, all Scripture references are from the *New International Version*.

Furthermore, different applications of the *regula* to changing contexts explains apparent variations in the fathers' theologies even while the christological core remains unchanged, demonstrating the consistency with which the early church maintained the faith given once and for all by Jesus Christ through his apostles.

The New Testament and the *Regula*

The concepts and ideas related to Jesus' inclusion in the unique divine identity are perpetuated in the *regula* with language that varies from author to author. All of the *regulae* incorporate basic functional statements identifying the essential aspects of Jesus' life, death, and resurrection. But the language expanding upon these foundational assertions can at times be more functional, delineating Jesus Christ's activity, or predominantly ontological, addressing his nature and being.

Thus, when Irenaeus' theology is described as functional, it refers to the predominantly biblical language that Irenaeus uses in developing such major themes as the *oikonomia* and recapitulation. These themes display the work of Christ prominently, but in doing so they provide a christological ontology through the concept of the unique divine identity much like what is seen in the New Testament. Jesus' actions may constitute the majority of the christological material, but the ontological concepts remain latent in his exercise of sovereignty, his participation in creation, and so forth.

Tertullian's use of metaphysical language begins to change the dynamic of functional and ontological language. In some of his writings he attempts, at least in part, to translate the christological ontology of the New Testament concept of the unique divine identity into the theological categories of the second and third centuries. The understanding of Jesus Christ's deity and its associated ideas are not changed, but the language used has to change to communicate to a changing church and world. New heretical challenges especially demand this conceptual translation. While Tertullian does this in part, Origen is more intentional and comprehensive in his use of developing categories and vocabulary, though even Origen is surpassed in the conciliar debates to follow.

Where Irenaeus generally utilizes functional terminology to communicate a conceptual ontology, Origen incorporates more ontological language, though this is not always the case. For example, Origen's understanding of the Son's eternal generation is framed largely in metaphysical or ontological language, but the Son's nature manifests itself most in his *epinoiai*, titles for Jesus Christ that are predominantly functional and dynamic. Irenaeus, in comparison, articulates some of the foundational principles behind the eternal generation of the Son such as his eternal existence with the Father, but he refuses to explain this existence, especially when it might require vocabulary foreign to Scripture.

Beyond the differences in functional and ontological emphases in vocabulary between the various authors of the *regulae*, the omission and addition of specific terms, phrases, and concepts even within the same author's *regulae* complicate the scene. It is widely acknowledged and easily seen that the text of the *regula* is not fixed. Tertullian, for example, gives us three versions of the *regula* of very different lengths and with important changes in emphasis. These variations pose some difficulties concerning the source or sources and the reliability of the *regula*, especially in light of numerous assertions of its significant authority in the early church. The first of these difficulties concerns the textual relationship between the *regula* and the New Testament and whether the latter is the source of the former.

It has been suggested that the *regula* is a summary or digest of Scripture. The most significant proposal defending this position rests on Roman law in which "a *regula* was a short summary of the contents of a statute" possessing the same authority as the statute itself.[4] The strength of this correlation rests in the fact that the summary's authority has its basis in the full text of the statute just as the *regula*'s authority depends on Scripture. Nevertheless, there is little evidence to support the theory historically or textually. The *regula* was already being cited as the canon of the New Testament was narrowing, and the early fathers themselves place the *regula* in the authoritative tradition coming directly from the apostles alongside of Scripture.[5]

That the formulation of the *regula* was independent of fixed textual sources is widely acknowledged, especially in light of the difficulties in tying it to declaratory creeds and the baptismal liturgy.[6] The *regula* simply does not match the creeds closely enough. Consequently, no other text besides Scripture remains as a potential source. Irenaeus' and Tertullian's account of the *regula* as an independent tradition parallel to Scripture, therefore, is generally accepted. In this understanding, the *regula* is "the summary of Christian doctrines and beliefs," or "what the Church has been preaching in uninterrupted continuity from the beginning."[7] In this view the tendency is to tie the *regula* loosely to the *kerygma* of the New Testament.[8] While there are difficulties with this view that will be ad-

---

[4] Gerald Bray, "Authority in the Early Church," *Churchman* 95 (1981): 50.

[5] Irenaeus *Adv. haer.* 1.10.2; Tertullian, *De praescriptione haereticorum*, in *The Ante-Nicene Fathers*, vol. 3, *Latin Christianity: Its Founder, Tertullian*, ed. James Donaldson and Alexander Roberts (United States: Christian Literature Pub. Co., 1897; reprint, Peabody, MA: Hendrickson, 1994), 19-21; Tertullian, "Prescription Against Heretics," in *The Library of Christian Classics*, vol. 5, *Early Latin Theology: Selections from Tertullian, Cyprian, Ambrose, and Jerome*, ed. and trans. S. L. Greenslade (Philadelphia: The Westminster Press, 1956); Tertullian, *Tertulliani Opera*, Corpus Christianorum: Series Latina (Turnhout: Brepols, 1954). All Latin quotations from Tertullian's works are taken from CCSL and all English quotations are taken from ANF unless otherwise noted.

[6] Cf. J. N. D. Kelly, *Early Christian Creeds*, 3d ed. (Singapore: Longman, 1981), 63; Eric F. Osborn, "Reason and the Rule of Faith in the Second Century AD," in *The Making of Orthodoxy* (Cambridge: Cambridge University Press, 1989), 43; Mitros, 452-3; Hanson, "The Church and Tradition," 27; Paul M. Blowers, "The *Regula Fidei* and the Narrative Character of Early Christian Faith," *Pro Ecclesia* 6 (spring 1997): 199-200; Paul M. Blowers, *Drama of the Divine Economy: Creator and Creation in Early Christian Theology and Piety* (New York: Oxford University Press, 2012), 76, 98.

[7] Mitros, 453; Hanson, "The Church and Tradition," 27-8; Blowers defines the *regula* as "a world-encompassing story or metanarrative of creation, incarnation, redemption, and consummation." Blowers, "The *Regula Fidei*," 202.

[8] Tertullian *Adv. Marc.* 4.2.1-2; 4.5.1.

dressed below, at a basic level the *regula* does function as a summary. It probably does not serve *primarily* as a summary and its intended purpose is likely more specific, but one of its effects is to mirror the essential content of the New Testament as a summary.

With this close relation in substance between the *regula* and the New Testament, the two operate in a unique hermeneutical relationship. Although Irenaeus and Tertullian will argue that the *regula* may be substituted for Scripture on occasion because of its essential content, the church fathers, including Irenaeus and Tertullian, rely upon Scripture to substantiate the authority of the *regula*.[9] In fact, "all of these fathers are anxious to prove the rule of faith from Scripture," especially as the chronological distance between the apostles and the church grows.[10] Although their genealogies differ, the basic substance of the *regula* and Scripture is the same, and verification of this fact substantiates the theologians' position, especially against the heretics.

The more significant relationship between the New Testament and the *regula* is seen in the use of the *regula* as a hermeneutical control on the interpretation of Scripture. The *regula*, with its brevity and pointedness, is more difficult to misinterpret and protects against the unintentional misreading of Scripture by neophyte believers and intentional manipulation by heretics. On account of these dangers, the proper interpretation of Scripture is restricted to "the Church, which has the key to its exegesis in the form of the original apostolic testimony, i.e., the rule of faith."[11] For Irenaeus, the church is the only qualified interpreter of Scripture because it is the sole possessor of the apostolic tradition.[12] Tertullian is even more adamant about the church's interpretive role. Those outside the church not only cannot interpret Scripture with authority, but they also cannot appeal to Scripture for any reason. The church alone has possession of Scripture.[13] The *regula*, therefore, is occasionally described as an adequate compendium of the faith suitable as a substitute for Scripture, but it is far more often used as a hermeneutical control on the proper interpretation of Scripture.

It should be noted that the question of priority between the *regula* and the New Testament is never an issue for the early fathers. They never ask which of the two, Scripture or tradition (in our case the *regula*), is superior or more authoritative.[14] The only hint of an answer rests in Origen's encouragement to look past the generally accepted opinions of the masses which are held as tradition in

---

[9] Irenaeus *Adv. haer.* 1.1.15; 1.1.20; 3.4; Tertullian *De praes. haer.* 19-21; Hanson, "The Church and Tradition," 26.

[10] R. P. C. Hanson, *Tradition in the Early Church* (Philadelphia: Westminster Press, 1962), 108.

[11] Mitros, 456.

[12] Irenaeus *Adv. haer.* 1.8.1; 4.26.5; 5.20.2.

[13] Tertullian *De praes. haer.* 19, 20, 31.

[14] Mitros, 455, 458.

order to examine the heart of the matter.[15] But even in this exhortation the intent is to measure what the majority call tradition against the true standard of the Scriptures and the original apostolic tradition. The intent is not to set the deliberated tradition of the fathers against the Scriptures.

The Christological Core

While the question of priority is a secondary query, what remains essential is the perpetuation of the basic christological assertions of the New Testament in the *regula fidei*, especially as these assertions include Jesus Christ in the unique divine identity. First, the fathers restate Christ's sovereignty over all that exists, usually in an eschatological context. Irenaeus speaks of Jesus' "coming from heaven in the glory of the Father [*en tē doxē tou Patros*] 'to gather all things in one.'" He will "raise up anew all flesh of the whole human race" and exercise "just judgment towards all" at the end of time.[16] Although he condescended in the incarnation, Jesus shall again "come in glory [*erchomenon en doxē*], the Savior of those who are saved, and the Judge of those who are judged."[17] In the present, God "by His Word and Spirit, makes [*faciens*], and disposes [*disponens*], and governs [*gubernans*] all things" in his work of providence.[18] Christ's exercise of authority over creation is most noticeable in the judgment, but his part in its providential care is no less significant.

Interestingly, while Irenaeus only describes Christ's sovereignty in the judgment, Tertullian not only considers his eschatological role in the judgment but also develops his sovereignty using Ps. 110:1. Long before Jesus comes "with glory to take the saints to the enjoyment of everlasting life and of the heavenly promises, and to condemn the wicked to everlasting fire" he "sat at the right hand of the Father" as the sovereign ruler of all.[19] Tertullian repeats the phrase "at the right hand of the Father [*ad dexteram patris*]" in all three of his *regulae*.[20] Of the three fathers, only Origen fails to make Christ's eschatological sovereignty explicit, largely because of other considerations bearing on his eschatology that will be addressed below. Origen simply hints at Jesus Christ's authority by means of several themes including creation and the incarnation, in which "divesting Himself (of His glory)" he "became a man" and "remained

---

[15] Origen, *Commentary on Matthew*, in *The Ante-Nicene Fathers*, vol. 9, ed. James Donaldson and Alexander Roberts (United States: Christian Literature Pub. Co., 1897; reprint, Peabody, MA: Hendrickson, 1994), 17.29. All English quotations from Origen's *Commentary on Matthew* are taken from ANF. Cf. Hanson, "The Church and Tradition," 28.

[16] Irenaeus *Adv. haer.* 1.10.1.

[17] Ibid., 3.4.2.

[18] Ibid., 1.22.1.

[19] Tertullian *De praes. haer.* 13.

[20] Tertullian *Adv. Prax.* 2; *De virg. vel.* 1.

what he was, God [*mansit quod erat, deus*]."[21] So while his deity is stated explicitly, Christ's sovereignty is implied in that deity and in "his glory."

Jesus Christ's participation in the creation of all things is the most detailed indicator of his inclusion in the divine identity held in common between the New Testament and the *regula*. All three fathers specifically associate Christ with the creation of the universe. In *Adv. haer.* 1.22.1, Irenaeus states four different times that God made everything by his Word. Later in the same work, Irenaeus repeats the statement and adds the possessive as he speaks of his [Christ's] creation.[22] Tertullian asserts Christ's involvement in creation similarly, citing his role as the instrumental cause.[23] Finally, Origen continues the emphasis with Jesus Christ's identification as "the servant of the Father in the creation of all things" and the appended quote from Scripture, "For by Him were all things made."[24] Jesus' involvement as the instrument or means of creation is an essential element and is indicative of his inclusion in the unique divine identity.

The attribution of the divine name to Jesus is easily identified in the explicit vocabulary of the fathers. In wording reminiscent of 1 Cor. 8:6, Irenaeus speaks of the church believing "in one God ... and in one Christ Jesus." Even more unambiguously, he calls Jesus Christ "our Lord [*kuriō*], and God [*theō*], and Savior [*sōtēri*], and King [*Basilei*]."[25] Both Irenaeus and Tertullian use the identification of the Word with God in John 1 to attribute to Jesus Christ inclusion within the divine identity.[26] Furthermore, Tertullian closely relates the Word with the title Son of God, though he confuses meanings in his attempt to contrast Son of God with Son of Man. His intent, nevertheless, is clearly to communicate Christ's divine identity since he equates Son of God with his deity and Son of Man with his humanity.[27]

Of the three fathers, Irenaeus is the most explicit in describing Jesus Christ as worthy of the worship due to God. He quotes Phil. 2:10-11 directly when he states that before Christ "'every knee should bow, of things in heaven, and things in earth, and things under the earth, and that every tongue should confess' to Him."[28] He also identifies Jesus as "having been received up in splendor" and as "the Savior of those who are saved," implying the obeisance due the rescuer

---

[21] Origen, *Traité des principes, Livres 1 & 2*, ed. and trans. H. Crouzel and M. Simonetti, 2 vols., Sources chrétiennes, nos. 252, 253 (Paris: Éditions du Cerf, 1978); Origen, *On First Principles*, in *The Ante-Nicene Fathers*, vol. 4, *Fathers of the Third Century*, ed. James Donaldson and Alexander Roberts (United States: Christian Literature Pub. Co., 1897; reprint, Peabody, MA: Hendrickson, 1994), pref., 4. Origen, *Origen on First Principles*, trans. G. W. Butterworth (New York: Harper & Row, 1966). All Greek and Latin quotations are taken from SC and all English quotations are taken from Butterworth's translation unless otherwise noted.

[22] Irenaeus *Adv. haer.* 3.4.2.

[23] Tertullian *De praes. haer.* 13; *Adv. Prax.* 2.

[24] Origen *De princ.* (ANF) pref., 4; John 1:3.

[25] Irenaeus *Adv. haer.* 1.10.1.

[26] Ibid., 1.22.1; Tertullian *De praes. haer.* 13; *Adv. Prax.* 2.

[27] Tertullian *De praes. haer.* 13; *Adv. Prax.* 2.

[28] Irenaeus *Adv. haer.* 1.10.1.

of men's souls.[29] Speaking of the barbarians, Irenaeus relates that they "expect the same advent of the Lord," portraying them as believers waiting upon Jesus just as the Scriptures command us to wait upon the Lord God.

Worship of Jesus Christ as divine is the least explicit identifier of the unique divine identity in Tertullian and Origen. That he is worthy of worship remains implied, nevertheless, within the substance of the *regula*. That Jesus Christ is included in binitarian and trinitarian statements of belief about God implies his worship. Belief, in this context, necessarily incorporates an element of worship since Christian belief is more than cognitive assent and involves the submission of oneself to God as an act of worship.

The extent to which the four identifiers of the unique divine identity are used christologically by Irenaeus, Tertullian, and Origen in the *regula* varies from explicit unanimity in reference to creation to the less obvious and often implied references to the divine name and worship. The consistent citation of the Son's exercise of sovereignty and his participation in creation argues forcefully for christological continuity in the *regula* from Irenaeus to Origen. The *regula* perpetuates a christological continuity, not necessarily in the restatement of biblical phrases and texts, but in the translation of christological monotheism from one mindset and vocabulary to another.

Irenaeus maintains this christological monotheism when he speaks of the church believing "in one God [*eis hena theon*]" while simultaneously addressing Jesus Christ as "our Lord, and God [*tōi Kurioi hēmōn kai theō*]."[30] This same Jesus Christ "Himself unit[es] man through Himself to God," an accomplishment only the "one God" could achieve.[31] Similarly, Tertullian begins with "the belief that there is one only God" and continues with an extensive statement concerning the Word, who was seen in the Old Testament and lived a life of ministry in the New Testament, all "under the name of God."[32] In *Adv. Prax.* 2 he writes of believers who have always believed "that there is one only God [*Vnum omnino Deum*]" and that Jesus Christ was incarnated, "being both Man and God [*hominem et Deum*]."[33] Finally, the christological monotheism of the *regula* can be no more obvious than when Origen writes "that there is one God [*quod unus est deus*]" and that Jesus Christ himself "became a man [*homo factus est*], and was incarnate [*incarnatus est*] although God [*cum deus esset*], and while made a man remained the God which He was [*mansit quod erat, deus*]."[34] Two things are abundantly clear in the *regulae* of Irenaeus, Tertullian, and Origen—first, that there is only one God, and second, that Jesus Christ is God. While emphases and vocabulary may change, when it comes to maintaining monotheism and the deity of Jesus Christ there is no equivocation among these early fathers.

---

[29] Ibid., 3.4.2.
[30] Ibid., 1.10.1.
[31] Ibid., 3.4.2.
[32] Tertullian *De praes. haer.* 13.
[33] Tertullian *Adv. Prax.* 2.
[34] Origen *De princ.* (ANF) pref., 4.

Besides portraying his deity, Christ's participation in creation, together with the other essential christological commonalities in the *regula*, perpetuates the New Testament's understanding of the atonement embodied in the belief that "Christ died for our sins, according to the Scriptures." That God created by means of his Word, the preincarnate Christ, confirms this "accord between the Scriptures and the Covenant made effective in the coming of Christ" that is in effect the *regula fidei*.[35] That Christ is the agent of both creation and re-creation substantiates the singular identity of the Creator and the Father of Jesus Christ (monotheism), the continuity between Old Testament prophecy and New Testament fulfillment, and the offer of salvation for all.

The manner in which Jesus Christ effected this salvation constitutes five of the remaining commonalities in the *regulae*, essentially the details of how "Christ died for our sins." First, Christ "became incarnate [*sarkōthenta*] for our salvation" by "uniting man through Himself to God."[36] He was "made flesh [*carnem factum*],"[37] or as Origen states more fully, the Son of God "became a man [*homo factus est*], and was incarnate [*incarnatus est*] although God, and while made a man remained the God which He was" as "He assumed a body [*corpus assumsit*] like our bodies."[38] The physical means for the incarnation, birth of a virgin, is the second of these commonalities.[39] The third consistent assertion in the *regulae* is that Christ "did truly suffer [*passus est in ueritate*], and did not endure this death common (to man) in appearance only [*non per phantasiam*], but did truly die [*uere mortuus*]."[40] While Irenaeus and Tertullian are not as explicit in their *regulae* as Origen concerning Jesus' death (Irenaeus, for example, mentions only his suffering), it is certainly implied, especially in light of the next commonality, the resurrection. Irenaeus speaks of "the resurrection from the dead" and of Jesus Christ "rising again," while Tertullian specifically cites its occurrence on the third day and that Jesus was "raised again by the Father."[41] Once again Origen emphasizes the physicality of the event with the modifier "truly," that "He did truly rise from the dead."[42] With the resurrection fulfilled, the remaining christological commonality in the *regulae* is Jesus Christ's ascent into heaven.[43]

These common statements, Christ's participation in creation, his incarnation, his birth of a virgin, the passion, his resurrection, and finally, the ascension, are the essential elements in the story of Christ's work, and therefore, humanity's

---

[35] Farmer, 167.

[36] Irenaeus *Adv. haer.* 1.10.1; 3.4.2.

[37] Tertullian *De praes. haer.* 13.

[38] Origen *De princ.* pref., 4.

[39] Irenaeus *Adv. haer.* 1.10.1; 3.4.2; Tertullian *De praes. haer.* 13; *Adv. Prax.* 2; *De virg. vel.* 1; Origen *De princ.* pref., 4.

[40] Origen *De princ.* (ANF) pref., 4.

[41] Irenaeus *Adv. haer.* 1.10.1; 3.4.2; Tertullian *De praes. haer.* 13; *Adv. Prax.* 2; Cf. *De virg. vel.* 1.

[42] Origen *De princ.* (ANF) pref., 4.

[43] Irenaeus *Adv. haer.* 1.10.1; 3.4.2; Tertullian *De praes. haer.* 13; *Adv. Prax.* 2; *De virg. vel.* 1; Origen *De princ.* pref., 4.

salvation. Without each event and Jesus Christ's inclusion in the unique divine identity underlying each activity, there is no basis for the atonement and the Christian faith. The truth of Christianity rests upon the historical reliability of these events and the historical continuity of the faith preached by the church.

The *Regula* as Composition in Performance

The *regula*'s ability to be flexible in form while consistently retaining the essentials enunciated above requires explanation. The fathers clearly describe the *regula* as uniform since it comes "from the apostles" and "was taught by Christ" himself.[44] It "is altogether one, alone immovable [*immobilis*] and irreformable [*irreformabilis*]."[45] Yet, the fathers clearly feel free to state this same irreformable confession in a variety of ways, depending on the circumstances. Tertullian uses only a handful of the same words in all three of his versions of the *regula*. His *regulae* are not dependent on one another or on a prior source for their vocabulary and grammatical structure. The same can be said of Irenaeus' *regulae*. In fact, both Irenaeus and Tertullian present the *regula* in bipartite and tripartite versions.

The natural question, therefore, is how the *regula* can be fixed enough to warrant the attribution of consistency and authority while allowing for its changing form and structural appearance. Identifying the *regula* as *only* a basic summary of Scripture, as the lowest common denominator per se, is one possible response. Nevertheless, this approach encounters problems since there exists a particularity in the *regula* that identifies it in contrast to other "summaries" of the faith. The texts at hand are "related to one another in such a way that they cannot be mere creations of the moment," and the manner in which they are presented seems to anticipate recognition by the reader.[46] The *regula* is more than a summary considering the significance granted to the *regula* in an ecclesiastical environment latent with other summaries.

At the other extreme, the *regula* is not a creed whether baptismal or otherwise. The obvious flexibility in the articulations of the *regula* is virtually antithetical to the structure inherent in a creedal statement. Even if authors cite a creed from memory with errors, the basic structure and outline of the creed will be evident in a comparison of several such citations since creeds have definite frameworks and particular vocabularies. Besides, baptism especially would provide little opportunity for the average believer to become familiar with such a statement since baptism was a private one-time experience. The average believer would not be exposed to multiple citations of the *regula* if it was associated only with baptism.

---

[44] Irenaeus *Adv. haer.* 1.10.1. See also Origen *De princ.* pref., 4; Tertullian *De praes. haer.* 13.

[45] Tertullian *De virg. vel.* 1.

[46] L. William Countryman, "Tertullian and the Regula Fidei," *The Second Century* 2 (Winter 1982): 216.

William Countryman provides a possible explanation consisting of what he calls composition in performance.[47] The *regula*'s flexibility discounts a fixed tradition, either oral or written, in which the text is passed on verbatim at baptism or some other occasion. At the same time, it does maintain a solid theological core independent of, but parallel to, Scripture.

Countryman suggests an oral-social theory in which the *regula* is "performed" before a Christian audience, most likely consisting of catechumens. In the performance the essential content remains the same but the performer has the flexibility to adjust the form to fit the context. Everyone can relate to the retelling of a familiar story which has never been placed in a fixed form but retains the same basic outline and content. One can hear such a story multiple times, know that it is without a doubt the same story, and yet come away from the events having heard different emphases each time. With such repetition, catechumens would learn "not only the basic content and structures but also the range of permissible variation—or, better, learning the former *through* learning the range of variation."[48] Such a retelling of the essentials of the faith would fit well in an oral catechetical environment involving several catechists, repetition, and the need to adjust to newly developing heresies.

The needs to protect against the second century heresies and to identify churches maintaining orthodoxy are both fulfilled in the *regula*'s balance between fixity and flexibility. Irenaeus speaks pointedly against the Gnostics when he asserts monotheism (a fixed element) against the powers of the Gnostic cosmology (a flexible element), for "there is no other God, nor initial principle, nor power, nor pleroma."[49] Origen likewise speaks against the Docetists when he emphasizes that "Jesus Christ was truly born, and did truly suffer, and did not endure this death common (to man) in appearance only, but did truly die; that He did truly rise from the dead."[50] Origen uses the fixed statements concerning Christ's birth, suffering, death, and resurrection, but the modifiers "truly" and "in appearance only" are certainly aimed at docetic teachings. Beyond these obvious examples are additional adjustments in vocabulary and structure that combat heretical views by means of asserting fixed concepts in flexible form.

This oral-social theory, though produced in an examination of Tertullian's *regulae*, could also explain the variations in *Irenaeus*' versions and, to a lesser extent, Origen's. With Origen the *regula* comes closer to being fixed than previously, though his *regula* in *On First Principles* was "very likely prepared for his advanced classes in the catechetical school at Alexandria" and as such would only constitute a historical development in Countryman's proposal.[51] Although any such theory explaining the perpetuation of the *regula fidei* necessitates substantial speculation, the oral-social theory with its "composition in performance"

---

[47] Ibid., 217-226.
[48] Ibid., 217-8.
[49] Irenaeus *Adv. haer.* 1.22.1.
[50] Origen *De princ.* (ANF) pref., 4.
[51] Albert C. Outler, "Origen and the *Regulae Fidei*," *The Second Century* 4 (1984): 138.

is a likely explanation for the *regula*'s historical development that allows for variation in form while maintaining essential doctrine.[52] Fortunately, in an examination of the *regula*'s Christology the question of the *regula*'s continuance and perpetuation of form bears on the argument primarily in relation to the *regula*'s purpose, which can also be ascertained at least in part by internal criteria. In the present study, what the authors themselves have to say about the *regula*'s role and the manner in which the *regulae* are stated will provide better source material concerning the *regula*'s purpose.

---

[52] In his article "The *Regula Fidei* and the Narrative Character of Early Christian Faith" Paul M. Blowers seems to criticize Countryman's proposal on at least two counts. "In the first place," he says, "the greater the brevity of an oral text, the more easily it is memorized and traditioned and the more unlikely it is to admit of variation in rendition" (206). Although true, this criticism only highlights the very problem that Countryman attempts to solve and that Blowers goes on to restate, that the fathers "are notoriously insistent on the Rule's originality, immutability, and irreformability" while their *regulae* "do show up differences of structure, wording, and length" (207). After additional discussion he states "The Great Church committed itself not to a universally invariable statement of faith but to variable local tellings of a *particular* story that aspired to universal significance" (208). With this statement Blowers seems to agree with Countryman more than he disagrees, with the most significant departure being his emphasis on narrative rather than catechesis. Where Countryman argues for an "oral composition" incorporating "old and familiar elements of Christian teaching," Blowers wants "the Christian canonical narrative tradition."

The second problem, according to Blowers, "arises from his [Countryman's] rather straightforward comparison of it to an epic" (209). Admittedly, the analogy may be poor, but after saying that the *regula* is "not a full-length narrative delivered in epic style" he drops the discussion with Countryman abruptly and engages in a discussion with Frances Young. He attributes to Young the idea that "they [the *regulae*] do not themselves qualify as genuinely narrative constructions" (209), while subsequently critiquing Young, who "overstates the extrinsic, particularistic, and non-narrative nature of the *regula fidei*" (210). Once again Blowers seems to agree more with Countryman than he seems willing to admit.

Overall, Blowers's narrative approach seems able to complement Countryman's general thesis. Both authors attempt to solve the dilemma concerning the *regula*'s "fixity and flexibility, conformity and freedom, unity and diversity" (227), Countryman by means of a catechetical context, and Blowers by the narrative form of the message. Who is to say that the narrative was not given as a performance in composition? Nevertheless, in the end, the argument for the *regula* as narrative runs into difficulties, especially with Tertullian whose *regulae* appear more like polemical timelines than narratives. Countryman's proposal, however speculative it may be, therefore, remains the most promising solution to the dilemma at present.

Part Two

Irenaeus' Functional Theology

Chapter 3

A Theology Confined by the *Regula*

Irenaeus was born about AD 130 in the Eastern Roman Empire, where in his youth he learned from Polycarp of Smyrna, who was himself a student of the Apostle John.[1] However long Irenaeus was near Smyrna and Ephesus, eventually he moved to Gaul where he was made a presbyter in the Lyons church. Sometime around 177 he was sent to deliver a letter from the church to the bishop of Rome. Pothinus, the bishop of Lyons, was martyred during Irenaeus' absence, and Irenaeus was named his successor upon his return to Lyons.

Irenaeus mentions Polycarp in order to highlight the zeal necessary to confront heretics like Marcion and to emphasize the continuity of the apostolic message. Irenaeus' connection with the Apostle John through Polycarp is illustrative of the doctrinal connections maintained by all of the churches. Consequently, we see in Irenaeus a pastor concerned especially with protecting the believers under his care from heresy. Irenaeus' major work, *A Refutation and Overthrowal of Knowledge Falsely So-Called*, shortened to *Against Heresies* (*Adversus haereses*) by Eusebius, focuses primarily on this pastoral concern. This pastoral focus, not only in his written work, but also in his general theological outlook, directly impacts his use of the *regula fidei*. With few exceptions, Irenaeus intentionally limits theological speculation in favor of doctrine more narrowly defined by the *regula fidei*.

There are four explicitly demarcated *regulae* in Irenaeus' works, *Adv. haer.* 1.10.1; 1.22.1; 3.4.2; and 5.20.1.[2] Each form of the rule is placed in a different context with varying implications. Nevertheless, Irenaeus' Christology is consistent throughout, not only between the various versions of the *regula*, but also in comparison to the New Testament. Irenaeus clearly includes Jesus within the unique divine identity, and he pointedly asserts the fulfillment of the Scriptures in the person of Christ and in his life, death, and resurrection.

---

[1] Irenaeus *Adv. haer.* 3.3.4.

[2] All quotations of Irenaeus' *regulae* in the Latin version or Greek, when available, are taken from SC. English quotations are taken from ACW for *Adv. haer.* 1.10.1 and 1.22.1, and from ANF for *Adv. haer.* 3.4.2 and 5.20.1. See appendix for complete texts.

The Christological Core in the *Regula*

Of Irenaeus' many theological themes, monotheism is easily the most dominant and foundational. He vociferously asserts the existence of only one God and his singular identity as Creator of the universe and Father of Jesus Christ. Each of his *regulae* begins with this assertion, whether it is that the church believes "in one God," that "all receive one and the same God the Father [*heni kai tōi autōi Theōi Patri*]," or "that there is one God Almighty [*unus Deus omnipotens*]." The christological monotheism of the New Testament, Jesus Christ's inclusion in the unique divine identity, is woven tightly into this driving theme of theological monotheism in both Irenaeus' overall theology and in his *regulae* specifically.

The first criterion for this christological monotheism, the exercise of divine sovereignty, is incorporated least in Irenaeus' shortest *regula* in *Adv. haer.* 5.20.1, where it is only implied with reference to the return of Christ. The rule of the Son of God is slightly more significant in 1.22.1 where it is first presented as an element within the more dominant theme of creation. God created through his Word, not by means of any angel or power "separated from His thought [*abscissas ab eius sententia*]." Above the Word, who is himself God, there is therefore, "no other god, nor a Beginning, nor a Power, nor a Fullness." Furthermore, having made everything, God disposes and governs all things through his Word and his Wisdom. By nature of his role in creation, the Word has absolute sovereignty over that same creation, a sovereignty in which he actively governs and sustains what is made.

Christ's eschatological sovereignty is brought out explicitly in *Adv. haer.* 1.10.1 and 3.4.2. First, in 1.10.1 he is specifically addressed as "our Lord and God, Savior and King," with each attribution adding slightly different connotations to the overarching idea of the divine rule. More than a transcendent Creator and Ruler as implied especially in "God," Jesus Christ is also the visible and present Redeemer, the Savior who rules the lives of men. He is king both of the world as a whole and of the redeemed individually. Second, he will return, "from heaven in the glory of the Father [*en tē doxē tou Patros*]." He does not possess a secondary, derived glory, but the glory of God himself. Third, he will come to "exercise just judgment [*krisin dikaian*] toward all," salvation for the righteous, and damnation for the wicked and godless. This judgment is based specifically upon whether or not one "kept His commandments" and "persevered in His love." Jesus possesses the authority and responsibility to reward or condemn based upon one's adherence to his rule and one's relationship to his person.

The *regula* in 3.4.2 further defines the judgments for salvation and condemnation in relation to Christ himself. His sovereignty is not passive but active. He is intimately involved in the lives of those he judges. On the one hand, he is "the Savior of those who are saved [*Sōtēra tōn sōzomenōn*]," thereby completing his work of recapitulation by restoring his creation and maturing it to the intended outcome. Only one with a sovereign right to creation and one intimately related to it could know the original intention of its making and transform it into such.

On the other hand, he is "the Judge of those who are judged [*Kritēn tōn krinomenōn*]," exercising his divine right to determine the end of those who despise the Father and his own coming.

This eschatological emphasis, especially in the *regula* of *Adv. haer.* 1.10.1, is the dominant means for Irenaeus' communication of Christ's sovereignty. The active sovereignty generally attributed to Christ results in a diminished emphasis upon predominantly static descriptions such as his being seated at the right hand of the Father. That is not to say that these depictions are absent, nor by any means is Irenaeus digressing from Scripture. Creator, Savior, and Judge are simply Christ's biblical roles that communicate most effectively in Irenaeus' conceptual framework based largely upon the *oikonomia*.

The Son's sovereign right to creation derives from his participation in the creation of all things, the second criterion for his inclusion in the unique divine identity. Due to the eschatological emphasis of *Adv. haer.* 1.10.1, Christ's role in creation is only implied in this version of the *regula* in the bestowal of "the gift of incorruption." Humanity originally lacked incorruption, even prior to the fall. It was to be given to mankind as a part of its maturation in God's continuing act of creation. Only the Creator would be capable of making the corruptible incorruptible.

In contrast to 1.10.1, the *regula* of 1.22.1 is dominated by God's creative work. The Word is repeatedly described as the instrument or means of creation. God "created all things through His Word [*omnia condidit per Verbum suum*]" and "[f]rom this *all* nothing is exempt." Being the means for the Father's creation, the Word exists in a unique relationship with the Father, for he is not "separated from His thought" as are all other powers and authorities. This unique relationship identified by the indistinguishable thought within the Godhead can be explained only within the context of christological monotheism, especially considering Irenaeus' dominant monotheism. Any other explanation would require something akin to the Gnostics' theories of emanation. An additional facet of this relationship is the inclusion of the Spirit in an analogous role. "The God of all things needs nothing" since "He made all things by His Word and Spirit" and exists in complete distinction from creation itself. The Son and the Spirit, the Word and Wisdom for Irenaeus, are often described as the hands of the Father.[3]

Irenaeus continues to describe the Son as the instrument of creation in the *regula* of *Adv. haer.* 3.4.2, though he goes further and explicitly names Christ Jesus as the Son of God. In fact, Christ Jesus, not the preincarnate Son of God, is said to be the means of creation. This synonymous use of appellations for Christ is likely due to the belief that the Son of God appeared in human form long before his birth of a virgin. This version of the *regula*, besides describing his instrumentality, also attributes possession of creation to Christ. "[B]ecause of His surpassing love towards His creation," he condescended to be made a man in order to unite man to God and God to man. The one who unites the Creator and

---

[3] Irenaeus *Adv. haer.* 4.preface.4; 4.20.1; 5.1.3; 5.5.1; 5.6.1; 5.28.4.

the creation in himself is himself the Creator who loves that which he has made and sustains.

The most definitive characteristic of the Son's participation in creation is unquestionably his place as instrumental cause, a role repeated numerous times.[4] This role correlates directly with Paul's christological statements in 1 Cor. 8:6 and Col. 1:15-17, the comments of the writer to the Hebrews in 1:2-3, and the prologue of John's Gospel. In fact, Irenaeus frequently quotes John's prologue as evidence of the Word's participation in creation, including one citation in the *regula* of *Adv. haer.* 1.22.1.[5] Similarly, there is little doubt that he was familiar with the christological passages in Paul's letters. Irenaeus' emphasis upon Christ's instrumentality in creation certainly perpetuates a similar thrust in the New Testament itself.

The attribution of the divine name to Christ, the third criterion for his inclusion in the unique divine identity, is not as explicitly identifiable as the preceding criteria, though it is by no means absent. The most obvious attribution of the divine name in the four *regulae* is in *Adv. haer.* 1.10.1, where Irenaeus refers to Christ as "our Lord and God, Savior and King." In addition to the direct attribution of "God" to Christ, the manner in which Irenaeus ties "Lord" and "God" together indicates the significance he applies to the title "Lord," a designation he uses in three of the four *regulae*.[6] Christ's lordship derives from the sovereignty discussed above, and if the apparent parallelism is intended, it surpasses simple transcendent kingship over creation and includes the rule of lives, especially his rule of the redeemed as Savior.

Irenaeus also refers to Jesus as the Son of God repeatedly in 1.10.1 and in two of the remaining *regulae*. Although his Sonship is not explained or developed in the *regula*, his relation to God the Father is explained elsewhere as incomparable. The Son is eternal and his generation is incomprehensible.[7] The uniqueness of the Son's generation and his Sonship are clear, even though Irenaeus considers it inappropriate to define distinctions within the Godhead prior to the *oikonomia*. A consequence of this uniqueness is that the title "Son of God" is an explicit statement of Christ's deity. Interestingly, this further contributes to the trend in the early church to associate "Son of God" with Christ's deity and "Son of Man" with his humanity. "Son of God," therefore, is another indicator of Christ's inclusion within the unique divine identity.

Several other titles incorporated into Irenaeus' *regulae* and applied to Christ also contribute more generally to including Jesus Christ within the unique divine identity. In *Adv. haer.* 1.22.1 he is called God's Word within the context of God's creative work. In *Adv. haer.* 3.4.2 he receives the titles of Savior and

---

[4] Ibid., 1.22.1; 2.2.4; 2.3.5; 2.6.2; 2.11.1; 2.27.2; 2.30.9; 3.8.3; 3.11.1; 3.24.2; 4.pref.4; 4.20.2, 4; 4.38.3; 5.1.3; 5.28.4; Irenaeus, *Démonstration de la prédication apostolique*, ed. and trans. Adelin Rousseau, Sources chrétiennes, no. 406 (Paris: Éditions du Cerf, 1995); Irenaeus, *On the Apostolic Preaching*, trans. John Behr (Crestwood, NY: St. Vladimir's Seminary Press, 1997), 6.

[5] Irenaeus *Adv. haer.* 2.2.5; 3.11.2, 8.

[6] See also ibid., 3.6.1; 3.8.3.

[7] Ibid., 2.13.2-6; 2.13.8; 2.25.3; 2.28.4-5; 2.28.6; 2.30.9; 3.19.1-2.

Judge as his eschatological roles are delineated. These titles reflect the previously discussed themes of Christ's divine sovereignty and his ownership of the universe as its Creator.

The final criterion for Christ's inclusion in the unique divine identity, the attribution of divine worship, occurs both implicitly and explicitly in Irenaeus' *regulae*. It is present implicitly in the manner in which believers, even barbarians, hold to faith in Christ and to the *regula* that states that faith. In *Adv. haer.* 3.4.2, that the barbarians hold allegiance only to Christ is manifested in the way that "salvation [is] written in their hearts" by the Spirit and in the fact that they "carefully preserv[e] the ancient tradition." If they were to hear anything contrary to the *regula* and their understanding of Christ, "they would at once stop their ears, and flee as far off as possible, not enduring even to listen to the blasphemous address." Considering the importance of the *regula* to early believers, its significance in Irenaeus' monotheistic theology, and Christ's prominent place therein, this elevated tradition indicates belief in Jesus' unique divinity by implication.

Aside from the significance of the *regula* as a whole, specific portions of the texts also contribute implicitly to the recognition of the worship of Christ as God. The barbarians await or "expect the same advent of the Lord," knowing that it will result in the exercise of his sovereignty in final judgment. Statements made in reference to this judgment in *Adv. haer.* 1.10.1 and 3.4.2 also portray Christ's status as worthy of divine worship. Those destined for eternal fire are those who "despise His Father and His advent," while life is given to "those who kept His commandments." One cannot easily separate obedience from worship, and the implication is that the obedient kept Christ's commands as the commands of God himself and thereby attribute worship to both. One can also connect adherence to the law with worship of Christ in light of Irenaeus' belief that the preincarnate Son of God was intimately involved in Old Testament patriarchal history and in the giving of the Mosaic law.

Consistent with the eschatological emphasis of the worship of Christ is a curious addendum to the *regula* in *Adv. haer.* 1.22.1 in which all of humanity finally acknowledges "the power of Him who raises them from the dead." The identity of "him" is not clear, though it might be argued that it refers to the Father since this entire version of the *regula* focuses on the Father as the primary subject. Yet, *Adv. haer.* 1.10.1 specifically identifies Christ as the one who raises the dead. Therefore, if this acknowledgement of authority by those raised is directed to the Father it still supports Christ's inclusion within the unique divine identity. Christ, in raising the dead, does what the Father does himself.

In a similar and more positive vein, Irenaeus quotes Phil. 2:10-11 in *Adv. haer.* 1.10.1, stating explicitly that "all flesh of the whole human race" will be raised "in order that to Christ Jesus, ... *every knee should bow* [*of those*] *in heaven and on earth and under the earth, and every tongue confess* Him." If there is any question as to Christ's worthiness of divine worship or to the attribution of such worship in the *regula*, this passage removes all doubt. In this biblical quotation the entire universe is displayed before Christ in worship and obeisance. None is exempt whether by time or place, for all people of all nations from all generations are raised from death to worship Christ as "Lord and God, Savior and King," whether or not they acknowledged him as such in life.

In Irenaeus' *regulae*, therefore, Christ is undoubtedly included in the unique divine identity. This is displayed in the exercise of his divine sovereignty, a sovereignty deriving in large part from his participation in creation as its instrumental cause. As Creator, Savior, and Judge, roles dominating the various dispensations of God's plan of salvation, the *oikonomia*, he is fully entitled to the divine name and the worship due to God alone. Essentially, Irenaeus continues in predominantly biblical terms the christological monotheism of the New Testament, especially as related to the four criteria presented above.

Together with the strict theme of monotheism, the *regula* adamantly proclaims the accord between the Scriptures and their fulfillment in the coming, death, and resurrection of Jesus Christ. In contrast to the belief of the Marcionites and Gnostics, the *regula* asserts the singular identity of the Creator God and the Father of Jesus Christ. Additionally, when Irenaeus reiterates implicitly the New Testament claim "that Christ died for our sins according to the Scriptures," he is further asserting a form of christological monotheism.

Irenaeus displays the singular identity of the Creator and the Father in the opening of each of his *regulae* and elaborates further with statements including the patriarchs, the prophets, and the apostles. *Adv. haer.* 1.10.1 begins with the statement that all Christians believe in "one God the Father Almighty [*Patera pantokratora*], the Creator [*ton pepoiēkota*] of heaven and earth." Besides the obvious fact that he is both the Father Almighty as seen best in the New Testament and the Creator in the Old Testament, this truth is received from the apostles of Jesus himself. The Creator of heaven and earth is the same God preached by the apostles and their successive disciples.

This persistent monotheism and the concord between the old and new covenants are also seen in the work of God's hands. In this version of the *regula* both the Son and the Spirit are seen working out God's unchanging purposes in the *oikonomia*. "Through the prophets," the Holy Spirit "preached the Economies, the coming, the birth from a Virgin, the passion, the resurrection from the dead, and the bodily ascension into heaven of the beloved Son, Christ Jesus our Lord, and His coming from heaven in the glory of the Father," and the final judgment. The Spirit prepared the way by declaring the events that were to come while the Son is continuing to fulfill the same events, all in accordance with the will of the Father. The same God who worked through the Spirit in the Old Testament is the same God who fulfills his promises in Jesus Christ.

In the *regula* of *Adv. haer.* 1.22.1 Irenaeus attacks the polytheism of the Gnostics even more vociferously than in the previous. He begins with the assertion that "there is one God Almighty, who created all things through His Word," and drives the point further with nearly every statement that follows. The initial association of God Almighty, the Creator, with the Word, Jesus Christ the Son of God, introduces the *regula*'s theme of the two testaments' alignment with the Son's involvement in creation and his relationship with the Creator God of the Old Testament. After citations from Ps. 33:6 and John 1:3, likely intentional references to both testaments supporting the same idea, "God Almighty" is called Father in the same context of creation. God is both the Almighty and the Father, and in both statements he is the initiator of the act of creation in which the Son serves as instrumental cause. Once again, after stating his uniqueness and absolute independence, God is declared to have "made all things [*omnia faciens*] by His Word and Spirit." Furthermore, this creative work is a continuing reality in which he is "disposing [*disponens*] and governing [*gubernans*] them [all things] and giving all of them existence [*omnibus esse praestans*]." Besides the initial act of creation in the beginning, God the Father continues to create and govern his creation through His Word and Spirit throughout both covenants.

If there is any doubt as to Irenaeus' point in the preceding, the conclusion to this rendition of the *regula* clarifies it entirely. After reiterating God the Father's identity as Creator, Irenaeus specifically identifies him as both the God of the patriarchs and the Father of our Lord Jesus Christ. The God of creation, whom he has already discussed repeatedly, "is the God of Abraham and Isaac and Jacob, above whom there is no other God, nor a Beginning, nor a Power, nor a Fullness." There is no being who can compare to this one God, but more importantly, "this is the Father of our Lord Jesus Christ" whom the Gnostics identify separately in their pleroma of divine entities. The driving point of *Adv. haer.* 1.22.1 is that the Almighty God is the Creator of all things and that he, being the only true God, is the same being as the Father of Jesus Christ.

The *regula* of *Adv. haer.* 3.4.2, being more concise, does not identify the Creator and the Father in as detailed or elaborate a fashion as that in 1.22.1, though it still does so in different forms. First, Irenaeus connects Jesus Christ with the Creator by naming him as the means for believing in the "one God, the Creator of heaven and earth." It is Jesus Christ who reveals the Creator God to his creation, allowing humanity the opportunity to know God himself. Then in an extraordinary phrase Irenaeus transforms the monotheism of the *regula* into christological monotheism. After naming Christ Jesus in relation to God the Creator, he explicitly assigns the creation to Christ's ownership when he speaks of "His [Christ's] surpassing love towards His creation." And if there is any question as to the identity of "His," the same person "condescended to be born of the virgin, He Himself uniting man through Himself to God." In this abbreviated version of the *regula*, therefore, Irenaeus not only presents clear biblical monotheism but modifies it to make monotheism christological.

Finally, in *Adv. haer.* 5.20.1, the brevity of the *regula* allows only an implied understanding of the relationship between the two testaments and the one God portrayed within them. According to "the sure tradition from the apostles, ... all receive one and the same God the Father, and believe in the same dispensation regarding the incarnation of the Son of God." The use of "dispensation" implies prior and successive dispensations all resting within one overarching *oikonomia*. This concise version of the *regula* does little to refute Gnostic polytheism. Nevertheless, it could easily be elaborated upon to explain a single God ruling over the entire expanse of time from creation to eschaton and incorporating the various dispensations of his plan of salvation.

Aside from identifying the Creator with the Father of Jesus Christ, the scriptural assertion "that Christ died for our sins according to the Scriptures" also declares the efficacy of Christ's salvific work for all peoples, both Jew and Gentile, according to the promises under the old covenant. In the *regula*, Irenaeus speaks of the church as "disseminated throughout the world, even to the ends of the earth."[8] This same church that "circumscribes the whole world" includes even "barbarians who believe in Christ."[9] All believers "receive one and the same God the Father, and believe in the same dispensation regarding the incarnation of the Son of God," having one way of salvation with no distinction between Jew and Gentile.[10] "The God of Abraham and Isaac and Jacob" is the same God who created all things, who sent Jesus Christ to earth, and who calls all to reconciliation with him.[11] All will receive life "who kept His commandments and who have persevered in His love."[12] Every other distinction between people was removed in the fulfillment of the Scriptures in the person of Jesus Christ.

Finally, "that Christ died for our sins," indicates the centrality of the cross in God's salvation plan. Although Irenaeus' theology moves some of the emphasis in salvation from the passion to the incarnation, the significance of the cross remains implicit in the shorter forms of the *regula* and explicit in the longer forms. On the one hand, Jesus' coming leads to the passion and his resurrection from the dead, the central events of "the Economies." On the other hand, the bodily ascension, Christ's second coming, and the final resurrection are dependent on Christ's resurrection as the first fruits.[13] Similarly, in *Adv. haer.* 3.4.2 Jesus Christ's sufferings and resurrection are centered between the incarnation and ascension. And when he speaks of the "salvation of the complete man," Irenaeus specifically includes the body, necessitating Christ's resurrection as the precursor to the general resurrection.

In summary, the Christology of Irenaeus' *regulae* conforms to that of the New Testament with only small variations in emphasis. Some of the New Testament themes of significance such as the offer of salvation for all and Christ's worthiness of worship are assumed by Irenaeus. At the same time, Christ's involvement in the creation of all things, especially as the instrumental cause, is dealt with extensively, as is his divine sovereignty both protologically and eschatologically. There can be no doubt that Irenaeus presents in his versions of the *regula fidei* a view of Jesus Christ as one who is fully included in the unique divine identity. Furthermore, his advocacy of the unity of God's salvation plan through both testaments and the singular identity of the Creator of all things and the Father of Jesus Christ clearly maintains a form of christological monotheism in direct contradiction to the Gnostic views of his time. In no way does Irenaeus

---

[8] Ibid., 1.10.1.
[9] Ibid., 5.20.1; 3.4.2.
[10] Ibid., 5.20.1.
[11] Ibid., 1.22.1.
[12] Ibid., 1.10.1.
[13] Ibid.

change the message of the New Testament. Apparent differences between his interpretations of the gospel message in the *regula* and the New Testament or between different versions of the *regula* can be attributed to variations in emphasis rather than to incongruities in substance.

Irenaeus' Variations in the *Regula*

The importance of context for the varying emphases of the different versions of the *regula* can be seen in Irenaeus' first and most thorough version in *Adv. haer.* 1.10.1. In the preceding chapter he deals with Gnostic errors in scriptural interpretation and theological method, accusing them of piecing together bits of Scripture to fit their own arbitrary structure.[14] As he continues, the *regula* serves not as a mere polemical device but as a corrective to their abuse of Scripture. The *regula fidei* not only shows the heretical theological structure for what it is, but it also "restore[s] each one of the passages to its proper order."[15] In order for the *regula* to function in such a general environment where a wide range of Scriptures and subjects may be involved it must contain all of the essential teachings of the faith, explaining the comprehensiveness of this first version in Irenaeus.

In contrast, Irenaeus' remaining versions of the *regula* are presented in more particular contexts. Of the four versions, the *regula* of *Adv. haer.* 1.22.1 is easily the most concerned with creation, the manner in which the creation was formed, and its corporeality. It separates an extensive treatment of Marcosianism from responses to a series of heresiarchs. Towards the end of the treatment of the Marcosians the subject turns to the various Gnostic deities and their origins, all within the context of the afterlife, which is thoroughly immersed in a material versus immaterial dualism. This version of the *regula*, therefore, serves as a direct answer to the Gnostics' series of divine emanations and their low view of the physical.

In response to the latter, Irenaeus repeatedly mentions God's role as Creator: The Almighty "created all things [*omnia condidit*]," "He both prepared and made [*et aptauit et fecit*] all things," "All things were made through Him [*Omnia per ipsum facta sunt*] and without Him was made not a thing [*et sine ipso factum est nihil*]," "the Father who made all things [*omnia per ipsum fecit Pater*]," "He made all things [*omnia faciens*] by His Word and Spirit," he "made the world [*mundum fecit*], which indeed is made up of all things," and he "fashioned man [*hominem plasmauit*]." In this relatively short passage God is explicitly cited as making or fashioning creation, the world, or humanity at least eight times. Furthermore, the corporeality of the creation is emphasized with very intentional modifiers aimed at the Gnostics. God made everything, "whether

---

[14] "After having entirely fabricated their own system, they gather together sayings and names from scattered places and transfer them, as we have already said, from their natural meaning to an unnatural one." Ibid., 1.9.1.

[15] Ibid.

visible [*uisibilia*] or invisible [*inuisibilia*], whether sensible [*sensibilia*] or intelligible [*intellegibilia*]," and the *all* of creation is stated repeatedly. God "made all things" and "from this *all* nothing is exempt," and the world is described as "made up of all things." Without question, God is the Creator of both corporeal and incorporeal realities in direct contradiction to the Gnostics' beliefs.

The other target of this version of the *regula*, the manifold divine emanations of the Gnostic pleroma, is dealt with by reasserting monotheism and by specifically excising the need for any subservient divine entities in creation. This one God "did not make [anything] through Angels or some Powers." Furthermore, above this God "there is no other God, nor a Beginning, nor a Power, nor a Fullness." He alone is God, no other has created from nothing as has he, and what he has created includes both the material and immaterial.[16]

In *Adv. haer.* 3.4.2 the *regula* comes closest to being a very concise narrative summary of the Christian faith. The context for this version is the tradition of the early church, apostolic succession, and the universality of the orthodox faith. Irenaeus provides the list of bishops at Rome to document the continuity of the church's tradition. The fact that believers from all over the Empire, having been taught in different local congregations, can come to Rome and agree on the teachings of the faith indicates the common source of their beliefs in Christ and his disciples. Even the "many nations of those barbarians who believe in Christ do assent." The result for the *regula* is a basic binitarian statement that identifies the essential events of the *oikonomia* especially in the life of Christ: creation, his birth of a virgin, his incarnation, passion, resurrection, and second coming. Since the context of this version of the *regula* is the unity of the church in the faith, there is little need for additional polemical emphases or for significant elaboration upon the basic content of the *regula*.

Irenaeus emphasizes the unity of the church in its basic understanding of the faith in his final version of the *regula* in *Adv. haer.* 5.20.1, though he is even less interested in specific details in this version than in the previous. In contradistinction to the Gnostics, the church possesses "the sure tradition from the apostles, and gives unto us to see that the faith of all is one and the same [*tōn patōn mian kai tēn autēn pistin*]." Only a brief Trinitarian statement recognizing each person of the Trinity follows, with the incarnation, the commandments, ecclesiology, the second coming of Christ, and man's final salvation mentioned only in passing. The preceding section of chapter nineteen sheds more light on the significance of the church's unity as Irenaeus parades through the constantly varying beliefs of the Gnostics. Although many of the Gnostics probably would have agreed with other forms of Gnosticism on varying points, Irenaeus presents no less than eight different opinions or segments of Gnosticism in this one section as a contrast to the unity of the church. Deviation is anathema, and it takes little elaboration in the *regula* to discover some of the heretics' deviations from

---

[16] "The attribute 'in need of nothing' (*adeētos*) is widely affirmed of god in the ancient world. Irenaeus includes the same claim in his rule of faith." Eric Osborn, *Irenaeus of Lyons* (Cambridge: Cambridge University Press, 2001), 64.

the church. The faithful, therefore, are admonished to adhere to the "one and the same way of salvation ... shown throughout the whole world."

In addition to the general changes in emphasis within Irenaeus' versions of the *regula*, the particular words, phrases, and concepts he uses reveal much of his interpretive method and his overall theology. One does not have to look far to find a strident dependency on Scripture and on scriptural language, especially in the explanations of the *oikonomia*. The significance of the *oikonomia* in Irenaeus' Christology reveals itself in the *regula* through its basic structure even before the specifically theological statements are evaluated. The *regula* in *Adv. haer.* 1.10.1 relates the christological statement to both the Son and the Spirit. The Spirit proclaimed all that the Son did in his redemptive work. The *oikonomia*, even in the incarnation, is not relegated solely to the Son but is a divine work of the Father as the Godhead manifested through both the Son and the Spirit.

Irenaeus tends to use functional rather than ontological language. Subjects are portrayed as effecting actions, most often in reference to some dispensation of the *oikonomia*, rather than constituting existential realities. The Father is the "Maker," the Holy Spirit "proclaimed," and the Son will "gather," "raise up," "execute judgment," "send" the wicked into "everlasting fire," "confer immortality," and "surround them with everlasting glory." The significant elements in the Son's recapitulation, "the birth from a virgin, and the passion, and the resurrection from the dead, and the ascension into heaven," while not predicates, are events implying action rather than portrayals of a state of being.[17] In *Adv. haer.* 1.21.1 God "made," "fashioned," "formed," "established," "makes," "disposes," "governs," and "commands." In 3.4.2 Jesus Christ "condescended to be born," "united man to God," "suffered," rose again, "received up in splendor, shall come in glory," and will send the condemned to hell. While there are certainly ontological implications for many if not all of these statements, the only explicitly ontological language speaks of the Son who "became incarnate" and God who effected specific actions. For example, "He who formed the world" is the God of the patriarchs and "is the Father of our Lord Jesus Christ."[18] Irenaeus, therefore, clearly works from the premise that one can know God only by what he does in relation to man, not by means of speculation into the intrinsic nature of God. Consequently, it is easy to see why he specifically rebuffs any attempt to explain the manner of the Son's generation from the Father or other issues related to the inner being of God.

Aside from the general form of the *regula* and the functional type of language used, Irenaeus' *regulae* also contain both implicit and explicit references to soteriology and the *oikonomia*. Irenaeus speaks of God who created and Jesus Christ "who was enfleshed for our salvation," displaying one of the more ontological phrases in an overtly functional context.[19] The Son of God changed his state of being in order to effect salvation. Furthermore, he did so "because of His

---

[17] Irenaeus *Adv. haer.* 1.10.1.
[18] Ibid., 1.10.1; 1.22.1.
[19] Ibid., 1.10.1.

surpassing love towards His creation."[20] God's love stands as the impetus behind the *oikonomia* even when it demands condescension, suffering, and death. Understanding this motive, there is no reason to speculate concerning the nature of the change in the Son's existence or any of the circumstances surrounding his state of being either preceding or succeeding the incarnation. The events of Christ's life and the assertion that the Holy Spirit revealed God to humanity through the prophets also serve this functional emphasis and reiterate the importance of the *oikonomia*.

As with the previous phrase that speaks of Christ's enfleshment, the Son's "uniting [*enōsanta*] man through Himself [*di heautou*] to God," though an ontological concept in and of itself, is thoroughly soteriological and represents the culmination of the incarnation as the pinnacle of the economy.[21] In addition to freeing man from enslavement to the devil and restoring humanity's pristine state through a life of obedience, Christ deifies man through the union of humanity and deity in his own person. Although ontological implications can be drawn concerning human redemption through union with Christ, the relation of the two natures in Christ is never addressed.

Furthermore, Christ, as the new man, replaces the first man Adam as the head of humanity, but how this takes place is explained little if at all. That humanity now finds communion with God possible in the person of Jesus Christ is a consequence of Christ's two natures, but how he can be both human and divine is not even a question for Irenaeus. All that matters is that Christ passed through every stage of our existence, was obedient to the point of death, and in so doing became "what we are [*quod sumus nos*], that He might bring us to be [*nos perficeret esse*] even what He is Himself [*quod est ipse*]."[22] No explanation of Christ's ability to be both human and divine is necessary. Scripture and tradition state the truth, and it is more a matter of acceptance or refusal than one of discovery and comprehension.

The *Regula* and Irenaeus' Hermeneutic

Irenaeus generally sees the *regula* as prescriptive in that only those things addressed in the *regula* and Scripture are to be considered. The *regula* is the road map for proper theological inquiry, and to deviate from this road map is to risk deviation from the faith given by Christ and his apostles. This authority of the *regula* is correlative to that of the Scriptures, though the Scriptures are far more thorough and all-encompassing.

---

[20] Ibid., 3.4.2.

[21] Ibid., 3.4.2.

[22] Ibid., 5.preface. See also ibid., 2.22.4-6; 3.18.7; 3.19.2; 3.22.3-4; 4.22.1; 4.33.4; 4.38.2; 4.39.2.

At the foundation of Irenaeus' hermeneutic is the sufficiency of Scripture and the tradition that accompanies it.[23] From a positive perspective this sufficiency identifies the Scriptures as the ultimate source of understanding for the believer who intently seeks wisdom and truth. Scripture is entirely sufficient for attaining true wisdom and understanding. In fact, close adherence to the obvious intent of Scripture is the "very method of discovery" without which one cannot gain truth.[24] The faithful believer has no reason to pass beyond the bounds of Scripture in order to gain understanding since such excesses will bring nothing but endless conjecture and speculation.

Speculation, in contrast, helps identify the sufficiency of Scripture from a negative point of view. The errors of speculation and allegorization are repeatedly identified, especially in reference to the misinterpretation of Scripture. Exceeding the bounds of Scripture's intent leads to "various systems of truth in mutual opposition to each other and setting forth antagonistic doctrines."[25] Furthermore, such speculation leads ultimately to a megalomania in which the inquirer "changes God Himself [*ipsum mutat Deum*], and exalts his own opinion above the greatness of the Creator."[26] Ironically, the inordinate pride and arrogance of those who seek to surpass God in his knowledge only serve to show the ignorance and stupidity of such endless inquiry. The extreme case is the person who cares to number the hairs on people's heads or the sands of the earth. Such a one would "labor in vain and would ... be justly declared mad and destitute of reason by all possessed of common sense."[27] In a practical sense, if one is unable to understand even the natural world, why then should he feel free to speculate on that which is above and beyond him and his finite abilities?[28] The wise, therefore, leave to God all questions not dealt with in Scripture and unexplainable to the natural intellect. In light of the priority of God's Word to us, "we should leave things of that nature to God who created us." The generation of the Son is a perfect example of a subject that should be left to God.[29]

---

[23] J. N. D. Kelly, *Early Christian Doctrines*, rev. ed. (New York: Harper & Row, Publishers, 1978), 38-9.

[24] Irenaeus *Adv. haer.* 2.27.2.

[25] Ibid., 2.27.1.

[26] Ibid., 2.26.3.

[27] Ibid.

[28] Ibid., 2.28.1-3.

[29] Ibid., 2.28.2. See also ibid., 2.28.3, 7, 8; 4.31.1. Although Irenaeus generally disdains speculation and philosophy, he does not reject entirely the works of the philosophers and shows himself to be familiar with some of their ideas. "Irenaeus, like Tertullian, says negative things about philosophers (2.14.3, 4) but then goes on to use, with discernment, the philosophers and the traditions which derive from them. These continue to attract interest, but do not indicate an engagement with contemporary philosophy such as we find in Clement of Alexandria and Origen." Osborn, *Irenaeus of Lyons*, 33. Irenaeus' writing also shows a certain familiarity with rhetorical forms, often expressing himself in such forms or utilizing rhetorical terms and concepts. Robert M. Grant, *Irenaeus of Lyons* (New York: Routledge, 1997), 47-53.

Of course the question then arises as to how one is to know whether a question or area of inquiry is appropriate or out of bounds, so to speak. That is where the church, tradition, and the *regula* come into play. Alongside the Scriptures, the church is the sole possessor of the authoritative tradition of the apostles. If the Scriptures themselves were unavailable, it would be possible "to follow the course of the tradition which they [the apostles] handed down to those to whom they did commit the churches."[30] The continuity of the church's tradition with the teaching of the apostles, as maintained in the continuous line of leaders in the church, provides the tradition with its authority. Therefore, hypothetically, if the Scriptures were unavailable, the founding of the church at Ephesus by Paul and the succession of leadership from John to Polycarp would provide that particular church with apostolic ties and the successive authority needed to provide "a true witness of the tradition of the apostles."[31] Of course these apostolic ties are only tangible manifestations of the more important fact that "where the Church is, there is the Spirit of God; and where the Spirit of God is, there is the Church."[32]

Nevertheless, a recognizable tradition is required if Irenaeus' argument in support of the apostolic tradition is to retain any value and significance. This recognizable tradition is the *regula fidei*, which he summarily presents in *Adv. haer.* 3.4.2 in the midst of discussing the church's tradition. Even those barbarians who cannot read the Scriptures can recognize the true Christian faith from their understanding of the apostolic tradition as embodied in the *regula*. More than a guide, the "rule is truth itself and saves us from being diverted in every direction."[33] It is the means by which we come to interpret and understand the Scriptures and the Christian faith as a whole.[34] Furthermore, it not only articu-

---

[30] Irenaeus *Adv. haer.* 3.4.1. "However, to inquire whether tradition or Scripture is the primary authority is to obscure the mind of S. Irenaeus by asking the wrong question. To him both are manifestations of one and the same thing, the *apostolic truth* by which the Christian lives. The authority within the Church is all one, '*the Apostolic*', however transmitted. The truth hangs by two cords, and he can speak of either as self-sufficient without intending to deny or subordinate the other." John Lawson, *The Biblical Theology of Saint Irenaeus* (London: The Epworth Press, 1948), 103-4. See also Jan Tjeerd Nielsen, *Adam and Christ in the Theology of Irenaeus of Lyons* (Assen: Van Gorcum, 1968), 49.

[31] Irenaeus *Adv. haer.* 3.3.4.

[32] Ibid., 3.24.1.

[33] Osborn, *Irenaeus of Lyons*, 41.

[34] In his discussions concerning scriptural authority and tradition Irenaeus also provides some very concrete principles for interpreting Scripture. Scripture, especially parables, should be interpreted according to the most obvious intent (Irenaeus *Adv. haer.* 2.27.1), especially since "the entire Scriptures, the prophets, and the Gospels, can be clearly, unambiguously, and harmoniously understood by all" (Ibid., 2.27.2). Similarly, eschatological texts should be taken literally and not allegorically, fitting in with Irenaeus' general distaste for allegory (Ibid., 5.35.1). Where difficulties remain in interpreting a text, types should be sought out (Ibid., 4.31.1), especially before allegory is utilized (Ibid., 5.35.2). Furthermore, plain texts should be used to interpret obscure texts (Ibid., 2.28.3).

lates the truth, but also sifts out the foreign matter and refuse concocted by the heretics.[35] The Scriptures, the tradition present in the *regula*, and the church, therefore, all have their parts to play in maintaining the continuity of the apostolic message and in confining the seeking intellect to the genuine truth that their message contains.

In summary, the believer need not and should not delve into questions outside the basic parameters of the *regula*, and one certainly must not exceed the bounds of Scripture. Of the three fathers being addressed, Irenaeus tends to stay closest to the biblical text, preferring scriptural vocabulary to develop ideas he sees as directly attributable, or at least conformable, to the *regula* and Scripture.

---

[35] Ibid., 1.9.4.

Chapter 4

A Functional Theology

Irenaeus' reliance upon biblical concepts and vocabulary places him solidly within the Pauline and Johannine traditions of the New Testament.[1] He draws extensively from Paul's Adam Christology to formulate his theory of recapitulation and follows such predecessors as Justin Martyr in utilizing the Logos Christology, though in a different form than that of the Apologists. This dependence on the New Testament, together with a strong emphasis upon the *oikonomia* and recapitulation, results in a high Christology that is largely defined in dynamic or functional terms. As anticipated in the analysis of Irenaeus' *regulae*, Jesus Christ is included within the unique divine identity while playing the most prominent role in the *oikonomia*, the saving work of God which "embraces both creation and the end, and puts the Christ-event in the middle."[2]

The *Oikonomia*

From the very beginning with creation by God through His Word and His Wisdom, the Son and the Spirit, the *oikonomia* is Irenaeus' way of maintaining and displaying the tension within Trinitarian theology. Irenaeus strictly adheres to a monotheistic faith, repeatedly stating both in his *regulae* and elsewhere that

---

[1] See Osborn, *Irenaeus of Lyons*, 186, 190.

[2] Aloys Grillmeier, *Christ in Christian Tradition: Vol. 1 From the Apostolic Age to Chalcedon (451)*, 2nd rev. ed., trans. John Bowden (Atlanta, GA: John Knox Press, 1975), 101. "Too large for exact definition, *oikonomia* can be taken as the ruling metaphor which holds Irenaeus' theology together." Osborn, *Irenaeus of Lyons*, 78. "The unfolding of this economy, salvation history, is centred on, and culminates in, Christ: what has gone before typifies its realization in him, as he realizes what will be wrought in those who follow him. For Irenaeus, both protology and eschatology are Christocentric: man, from his initial formation and throughout the pedagogy of the economy, can be understood only in the light of Christ." John Behr, *Asceticism and Anthropology in Irenaeus and Clement* (New York: Oxford University Press, 2000), 85. Cf. Alfred Bengsch, *Heilsgeschichte und Heilswissen* (Leipzig: St. Benno-Verlag, 1957), 74; F. R. Montgomery Hitchcock, *Irenaeus of Lugdunum* (Cambridge: University Press, 1914), 128.

there is "one God the Father, who made all things by Himself."[3] Distinguishing himself from the Gnostics and polytheism, Irenaeus never compromises on the Christian belief in the singularity of the Godhead.

Nevertheless, it is equally clear that the inclusion of the Son of God in the unique divine identity results in christological monotheism and multiplicity within the Godhead. Creation is a work of the Trinity, enacted by the Father through the Son and the Spirit. He is the "one only God, the Creator ... who made those things by Himself, that is, through His Word and His Wisdom." The Son and the Spirit are his hands, the instruments of creation, and clearly God himself. The fact that "the Son eternally co-exist[s] with the Father [*semper autem coexsistens Filius Patri*], from of old, yea, from the beginning [*ab initio*]" only confirms his inclusion in the unique divine identity. So in the same passages on creation both the oneness of God and his threeness are asserted without hesitation.[4] It is not surprising, therefore, when "one God and his Son" or "one God and his Word" become common statements of God's multiplicity within singularity.[5]

The work of God through his hands does not end with creation but continues through all the dispensations of the *oikonomia*. All of creation is ruled and sustained by God's Word and Wisdom, just as Enoch and Elijah were taken into heaven by the same hands that created them.[6] God's actions throughout history from creation until the eschaton are the result of God's hands, his Word and Wisdom, at work. In the midst of this history, at the pinnacle of the *oikonomia*, "by the good pleasure of the Father, His hands formed a living man [i.e. Jesus Christ], in order that Adam might be created again [*ēenētai ho Adam*] after the

---

[3] Irenaeus *Adv. haer.* 4.36.1. See also ibid., 1.10.1; 1.22.1; 3.4.2; 5.20.1; 2.30.9; 3.6.4; 4.20.4.

[4] Ibid., 2.30.9. See also ibid., 3.24.2; 4.20.1-2; 4.20.4; 5.18.2; John Behr, *Asceticism and Anthropology*, 38; M. C. Steenberg, *Irenaeus on Creation: The Cosmic Christ and the Saga of Redemption* (Boston: Brill, 2008), 63-65.

[5] Irenaeus *Adv. haer.* 3.1.2; 3.6.5; 3.12.8; 3.15.3; 3.16.6; 4.pref.4; 4.1.1; 4.6.7; 4.28.2; 5.18.2. Albert Houssiau evaluates this Trinitarian tension in Irenaeus and shows the connection that he makes between creation and salvation. "The responses of Irenaeus are eminently varied. Two series of texts are presented to us. The first demonstrates the transcendence of creator God, who created all things by himself, that is to say through his Word; God is therefore 'not necessitous': he does not need instruments distinct from himself.

... The second series of texts presents to the contrary an immediate concern for the study of Christology; it exploits directly the double role assigned to the Word by the prologue of John: ...

The oneness of God proceeds therefore to the role of the Word in creation and salvation: in both venues God works through the Word or, more simply, the Word works in both venues. The union and the distinction of the two orders, this concerning creation and that concerning salvation, are expressed in the relation between the creator Word and the incarnate Word" [trans. mine]. Albert Houssiau, *La christologie de Saint Irénée* (Louvain: Publications Universitaires de Louvain, 1955), 107.

[6] Irenaeus *Adv. haer.* 5.6.1.

image [*eikona*] and likeness [*homoiōsin*] of God."[7] The enactment of God's plan of salvation, therefore, is the distinct work of the three persons of God according to his single will.

Among the most significant functions of this distinct work are the revelation of God to humanity and the facilitation of humanity's intimate knowledge of God. The most obvious form of this revelation was the incarnation of the Son of God, when Jesus Christ himself bore witness "that in Himself they [the disciples] had both known and seen the Father."[8] Some form of incarnation was essential for humanity to know the Father since "no other being had the power of revealing to us the things of the Father, except His own proper Word."[9] The invisible became visible so that finite man might know the invisible Father. But the revelation of God by the Word was not limited to the incarnation, "for by means of the creation itself, the Word reveals God the Creator." Furthermore, the Law and the Prophets are the preaching of the Word of God that reveal both the Father and the Word himself to those who hear. Essentially, every witness to God is a result of the work of the Word, the Son of God, whether preincarnate or incarnate.[10]

Besides revealing the Father in a visible, tangible form, the Son grants humanity the opportunity to know and love the Father in an intimate way. It is the Son of God who enables humans to respond to God's revelation of himself, for not "without the agency of the Son [*tēs diakonias tou Uiou*], can any man know God [*gnōsetai tis ton Theon*]."[11] This intimate knowledge of God is life itself, and the means for granting this life is the Son of God himself. The Son leads those who believe in him to the Father, and seeing the Father, believers receive the splendor of God and are vivified. To know and see God intimately through faith in the Son of God, therefore, is to receive "the means of life ... found in fellowship with God."[12]

Everything that the Son of God does in revealing God to humanity and restoring humanity to fellowship with God is done according to the will and fore-

---

[7] Ibid., 5.1.3. See also Hitchcock, 108, 111.

[8] Irenaeus *Adv. haer.* 3.13.2; John 14:7-10.

[9] Irenaeus *Adv. haer.* 5.1.1. "Christology is the place for the revelation of the eternal Trinity" [trans. mine]. Bernard Sesboüé, *Tout récapituler dans le Christ: Christologie et sotériologie d'Irénée de Lyon* (Paris: Desclée, 2000), 66.

[10] Irenaeus *Adv. haer.* 4.6.6; 2.9.1; 4.7.2-3. "He is not saying that only Christ is a revelation of the Father, to the exclusion of revelation in nature, but he is insisting that all the forms of divine self-revelation are by the agency of the Son. He is thus clear witness to the absoluteness of Christ in the knowledge of the Father. Although he never specifically addressed the question, it is clear that Irenaeus would not conceive of revelations found in non-Christian religions as *alternative* means of knowing God *apart from* revelation through the Son. Whatever knowledge of God might be had by means of Hinduism or Buddhism would have to be mediated by Christ and be the result of the Father's will to make himself known to them for salvation." Terrance L. Tiessen, *Irenaeus on the Salvation of the Unevangelized* (Metuchen, NJ: Scarecrow Press, 1993), 131.

[11] Irenaeus *Adv. haer.* 4.7.3.

[12] Irenaeus *Adv. haer.* 4.20.5.

knowledge of the Father. The *oikonomia*, God's plan of salvation, is thoroughly trinitarian, "the Father planning everything well and giving His commands, the Son carrying these into execution and performing the work of creating, and the Spirit nourishing and increasing [what is made]."[13] This great plan of God, beginning with creation and culminating in the *anakephalaiosis* or recapitulation in Christ as the second Adam, will conclude with the return of Christ, judgment, and the bestowment of immortality upon man. At that point "the Son will yield up His work to the Father" and the *oikonomia* will be complete according to the original will and desire of God as spoken by the Father through his hands, his Word and Wisdom.[14]

The *Logos* and the Son of God

Although the *oikonomia* obviously influences the self-revelation of the Son of God as he manifests himself in different ways, it is not determinative for his being as God. Instead, the Son's involvement in the events of the *oikonomia* portrays elements of his eternal nature and being. This is most obvious in the Son's role as savior and redeemer. Humanity's need for a savior did not determine or demand that the Son take on the nature of a savior. On the contrary, since "He had a pre-existence as a saving Being [*prouparchontos gar tou sōzontos*]" humanity was created in order that God might express himself through the Son as Savior.[15]

More significant than this preexistence as a saving being is the eternality of the Word, the Son of God. The Word is not a created being but a participant in the unique divine identity. Those err who attempt to assign "a beginning [*prolationis initium*] and course of production [*genesim*]" to him since it is little more than an attempt to "transfer the generation of the word to which men g[i]ve utterance [*generationem prolatiui hominem uerbi*] to the eternal Word of God [*Dei aeternum Verbum*]."[16] Humanity's concept of the spoken word is insufficient to describe the eternality of the Word who became incarnate as Jesus Christ. The analogy of human speech fails to communicate that God's Word precedes all of creation, is himself uncreated and has no beginning, and eternally co-exists with the Father.[17]

The Word's eternal preexistence prompts speculative questions for many as to the nature of his being, but for Irenaeus the existence of the *Logos* and his generation is to be left as a mystery except where specifically addressed by Scripture. Even our inability to find an adequate word or phrase shows that "no man understands that production [*prolationem*], or generation [*generationem*],

---

[13] Ibid., 4.38.3. See also ibid., 3.16.7.
[14] Ibid., 5.36.2.
[15] Ibid., 3.22.3. Cf. Behr, *Asceticism and Anthropology*, 60; Osborn, *Irenaeus of Lyons*, 219; Steenberg, *Irenaeus on Creation*, 34.
[16] Irenaeus *Adv. haer.* 2.13.8.
[17] Ibid., 2.25.3; 2.30.9; 4.14.1; 4.20.1, 3.

or calling [*nuncupationem*], or revelation [*adapertionem*], or by whatever name one may describe His generation, which is in fact altogether indescribable [*inenarrabilem*]."[18] Therefore, "we should leave things of that nature to God who created us" and depend entirely upon the Scriptures, the words of which have been given by the Son and the Spirit.[19] On the matter of the Son's generation Irenaeus sees Scripture as particularly clear when he reads "Who shall describe His generation?" and interprets it as a rhetorical question with the answer "no one."[20]

Despite this perceived prohibition against speculation, Irenaeus' exploration into the existence of the Son of God, especially in his preincarnate state, incorporates portions of the Logos Christology of Justin Martyr and the Apologists. Nevertheless, he does little to develop this christological perspective and limits its use in comparison to many of his predecessors. The idea of an innate Word within God is adjusted to say that God is "all Mind [*totus exsistens Mens*], and all Logos [*totus exsistens Logos*]," he "both speaks [*loquitur*] exactly what He thinks [*cogitat*], and thinks [*cogitat*] exactly what He speaks [*loquitur*]." The emphasis, therefore, is not that the Word is distinct within the mind of God but that he *is* God. The distinction between the *Logos endiathetos* and the *Logos prophorikos*, the innate word and the spoken word, in its concern with the preexistent being of the Son, is speculative and inappropriate. It draws too extensively from the common analogy between man's *logos* and the *Logos* of God. The one attempting to find congruity between the words of God and human words not only reveals his ignorance of the divine, but also evidences his ignorance of the mundane.[21]

It is enough to know from Scripture that the Son was with the Father from the beginning and that they eternally co-exist. That the Son "was always with" the Father seems to imply the eternal generation of the Son, but that later theological language is not part of Irenaeus' conclusions, and there is no attempt to define the Son's preexistence beyond the mere statement of fact. One is left with an essentially economic understanding of the relationship between the Father and the Son and the Son's generation. Substantial ontological inquiry would lead to "another" god when one should lean on Scripture to know that "the Son was as a beginning for God before the world was made, but for us [*nobis autem*], [his beginning was] at the time of His appearance [*manifestatus est*], but before that He did not exist for us [*ante hoc autem nobis non erat*], in that we knew Him not [*qui non cognoscebamus eum*]."[22] What can be known about God has been revealed in God's *oikonomia* through the Son's incarnation and the work of the Spirit.

---

[18] Ibid., 2.28.6.
[19] Ibid., 2.28.2.
[20] Ibid., 2.28.5; *Dem.* 70. Cf. Isa. 53:8.
[21] Irenaeus *Adv. haer.* 2.28.4-5. Cf. Robert M. Grant, *Jesus after the Gospels: The Christ of the Second Century* (Louisville, KY: John Knox Press, 1990), 101; Houssiau, 165; Osborn, *Irenaeus of Lyons*, 90, 111; Tiessen, 128.
[22] Irenaeus *Dem.* 43.

Creation

While the *oikonomia* is not fully revealed until the incarnation, there are traces of it throughout the Old Testament beginning with creation. This saving plan of God explicates an economic Trinity manifested especially through the work of the Son and the Spirit. The Father is on the one hand transcendent, the source and fount of the Godhead, and unapproachable from a human perspective. In this respect, the Son and the Spirit are the means by which God reveals himself to mankind. On the other hand, the Father's immanence is evident in works like creation, where his intimate involvement contrasts with the distance of the Demiurge and other heretical notions of God.

The *oikonomia* begins with the creation of the universe by "the only God, the only Lord, the only Creator, the only Father, alone containing all things [*solus continens omnia*], and Himself commanding all things into existence [*omnibus ut sint ipse praestans*]."[23] There is no other being with whom God can be compared, for he formed everything, whether visible or invisible, without necessity and *ex nihilo*. He made all things freely, desiring only "that He might have some one upon whom to confer His benefits."[24] Creation was a gracious benevolent act of God for which there was no necessity. Furthermore, he created *ex nihilo*, having no preexisting substance with which to work. This contrasts with the Gnostic deities that created by means of emanations from their own being or from emissions of passion and feeling.[25] Similarly, God has "from Himself the model and figure of those things which have been made" and does not require a form for creation, unlike the Gnostic Demiurge who needs a form to shape the matter before him as would a simple craftsman. While Gnosticism is unable to explain the origin of form and has great difficulty with the origin of matter, the true origin of both rests within the mind of God who created without compunction and resource.[26]

This one true God "made and fashioned everything, and brought being out of nothing" by means of "His own hands." "The Word and Wisdom, the Son and the Spirit," are his hands "by whom and in whom ... He made all things" with-

---

[23] Irenaeus *Adv. haer.* 2.1.1. See also ibid., 2.30.6, 9.

[24] Ibid., 4.14.1. See also ibid., 2.2.4-5; 2.30.9.

[25] Ibid., 2.10.4; Osborn, *Irenaeus of Lyons*, 52. "In the recounting of the Nag Hammadi codex, the demiurge is ultimately powerless to create an image of God, and as such he produces only lifeless, material objectifications of his personal defect.... In the scriptural text, however, it is precisely the 'true God' who does fashion the creature, and who does so as an iconic manifestation of his own being. The same God who had the power to create the cosmos, not from previously existing matter but *ex nihilo*, out of nothing (the chief witness of his omnipotence), is he who now fashions the human person in his own image." M. C. Steenberg, *Of God and Man: Theology as Anthropology from Irenaeus to Athanasius* (New York: T&T Clark, 2009), 32.

[26] Irenaeus *Adv. haer.* 4.20.1.

out necessity.[27] The Word is clearly the instrument of God's creative work as Irenaeus interprets the prologue of John and David's words in the Psalms.[28] But the Word is more than the instrumental cause of creation and the means for the self-revelation of God. The Word "contains all things [*sunechōn ta panta*]," an action that is elsewhere attributed to the one God alone.[29] All things exist and move according to the divine will and desire of the Word of God. Furthermore, he is "always present with mankind [*aei sumparonta tē anthrōpotēti*]" as is most evident in his incarnation and work of recapitulation.[30]

The redemption of humanity in Jesus Christ is a re-creation that bears with it several analogies with the original creation. When the Son of God comes as the second Adam to recapitulate humanity, he is born without a human father just as he himself created the first Adam without a human forebear. As Creator of the first man the Word is himself ideally suited in his incarnate state to bring humanity to its intended existence as the second Adam. In fact, the re-creation of humanity is predestined before creation and prefigured within the original creation. Before the Word created, God "predestined that the first man should be of an animal nature [*ton psuchikon anthrōpon*], with this view, that he might be saved by the spiritual One [*hina hupo tou pneumatikou sōthē*]."[31] In a sense, God did not become man in order to fix the original creation; rather, he created in order to provide for the completion of his plan in Christ's work of recapitulation ultimately fulfilled in the eschaton.

Incarnation and Recapitulation

The incarnation, the central activity of the *oikonomia*, did not take place in a vacuum. The Word contains all things and is continually active in human history. Prior to the incarnation he revealed himself to the patriarchs and prophets and provided the words of the Law and Prophets that make up Scripture.[32] He is the same Word of God who "produced both covenants, ... who spoke with both

---

[27] Irenaeus *Dem.* 4; *Adv. haer.* 4.20.1. See also *Adv. haer.* 4.pref. 4; 5.1.3; 5.6.1; Osborn, *Irenaeus of Lyons*, 53; Steenberg, *Irenaeus on Creation*, 80-84. The close relationship between the Son and the Spirit ("His own hands") is also seen in the incarnation through the Spirit's anointing of Jesus' human nature and the Spirit's ongoing participation in salvation. Anthony Briggman, *Irenaeus of Lyons and the Theology of the Holy Spirit*, (New York: Oxford Univ. Press, 2012), 73-77.

[28] Irenaeus *Adv. haer.* 2.2.5; 3.8.3; 3.11.2; Ps. 33:6, 9; 115:3; 148:5; John 1.

[29] Ibid., 3.11.8. See also ibid., 2.1.1; 4.20.2.

[30] Ibid., 3.18.1.

[31] Ibid., 3.22.3.

[32] Irenaeus distinguishes between four phases of the Word's activity beginning with his self-revelation to the patriarchs and through the Law. The third and fourth phases are the incarnation and the sending of the Spirit following Christ's ascension. D. Jeffrey Bingham, *Irenaeus' Use of Matthew's Gospel in Adversus Haereses* (Louvain: Peeters, 1998), 83.

Abraham and Moses, and who has restored us anew to liberty."[33] These two covenants are not separate works connected by a common author. They work in unity, "for the fundamental exigency of the law is the same as that for the gospel, 'to accompany the Word;' and more, the law itself is to concede to the Word, the bestower of the two testaments, who is the author of servitude as he is of freedom; the servitude of the law ceases with the incarnate presence of its Lord" [trans. mine].[34] Not only is the Creator of the world the Father of Jesus Christ, but the Son of God is himself the Creator, the lawgiver, the source of prophecy, and the fulfillment of each respectively. In becoming incarnate the Son of God fulfills the prophecy he inspired, in his life and death he completes the law he commanded, and by means of his perfect life as both God and man he perfects the creation he made.

Jesus Christ, the only begotten incarnate Son of God, is both fully divine and fully human. Against the Ebionites who deny his deity, Jesus Christ is the eternal Word of God who created all things and gave life to humanity.[35] At the other extreme, the Gnostics are in error to deny Christ's complete humanity, suggesting instead that he only appeared to be human or distinguishing between a human Jesus and a spiritual Christ. The angels correctly informed the shepherds of the real birth of the child Jesus, and Paul knew only the completely physical and human Christ who "died for our sins, according to the Scriptures."[36] His saving work would have been without value if he had only appeared to eat, fast, bleed, suffer, die, and rise again.[37] Likewise, at the baptism Christ did not "descend upon Jesus, neither was Christ one and Jesus another: but the Word of God ... was made Jesus Christ."[38] Jesus Christ is one undivided person, both God and man, and those who teach otherwise are wolves in sheep's clothing seeking to devour believers.[39]

Christ's humanity was formed in the exact manner as was the original man's, "by the Will and Wisdom of God [*voluntate et sapientia Dei*], ... according to

---

[33] Irenaeus *Adv. haer.* 4.9.1. See also ibid., 3.6.1; 4.2.3; 4.5.2-4; 4.10.2; 5.17.2; Bingham, 171, 181.

[34] Houssiau, 114, 117.

[35] Irenaeus *Adv. haer.* 5.1.3.

[36] Ibid., 3.10.3; 3.18.3.

[37] Ibid., 3.22.1-2; 5.1.2.

[38] Ibid., 3.9.3. See also ibid., 3.16.2, 6. "No variance of essence exists between the Word, Saviour, universal ruler, Jesus, the one made flesh, and the one anointed by the Father with the Spirit." Bingham, 118.

[39] Irenaeus *Adv. haer.* 3.16.8. Even though Chalcedonian language is not yet available, Irenaeus also affirms Jesus Christ's continuing existence in two natures in his understanding of Jesus' anointing by the Holy Spirit. Jesus "needed the anointing of the Spirit to empower his humanity so that he could fulfill the Messianic mission, but he did not need a similar empowerment with respect to his divinity." Briggman, 62.

the image and likeness of God [*secundum imaginem et similitudinem Dei*]."[40] The Will and Wisdom of God refer to the hands of God, revealing the participation of the three in the virginal conception. Humanity's pristine state was completely recreated in the incarnation. Christ's life was then lived in direct opposition to Adam's, bringing about the incorruptibility and maturity of the fully human. One, therefore, cannot say that Adam preceded Christ, for "in Adam the Word prefigured, sketched out in advance, the fullness of the human being that would be manifested in the economy of the Incarnation."[41] Adam was modeled after the true human being, Jesus Christ, who is the true beginning as both the Creator of humanity and the fulfillment of his intent for humanity.

The birth, life, death, and resurrection of Jesus constitute the climax and pinnacle of the *oikonomia*, the means by which Jesus Christ recapitulates mankind, and his central contribution to the *oikonomia*. In the incarnation Jesus Christ recreates humanity and provides the possibility of incorruptibility lost in the garden of Eden by uniting humanity and deity in himself and passing "through every stage of life, restoring to all communion with God."[42] He experienced everything that humanity experiences from birth through old age, living to be fifty years old according to Irenaeus, in order that he might save all in accordance with their circumstances.[43]

In taking up humanity in himself, the Son of God relives Adam's life in obedience to God according to the original intent. On the one hand, Adam, the seminal head of the human race, disobeyed and received death as a result of eating from the tree. Jesus Christ, the second Adam, on the other hand, recapitulates humanity in a life of obedience and brings life to humanity by partaking of death on a tree.[44] By this obedience he fulfills "all the conditions of human nature," summing "up in Himself the whole human race from the beginning to the end," including humanity's death.[45] Even more, the incarnation and Jesus' life, death, and resurrection are the "summing up [of] all things in Himself" so that he might be sovereign and supreme over both the invisible and visible, incomprehensible and comprehensible, and the impassible and changeable.[46] The single life that

---

[40] Irenaeus *Dem.* 32; *Adv. haer.* 3.21.10. "His birth of the Virgin Mary testifies to Christ's humanity. If God had allowed Jesus to be born as the son of an ordinary husband and wife, as all the descendants of Adam were born, His birth would have been unlike Adam's, and would have had no similarity to the creation of man. Mary's virginity bears witness to Christ's resemblance to Adam, i.e., to His humanity." Gustaf Wingren, *Man and the Incarnation: A Study in the Biblical Theology of Irenaeus*, trans. Ross Mackenzie (Edinburgh: Oliver & Boyd, 1959), 97.

[41] Behr, *Asceticism and Anthropology*, 58, 61-2. See also Sesboüé, 187; Steenberg, *Irenaeus on Creation*, 110.

[42] Irenaeus *Adv. haer.* 3.18.7. Note the important distinction that "the union of man with God does not produce the person of Christ; rather, it is the mediation of Christ, which brings together God and man." Osborn, *Irenaeus of Lyons*, 113.

[43] Irenaeus *Adv. haer.* 2.22.4-6; 3.18.7; 4.38.2; Grant, *Irenaeus of Lyons*, 33.

[44] Irenaeus *Adv. haer.* 3.18.6; 5.16.3.

[45] Ibid., 3.17.4; 5.23.2. See also ibid., 3.22.3.

[46] Ibid., 3.16.6. See also ibid., 3.21.9; 4.38.1; 5.18.3; 5.21.1.

fulfills prophecy and perfectly adheres to the law is the same lived life that confirms the Son's absolute sovereignty over all of creation.

It is this dominion over both the mutable and immutable that allows the Son of God the unique ability to "accustom man to receive God [*ethisē ton anthrōpon chōrein Theon*], and God to dwell in man [*ethisē de kai ton Theon skēoun en anthrōpōi*]."[47] Apart from Jesus Christ, humans are unable to comprehend the Father much less enjoy communion with him. In his incarnation Jesus Christ became "what we are [*gegonoti touto hoper esmen hēmeis*], that He might bring us to be [*hēmas inai katartisē*] even what He is Himself [*estin autos*]." In so doing he gives us the capacity not only to endure the glory of the Father, but also to comprehend it and flourish within it.[48] In fact, Jesus Christ bestows on humanity the incomprehensible opportunity "to partake of the divine nature [*chōrein Theou*]."[49] The union of God and man in the person of Jesus Christ means far more for humanity than the simple paying of a ransom, a legal description of justification, or victory over an adversary, though it entails all that and more.[50] In the intimate communion realized in Jesus Christ man finds the source of all meaning and purpose, the restoration of his nature not to its pristine state but to its intended state of maturity.

By "attaching man to God [*eis Theon de palin anagagontos ton anthrōpon*] by His own incarnation [*dia tēs idias sarkōseōs*]" Christ bestows upon humanity the immortality and incorruption that comes with partaking of the divine nature and communion with God.[51] Even in his pristine state man was unable to bear the glory of God or possess immortality and incorruptibility in his own nature. It is only by means of union with the immortal and incorruptible that humanity can receive it, and that can only take place when incorruptibility and immortality are brought to humanity and not vice versa.[52] Man cannot achieve it on his own effort or merit because of his mortal nature, presumably even in his pristine state. For people to know God it is necessary for God to condescend to their level and reveal himself to them in an intimate way.

---

[47] Ibid., 3.20.2. "Apart from the designating conditions in the preliminary remarks of the true humanity (Incarnation) and the true human being (Obedience) the Redeemer must fulfill an additional condition, in humanity (and the Creator altogether) to be able to find salvation. He must be *true* God, then God can redeem all. Jesus Christ fulfills all three conditions, and therefore is the *mediator* between God and men" [trans. mine]. Daniel Wanke, *Das Kreuz Christi bei Irenaeus von Lyon* (New York: Walter de Gruyter, 2000), 189.

[48] Irenaeus *Adv. haer.* 5.pref. See also ibid., 4.20.4; 5.35.1.

[49] Ibid., 5.32.1. See also ibid., 4.28.2; 4.33.4.

[50] "The complexity of the concept [recapitulation] is formidable. At least eleven ideas–unification, repetition, redemption, perfection, inauguration and consummation, totality, the triumph of Christus Victor, ontology, epistemology and ethics (or being, truth and goodness)–are combined in different permutations. Are all these ideas necessary to the concept? Even together they are an understatement, because everything that God does is part of his economy and every part of his economy is defined in relation to its recapitulation." Osborn, *Irenaeus of Lyons*, 97-8.

[51] Irenaeus *Adv. haer.* 5.1.1. See also ibid., 3.5.3; 4.20.2; 5.32.1.

[52] Ibid., 3.19.1; 4.38.4.

In condescending to humanity and restoring communion God effectively "abolished death, vivifying that man who had been in a state of death."[53] This vivification takes place as humanity sees God, is in God, and receives God's splendor, for it is God's presence, his glory, that grants real life and being just as it renders humanity incorruptible.[54] Christ's atoning death not only results in humanity's revivification and the end of death, but it also frees us from enslavement to the devil. Since man lost his freedom as a result of disobedience and sin, the cords by which Satan holds him, it is through Jesus Christ's obedience as a man in the face of Satan's temptation that Satan himself is bound and man is freed.[55] When Satan is bound humanity receives back "what we had lost in Adam—namely, to be according to the image and likeness of God," and to receive our adoption as the sons of God.[56]

Whether it is described as ransoming captives, victory over Satan, adoption as sons, justification, revivification, or the granting of incorruptibility and immortality, the salvific work of Jesus Christ finds its completion in his ultimate sovereignty over all of creation. "Even as the Word of God had the sovereignty in the heavens, so also might He have the sovereignty in earth" by his sinless life, his death, and his status as the first-born from the dead.[57] The incarnation of the Son of God and his recapitulation of humanity fulfill both prophecy predicting his coming and the requirements of the law. But more importantly, in his coming Christ perfects his own creation, thereby completing what was originally intended. In so doing, the Son of God "joined the beginning to the end [*tēn archēn tōi telei sunēte*], and is the Lord of both," showing again that he is not only the Savior and Revealer of God to humanity, but also the instrumental cause of creation, its sustainer, its perfecter, and its sovereign Lord.[58]

The Eschaton

While Jesus' work of redemption is complete with his ascension, the recapitulation of humanity and the *oikonomia* are not complete until the return of Christ and the judgment. The Creator's intent for human beings—a state of incorruptibility, immortality, and participation in the divine nature—is fulfilled in the eschaton when Jesus Christ stands as judge of creation and finishes what he started.

The judgment he presaged in his life on earth, and which he enacts eschatologically, "is more severe than any other, yet more gentle than any other." Its severity is in its eternal nature and in the fact that it is judgment of thoughts and words in addition to actions. At the same time Christ's judgment, especially in

---

[53] Ibid., 3.23.1, 7.
[54] Ibid., 4.20.5.
[55] Ibid., 3.23.1; 5.21.3; *Dem.* 31, 34, 38.
[56] Irenaeus *Adv. haer.* 3.18.1. See also ibid., 3.10.2; 3.19.1.
[57] Ibid., 4.20.2.
[58] Ibid., 4.34.4; 4.20.4.

his earthly ministry, is tempered by the love in which he invites the poor and destitute to come to himself.[59] In his incarnation "He did not judge according to glory" but preached repentance and granted forgiveness to the humble and those who mourned.[60] Nevertheless, the day is quickly coming when he will exercise his sovereign rule and responsibility and hold all accountable for their actions. At present he sits at the right hand of the Father in the place of authority and sovereignty, "supreme over all the living and dead."[61] But at the appointed time Christ will return "in the same flesh in which He suffered" in order to bring all things to their proper conclusion.[62]

At the end, the Son of God will "descend from heaven in His Father's power and pass judgment upon all."[63] Since the Judge is the same Son who came to reveal the Father, all will recognize him, those judged for their sins and those granted his gift of glory.[64] All will be raised to receive the consequences of their own free decisions, the believing to receive life in communion with God, the unbelieving to receive separation from God and the damnation they have freely chosen. This separation from God "is death, and separation from light is darkness; and separation from God consists in the loss of all the benefits which He has in store."[65] The righteous, on the other hand, will be resurrected to a life of eternal communion with God and endowed with immortality and incorruptibility. Jesus' miracles of resuscitation and his own resurrection are guarantees of the believer's bodily resurrection. The same Creator who formed humans in the beginning will restore them on the day of judgment and raise each one bodily to a new life in communion with God.[66]

This final judgment will bring the *oikonomia* to completion. The end will be as God designed in the beginning, six thousand years for Irenaeus, "for in as many days as this world was made, in so many thousand years shall it be concluded."[67] In this conclusion humanity will have ascended to the Son through the Spirit and to the Father through the Son, and finally, at the end the Son will return his authority and labors to the Father, fulfilling the divine plan of salvation.[68]

---

[59] Wingren, 136-7. See also Bingham, 235.
[60] Irenaeus *Adv. haer.* 3.9.3.
[61] Ibid., 3.16.3. See also ibid., 2.28.7; 3.10.5; 3.12.13; 3.16.9.
[62] Ibid., 3.16.8.
[63] Ibid., 3.5.3.
[64] Ibid., 3.9.1. "Irenaeus seeks to resolve the theological problem of the justice and the goodness of God in presenting the two comings of Christ as complementary. In the one, Christ comes with mildness, in the other he appears as Judge. The mildness of Christ in his human life compensates for his severity in his glorious coming. In reality it is in the same judicial coming and in the idea of judgment that Irenaeus finds the solution" [trans. mine]. Houssiau, 137. Cf. Wingren, 136-7.
[65] Irenaeus *Adv. haer.* 5.27.1-2
[66] Ibid., 5.3.2; 5.7.1; 5.31.2.
[67] Ibid., 5.28.3.
[68] Ibid., 5.36.2. See also Behr, *Asceticism and Anthropology*, 57.

The *Regula* and Economic Language

The dominant place of the *oikonomia* in Irenaeus' theology is one factor contributing to the predominance of functional language in his theology. Tertullian and Origen rely upon the same christological core, but to varying degrees they explain it using additional metaphysical vocabulary. Irenaeus' hermeneutic also helps to explain his functional emphases and his distaste for the speculative. This refusal to speculate and his correlative reliance upon concrete concepts are not necessarily deficiencies in Irenaeus' theology.

The strong soteriological emphasis of Irenaeus' theology, a point closely related to his understanding of the *oikonomia*, also explains in part his distaste for speculation. Irenaeus' polemic against the Gnostics and other heretics is not intended as a defense of a body of knowledge for its own sake. This polemic is meant to defend the truth "so that men and women no longer may be led astray."[69] His primary concern is the salvation of people who otherwise might be led to destruction by the false teachings of the heretics. Irenaeus is not as concerned with who God is as much as he is concerned that God is *for humanity*. Preeminent in this concern is Jesus Christ's existence as both God and man. *That* he is both God and man is essential soteriologically since man's obedience and maturation is required for salvation and God alone is able to fulfill his righteous requirements and enable participation in the divine nature. Nevertheless, explaining *how* Christ can be both God and man is inconsequential when its truth can be accepted with authority from the Scriptures and tradition. Economic language, therefore, naturally dominates much of Irenaeus' theology, especially when soteriology is involved.

Irenaeus' acceptance of Scripture's authority, together with his ties to the still strong oral tradition of the apostles, adds to his strong reliance upon economic or functional language. His relatively close temporal proximity to the apostles increases the value of simply repeating their words where others later would have to interpret, paraphrase, and translate their words more extensively. The dominance of functional language in the New Testament, therefore, easily carries over into Irenaeus' theology. Furthermore, his early place in doctrinal development and explication leaves him fewer challenges to address. Heresies such as modalism and Arianism, which are often couched in metaphysical language and categories, are not yet on the theological scene, at least in definitive forms. Irenaeus can address the concerns of his period adequately by simply disclosing the errors of his opposition and pronouncing the truth through quotations from Scripture and the apostles.

Irenaeus' strong reliance on the *regula* can be explained by his soteriological emphasis and his belief in the authority of Scripture and its sole possession by the church. The *regula*, a reliable, authoritative, and tangible part of the church's tradition, serves as a hermeneutical tool for the proper understanding of Scrip-

---

[69] Irenaeus *Adv. haer.* 1.pref.3.

ture. It lays out in very concrete, functional terms the basic beliefs of the Christian faith, thereby stating the standard by which Scripture should be interpreted. Furthermore, it functions as a basic explanation of the way of salvation, driving Irenaeus' soteriological intentions. Even apart from the Scriptures one might come to salvation by means of the tradition. The barbarians spoken of in *Adv. haer.* 3.4.2 recognize misleading heresy with only the *regula*. More importantly, they are able to draw from the tradition "the water of life" and receive for themselves the salvation given by God in Christ. The *regula*, one strain of "the preaching of the Church," is their source of authority and life and "is true and steadfast, in which one and the same way of salvation is shown throughout the whole world."[70]

The *regula fidei*, a control on the interpretation of Scripture and the essential content of the Christian faith, is critical to the early interpretation of Scripture, the resulting theology, and the manner in which it is communicated and sustained in the church. For Irenaeus it provides the basic parameters for weeding out heresy and carries the content of the faith that is common in all the churches throughout the world. In Irenaeus' pastoral hands its use in interpreting Scripture results in a theology dominated by economic language that emphasizes soteriology and relies on Scripture extensively. His language is remote from the language later used in the christological controversies; nevertheless, he "anticipates for his part Ephesus (the unity of Christ) and Chalcedon (the unity of the two natures)." In so doing he "leaves behind him an immense speculative quarry" [trans. mine] from which others may work.[71] Some of this remains the case in Tertullian, though his place in history moves him closer to the conciliar conclusions to come, and differing contexts and varying styles adjust some of his emphases.

---

[70] Ibid., 5.20.1.
[71] Sesboüé, 81. See also ibid., 67.

Part Three

Tertullian's Transitional Theology

Chapter 5

Theological Elaboration Upon the *Regula*

As with the bishop of Lyons, Tertullian often addresses heresy, though from a different perspective. Where Irenaeus is a bishop with pastoral concerns, Tertullian is more blatantly polemical. He has a sharp and biting style that he uses to good effect in his apologetical and polemical works. Tradition has identified him as a lawyer, in part because of this aggressive style, but this has never been confirmed. He was born in the middle of the second century into a pagan family in Carthage, but converted to Christianity as a middle-aged adult. Sometime around the turn of the third century he joined the Montanists, a schismatic group that emphasized the work of the Spirit and followed the leadership and teachings of Montanus and two prophetesses, Priscilla and Maximilla. Several of his extant works are from this Montanist period.

Whatever his occupation, Tertullian is well educated, showing an awareness of the philosophies of his day and demonstrating rhetorical skill. Some of his works are addressed to fellow believers, exhorting them to remain holy in a pagan culture. Other writings, like his *Apology*, are directed to non-Christians in defense of the Christian faith. Tertullian's polemical works, though, are the primary context for his versions of the *regula fidei*. *Prescription Against Heretics* (*De praescriptione haereticorum*) is his prominent work dealing with heresy and scriptural interpretation. *Against Praxeas* (*Adversus Praxean*), prompted by Praxeas' version of modalism, is his most christological work. The exception to this heretical context for the *regula* is his briefest version in *On the Veiling of Virgins* (*De virginibus velandis*), which addresses custom in the church.[1]

Prescription Against Heretics outlines the proper relationships between the *regula*, the church's interpretation of Scripture, and heretics. In brief, the Scriptures belong solely to the church, whose members are defined by adherence to the *regula*. Heretics have no proper claim to the Scriptures or their interpretation. The *regula* as a delineation of basic Christian belief, therefore, serves not

---

[1] The present concern is to evaluate Tertullian's *regulae* as a whole in comparison to those of Irenaeus and Origen. Nevertheless, it should be noted that even in his own versions of the rule there is "a real progress in the Trinitarian reflection of Tertullian, a progress in its explication ... but not in the faith itself" [trans. mine]. Joseph Moingt, *Théologie trinitaire de Tertullien* (Paris: Aubier, 1969), 69.

only as a barrier against heresy, but also as a guide to the proper interpretation of Scripture, though how this guide functions can vary.

Against Praxeas also has an anti-heretical purpose, but this more focused work deals directly with a particular manifestation of heresy, a version of modalistic monarchianism contemporary to Tertullian. This polemic against Praxeas is the context for Tertullian's most significant articulations of Trinitarian theology and Christology. As with Irenaeus, Tertullian's desire in this debate is to remain true to Scripture; but since his context involves different categories of communication and new heretical developments, new expressions of biblical truth are necessary. As he addresses Praxeas' heresy, the purely functional and biblical vocabulary of Irenaeus appears to be inadequate for communicating the biblical truths involved. Tertullian, therefore, begins to incorporate additional categories and modes of thinking in order to communicate effectively the New Testament's view of Christ's inclusion in the unique divine identity. These categories tend to include more ontological vocabulary than those utilized by Irenaeus. Nevertheless, the result is a consistent delineation of biblical christological monotheism continuous with both the New Testament and Irenaeus.

The Christological Core in the *Regula*

Tertullian, like Irenaeus, begins each rendition of the *regula* by asserting the existence of only one God who is the Creator of the universe.[2] Monotheism is foundational, and the *monarchia*, the single rule of God, and the *oikonomia*, the dispensation of the three in one, are used to modify and explicate this understanding of monotheism. Although some of his philosophical ideas borrowed from Stoicism impact his understanding of deity, the biblical understanding of the singular existence of God remains essential and basic to Tertullian's theology and the *regula*. He says as much when he mentions simple believers whose "rule of faith [*regula fidei*] withdraws them from the world's plurality of gods [*a pluribus diis saeculi*] to the one only true God [*ad unicum et uerum Deum*]."[3] However God may manifest himself in the *oikonomia*, his unity remains basic.[4]

Within this monotheism God is quickly identified as the Father of Jesus Christ the Son of God, and the Son's inclusion in the unique divine identity is revealed. Tertullian's emphasis on monotheism remains primary despite his need to differentiate between the three *personae* in order to combat Praxeas and other modalists. This emphasis, together with a developing stress on the distinc-

---

[2] All quotations of Tertullian's *regulae* in the original Latin are taken from CCSL. English quotations are taken from ANF, unless otherwise noted. See appendix for complete texts.

[3] Tertullian *Adv. Prax.* 3.1.

[4] The foundational importance of monotheism is best seen in Tertullian's denunciation of Marcion. The phrase "one and only God" dispatches not only Marcion's claim of two gods, but also his sharp distinction between law and gospel from which it is derived. Farmer, 162-3.

tions within the Godhead, necessitates a clearly delineated christological monotheism that maintains the deity of the Son without questioning the singularity of God. Tertullian articulates this christological monotheism by means of the same basic categories discussed above, and he does so especially well by reemphasizing a significant biblical phrase.

That Christ "is sitting at the right hand of the Father [*ad dexteram patris*]" reiterates the New Testament claim to Christ's divine sovereignty and authority over all things, the first identifier of his inclusion in the unique divine identity. Jesus Christ, the risen and glorified Son of God, sits in the place of authority and majesty at the right of the Father. He wields an authority that only God himself possesses. All three *regulae* incorporate the phrase, even the abbreviated version in *On the Veiling of Virgins*, and its significance for Tertullian can hardly be underestimated. Interestingly, Christ's place at the right of the Father communicates both the single rule of God as well as the distinctions between the *personae*. At present it is enough to say that the phrase clearly substantiates the Son's sovereignty and ties Tertullian's Christology closely to the New Testament.

His *regulae* also incorporate the eschatological exercise of this sovereignty. From his place of sovereignty at the right hand of God, Christ "will come with glory [*uenturum cum claritate*]," a divine glory that accompanies the one who has the power to restore and condemn. In this glory, he is destined "to judge the quick and the dead" and "to condemn the wicked to everlasting fire," fulfilling his role as the ultimate authority.

Although Christ's authority is most evident eschatologically, a form of it is seen in his life and ministry, especially in his preaching of "the new law [*nouam legem*] and the new promise [*nouam promissionem*] of the kingdom of heaven [*regni caelorum*]."[5] While preaching the law and the promise of the kingdom is not an activity requiring divinity, the manner in which Christ initiates it is an activity requiring authority. When Christ preaches "you have heard it said ... but I say to you," he not only supersedes the law given by God to Moses, but he also institutes a new law which culminates in his own activity (his death, burial, and resurrection) and in his own person. Furthermore, only the monarch himself may extend the promise of the kingdom, though he may do so through messengers as does Christ when he sends out his disciples.[6]

Whether or not Christ's life and ministry convincingly exhibit his divine sovereignty, his current place at the Father's right hand reveals his authority. Christ's sovereignty is also closely connected to his participation in creation. In continuity with the New Testament and Irenaeus, Tertullian asserts Christ's involvement in the creation of all things as the instrumental cause. The one only God is "none other than the Creator of the world [*praeter mundi conditorem*], who produced everything from nothing [*uniuersa de nihilo produxerit*] through

---

[5] Tertullian *De praes. haer.* 13.

[6] For an analysis of Tertullian's view on Christ's divine sovereignty expressed through his ministry see Roy Kearsley, *Tertullian's Theology of Divine Power* (Carlisle, UK: Paternoster Press, 1998), 71-74.

his Word."[7] The Word, subsequently designated the Son of God, is the means for creation, the instrument of God in the making of everything. Christ, in being the instrumental cause, is distinct from the material of creation. Neither was there any preexistent matter for creation from which the Son worked only as a master craftsman, nor was creation the result of an emanation from his being. God made all things through the Son out of nothing.[8]

The *regula* in *Adv. Prax.* 2 reemphasizes the inclusion of all things in God's creation through the Son. Nothing was created apart from the Son's work. Creation did not include any division of responsibilities between the *personae* of the Godhead by which each *persona* would have different responsibilities and therefore different measures of authority. All things are subject to the Son because all things were created through the Son. In an important side note, this version of the *regula* also mentions the Son's procession in close relation to his participation in creation, anticipating the significance of creation in the relationship between the *monarchia* and the *personae* of the Godhead. Tertullian sees the threeness of God as an economic manifestation of God's will to create, not necessarily as an eternal ontological principle within God's nature. Nevertheless, the Son of God remains the sole means of creation despite Tertullian's difficulties in delineating his eternal nature.

Unlike the longer forms, the abbreviated form of the *regula* in *On the Veiling of Virgins* does not explicitly assert the Son's involvement in creation. Yet, it is implied in his judiciary role insofar as his judgment of the quick and the dead is accomplished "through the resurrection of the flesh as well as of the spirit." For Christ to be able to resurrect *all* flesh and spirit would require him to have the sovereignty that can come only through his involvement in creation. The authority over all things that is implied in this resurrection, therefore, assumes what is explicitly stated elsewhere, that Christ is the instrumental cause of *all things*.

The third criterion for Christ's inclusion in the unique divine identity, the attribution of the divine name, is the criterion that becomes more explicit from Irenaeus' versions of the *regula* to Tertullian's versions. In the two longer versions the Word, the Son of God, is specifically identified as God. In *De praes. haer.* 13, Tertullian first states that the Word is called the Son of the Creator God and follows with the assertion that the Son relates to the patriarchs and the prophets "in the name of God [*in nomine Dei*]." Tertullian's understanding of the *monarchia* explains the unusual description of the Son's functioning *in* the divine name. As a river flows from a spring or sunlight streams from the Sun, so the Son extends from the divine Godhead.[9] In his existence as a distinct *persona*

---

[7] Tertullian *De praes. haer.* (LCC) 13.

[8] Tertullian's understanding of creation *ex nihilo* by means of the Word clearly draws "from Irenaeus and, by implication, from an established Church tradition." Kearsley, *Tertullian's Theology of Divine Power*, 36. Kearsley says that "every major tenet of the *regula fidei*" hung on the outcome of *creatio ex nihilo* (46), and he sees most of Tertullian's theology either referencing or dependent upon the doctrine. See also Robert H. Ayers, *Language, Logic, and Reason in the Church Fathers: A Study of Tertullian, Augustine, and Aquinas* (New York: G. Olms, 1979), 35.

[9] Tertullian *Adv. Prax.* 8.

within the one substance of God, he works in the name of the one God, meaning the single rule or *monarchia* of the Godhead.[10]

The attribution of the divine name in *Adv. Prax.* 2 is clearer and more blatant, partly because of its christological context. The Son's procession from the Father is described in the statement on the Father where he is called the Word, and the Son's deity is explicitly affirmed within the christological statement. This christological statement transitions from God's creative work through the Word to the virgin birth and subsequently affirms the deity of Christ in his incarnation. The Word is "both Man and God [*hominem et Deum*], the Son of Man [*Filium hominis*] and the Son of God [*Filium Dei*]" and is specifically identified as Jesus Christ. In addition to the direct attribution of *God* to Jesus Christ, the parallelism of this statement reveals the early tendency to identify "Son of God" with Christ's deity and "Son of Man" with his humanity. When he addresses the two natures of Christ this identification is assumed and is often used to delineate the distinction between the natures.

With this developing interest in the two natures of Jesus Christ, the Trinitarian implications involved, and their application against heresy, one would expect additional ontological language in the identification of the Son. Yet, the attribution of christological titles in Tertullian's *regulae* is restricted to Word, Son, and Christ, with most of the descriptions of Jesus Christ being functional portrayals of his activity. Even in the names used for Christ, therefore, one can see the transitional nature of Tertullian's theology. He is willing to delve into speculative issues more than Irenaeus while maintaining most of the same emphases in functional and biblical language.

The best example of Tertullian's use of biblical language is the reference to Jesus "sitting at the right hand of the Father." This reference also contributes to the final identifier for his inclusion in the unique divine identity.[11] Jesus Christ's place at the right hand of the Father identifies him as worthy of the worship attributable only to God himself. All three of Tertullian's *regulae* incorporate the phrase and thereby assert his sovereignty and his worthiness of worship. In addition, prior to his incarnation he was received with worship and honor by the patriarchs and the prophets, and eschatologically he will return with glory as the judge of humanity.[12]

Tertullian's articulation of the rule consistently maintains the christological monotheism of the New Testament. Jesus Christ not only possesses the name *God*, but he also receives the worship attributable only to the divine. More importantly, he possesses the characteristics from which this name and worthiness of worship derive—he is the Creator of all that exists and he holds absolute sovereignty over creation in its entirety. In his place at the right hand of the Father he is both man and God, the savior and the future judge of all creation. So within the moderate speculation that ensues concerning the existence of the Son in two

---

[10] Ibid., 16.

[11] Christ's place at the right hand of God also accords him the divine title of "the Most High," which states explicitly his worthiness of worship. Ibid., 17.

[12] Tertullian *De praes. haer.* 13.

natures, the foundation remains the New Testament and its christological monotheism.

Not only is monotheism foundational to Jesus Christ's inclusion in the unique divine identity, but monotheism is also basic to the *regula*'s central assertion that the two covenants are in accord. Each version of Tertullian's *regula* begins with the existence of one only God and then ties that monotheism to two beliefs, his identity as Creator and the existence of his Son. The shortest *regula* is the most concise and direct, saying that Christians believe in one God, the Creator, and his Son Jesus Christ.[13] *De praes. haer.* 13 makes the same connection between the God of the Old Testament and the God of the New Testament but does so in more detail. The Creator God sent forth his Word, and his Word is subsequently equated with the incarnate Jesus Christ once the *regula* proceeds through the historical sequence of creation, Old Testament theophany, and incarnation. *Adv. Prax.* 2 is similar, though creation is seen through the instrumentality of the Son. The order, therefore, is all that changes as the Son proceeds from the one God, serves as the instrument of creation, and is finally identified as Jesus Christ after the incarnation. Despite the differences, all three versions effectively equate the Creator God with the Father of the New Testament, refuting the contentions of many heretics that they are two different beings and that the Old Testament may be discarded.

The concept of creation and redemptive history as a *dispensatio* or *oikonomia* also contributes to this accord between the two covenants. Monotheism is the foundational principle, yet God has formulated a divine plan, an *oikonomia*, which includes not only redemption in the Son's incarnation and atoning work, but also creation, and for Tertullian, the procession of the Son.[14] All of history, from the procession of the Son to the final judgment, is a part of God's all-encompassing plan, the enactment of his single undifferentiated divine will. To suggest that the two covenants are divergent, therefore, is contrary not only to monotheism, but also to the single *oikonomia* of the one God.

The particulars of the *oikonomia* also bear testimony to the unity of the old and new covenants. It was the same Son of God who was seen "by the patriarchs, heard at all times in the prophets," and born of the virgin Mary as Jesus Christ.[15] Not only is the same God active in both covenants, but his Son also fulfills responsibilities in both time periods. Among these responsibilities is the atonement. That Christ "suffered [*passum*], died [*mortuum*], [was] buried [*sepultum*], according to the Scriptures [*secundum scripturas*]," and was subsequently raised reiterates Paul's assertion in 1 Cor. 15:3 and declares the essential core of the *regula*.[16] Jesus Christ, the Word, the Son of God is both the instrument of the

---

[13] Tertullian *De virg. vel.* 1.

[14] Tertullian *Adv. Prax.* 2. Tertullian describes the differentiation between the Father and the Son as "procession" as a result of his understanding of the *logos endiathetos* and *logos prophorikos*, the internal Word of God spoken. The eternal generation of the Son will not be spoken of until Origen proposes it some decades later.

[15] Tertullian *De praes. haer.* 13.

[16] Tertullian *Adv. Prax.* 2.

Creator God and the Son of the gracious loving God of the New Testament. In place of the heretics' radical dualism is an extraordinary unity of divine character, will, and fulfillment that can be defined best as christological monotheism.

In summary, Tertullian's *regulae* maintain the christological continuity that begins in the New Testament and continues in Irenaeus' *regulae*. With a renewed emphasis on the New Testament's placement of Christ at the right hand of the Father, these *regulae* confirm Christ's sovereignty and his worthiness of worship. This sovereignty undoubtedly derives most from his involvement in creation as its instrumental cause. In addition, Tertullian attributes to the Son the divine name, explicitly naming him God. In the process he begins to raise the issues of the relationship of Christ's two natures and his place in the Trinity. Tertullian, therefore, includes all four of the identifiers for Christ's inclusion in the unique divine identity in his versions of the *regula*. Furthermore, these *regulae* maintain the unity of the two covenants. Christ, the Son of God, is included in the unique divine identity and is the fulfillment of the Scriptures in his death, burial, and resurrection.

Tertullian's Variations in the *Regula*

Tertullian's *regulae* display many aspects of his transitional theology. The most general aspect of this transitional theology is the use of *dispensatio* or *oikonomia* to portray God's divine plan encompassing everything from the procession of the Word to the final judgment. While the *oikonomia* overall is articulated using functional language as in Irenaeus, Tertullian's delineation of the divine plan develops out of features pertaining to the procession of the Son from the Father.[17] He is "sent forth" in order to fulfill the functions of creator, redeemer, and judge. Speculations apart from the *regula* concerning the nature of his procession and his continuity of substance with God show the development of issues addressing the Son's being and nature in addition to his work. Elaboration on such features as his designation as Son specifically in relation to God as Father also contribute to this development.

While the *oikonomia* primarily defines the divine acts of redemption in Irenaeus, Tertullian intentionally builds his ontological understanding of the threeness of God on the concept of the *oikonomia*. Both theologians incorporate the Trinity and the plan of redemption in the *oikonomia*, but Irenaeus emphasizes the acts of God while Tertullian's emphasis is God's manifestation of himself as three in one. This transition to an understanding of the *oikonomia* incorporating ontological categories develops especially out of the polemic against Praxeas. While Irenaeus does not have a specific opponent in mind in delineating the *oikonomia* as the acts of the Triune God, modalism motivates Tertullian to reverse the emphasis and define the *oikonomia* as the Triune God acting through creation, redemption, and judgment.[18] It is natural, therefore, for the *regula* in

---

[17] See ibid.
[18] See ibid., 2-3.

Against Praxeas to state specifically the procession of the Son as a precursor to creation and the rest of God's activities.

This change in emphasis does not discard the functional elements of God's divine plan, but it does reorient them to support more directly the ontological distinctions within the Godhead that are more significant for the debate with Praxeas. The resurrection of the Son "by the Father" (a phrase found only in Tertullian's *regula*), a seemingly straightforward reiteration of Christ's return from death, is subsequently used to substantiate the existence of *personae* within the unity of the divine substance.[19] Modalism asserts that the Father became the Son, contradicting the belief that the Father raised the Son, a statement requiring two distinct persons, both subject and object. The simple addition of the phrase "by the Father," therefore, not only denies patripassionism, the belief that the Father died on the cross, but also substantiates the distinctions between persons of the Godhead. Consequently, the phrase "by the Father" is used primarily to delineate an aspect of the ontological existence of God—that he exists as more than one *persona* at one point in time. It is used only secondarily to describe the action of God.

The virginal conception of the Son described in the *regula* functions in a similar way when the Son is "sent by the Father" and brought down by "the Spirit and Power of the Father." All three persons of the Trinity are involved in the virginal conception. The Father is the sending agent, the Spirit is the instrumental agent, and the Son is the one sent and conceived. Again, the same distinction between agents is involved when Christ "sent in his place the power of the Holy Spirit."[20]

The most significant example of this delineation of God's threeness by means of the divine activities is the seating of the Son "at the right hand of the Father [*ad dexteram Patris*]." The phrase is one of the few that occurs in all three of Tertullian's *regulae*. The form of *sedere* changes with each version ["sat," "to be sitting," "now sitting"], revealing that it is a persisting state of existence. Consequently, the impact is the same as above with respect to the distinctions between *personae* within the Godhead. The Father and the Son coexist simultaneously, ruling together in the one *monarchia*, thereby refuting Praxeas' modalism while maintaining the single rule of God.

This attention to heresy and the concomitant change in the emphasis of the *oikonomia* affects soteriology. The soteriological emphasis is not as explicit in Tertullian's versions of the *regula* as in Irenaeus'. Tertullian nowhere explicitly designates the salvation of humanity to be the purpose of the *oikonomia*, and the *regula* is given only as a statement of the truth about God that is to be believed. Those who believe will enjoy eternal life, but that is only the final result, not the overarching theme of the *regula*. Nevertheless, Tertullian does include specifics detailing the manifestation of the *oikonomia*. The Word is specifically equated with the Son and with Jesus Christ in the two longer *regulae*. This identification

---

[19] Ibid., 2, 28, 29.
[20] Ibid., 2; *De praes. haer.* (LCC) 13.

indicates the participation of the second person of the Trinity in all of the *oikonomia* and his interaction with the Father and the Spirit in a variety of contexts.

Aspects of the Son's participation in the *oikonomia* unique to Tertullian's *regulae* include being seen "in diverse manners by the patriarchs" and preaching "the new law and the new promise of the kingdom of heaven."[21] Irenaeus addresses the God of the patriarchs but does not pointedly refer to his interaction with the patriarchs in the *regula*. Tertullian may have Jews in mind when he places the Son and the patriarchs in the same context. Although this connection may not be intentional, the concept of the new law preached by Christ is certainly an addition of Tertullian's to the *regula* aimed at the Jews of the time. In *Against the Jews* he calls the new law a law of forgiveness and peace in contrast to the old law of vengeance proscribed in the old covenant.[22] Not that the new law contravenes the old law; rather, the new law supersedes the old law, fulfilling its obligations and bringing reconciliation. Tertullian sees indication that the new law fulfills the old law in the fact that the new law is foreseen in the Law and the Prophets.[23] Interestingly, the new law is also used against Marcion to maintain the continuity of the two testaments and the singular identity of the Creator God and the Father. While the dichotomy of the old and the new would appeal to Marcionites and Gnostics, that both are laws is a setback to their theologies, especially when their continuity can be shown.[24]

Tertullian is also unique in explicitly stating in the *regula* the mode of Christ's death.[25] Irenaeus and Origen do not avoid the crucifixion but refer to it using such general terms as passion, suffered, and die. Furthermore, Tertullian is the only one of the three to specifically refer to Christ's burial, though it is implied in any statement of his death and resurrection.[26] One statement in common with Irenaeus that bears mentioning is the inclusion in the *regula* of Pontius Pilate's role in the crucifixion, mentioned in *On the Veiling of Virgins*. Tertullian believes the story in the early church that Pontius Pilate, after sending Christ to be crucified, was converted and sent word to Caesar concerning Christ.[27] Yet, Tertullian's intent for including Pilate is most likely the same as Irenaeus', to place Christ solidly within world history against the Gnostics and others whose tendency is to spiritualize events. This is even more likely considering the brevity of this version of the *regula*.

While much of Tertullian's theology addresses ontological ideas in functional and economic categories and terms, this does not preclude him from using ontologically oriented concepts and vocabulary. He does this most explicitly in the inclusion of the two-natures doctrine, that Christ is "both Man and God, the

---

[21] Tertullian *De praes. haer.* 13.

[22] Tertullian *Adversus Judaeos* 3.

[23] "And, primarily, we must lay it down that the ancient Law and the prophets could not have ceased, unless He were come who was constantly announced, through the same Law and through the same prophets, as to come." Ibid., 6.

[24] Tertullian *Adv. Marc.* 4.9; *De Monogamia* 7.1-2.

[25] Tertullian *De praes. haer.* 13; *virg. vel.* 1.

[26] Tertullian *Adv. Prax.* 2.

[27] Tertullian *Apol.* 21

Son of Man and the Son of God."[28] Naturally, the incarnation is an essential component of every version of the *regula*, but Tertullian brings direct attention to the inclusion of both natures while Irenaeus is more generic in his delineation of the incarnation. The relationship between the two natures is not directly addressed in the *regula* since the categories and vocabulary needed to state the truth concisely are being developed in his own work and in the work of those to follow. Nevertheless, the subsequent discussion in *Against Praxeas* makes it clear that the Son's state of being is in the author's mind as he articulates the *regula*. He has a very definite Christology however primitive it may seem in retrospect.

Tertullian's *regulae* anticipate details of his subsequent work, at least providing hints of his emphases. He maintains many of Irenaeus' functional aspects, but on several issues he delves into ontological features by means of these functional aspects. Essentially, Tertullian's reversal of emphasis in the *oikonomia* and his elaborations upon some of the same activities of God mentioned by Irenaeus are aspects and indicators of a transitional theology. This transitional theology addresses issues couched in ontological categories with truths stated in biblical and functional language.

The *Regula* and Tertullian's Hermeneutic

Underlying Tertullian's exegetical practices is his general understanding of the relationships between Scripture, the church, and the apostolic tradition. All three entities are closely intertwined and support the same basic content and faith. Individual believers who make up the church are defined by their adherence to the *regula*.[29] Anyone disputing the *regula* places himself outside of the church. In addition, the church as a whole has a common origin with the Scriptures in the apostolic preaching that comes from Christ.[30] The church in turn has sole possession of Scripture and keeps for itself the privilege and authority to interpret it. Only believers within the church, therefore, may use Scripture; it is off limits to heretics since they pick and choose what is included in the canon and do so without regard to the *regula*.[31] As believers interpret Scripture, interpretations must be strictly within the bounds of the *regula*, though the strictness with which interpretations must conform to the *regula* seems to change with the context. Regardless, one's interpretation of Scripture at minimum cannot contravene the *regula* since the *regula* "was taught by Christ" and leads one to genuine faith.[32]

---

[28] Tertullian *Adv. Prax.* 2.
[29] Tertullian *De praes. haer.* 12, 14.
[30] "What we are ourselves, that also the Scriptures are (and have been) from the beginning." Ibid., 38.
[31] Ibid., 15, 19, 37.
[32] Ibid., 13-14. See also Kelly, *Early Christian Doctrines*, 39-41.

Several exegetical principles help maintain this interpretive integrity, especially against the heretics.[33] First, where the heretics grant themselves the authority to piecemeal their own Scriptures together, eliminating the portions they cannot twist to their purposes, believers must interpret within the context of Scripture as a whole. Not only are the two testaments a unified whole (against Marcion and the Gnostics), but the gospels and the epistles of the New Testament also teach a consistent message.[34] Portions of Scripture cannot be set against each other; rather, harmony is found throughout Scripture when it is properly interpreted.

Closely related to the unity of Scripture is the principle that Scripture interprets Scripture, that clear passages illuminate those that are not as easily interpreted and that occasional statements should be understood "in the light of the many [*secundum plura*]."[35] Heretics often take vague, elusive, and isolated passages of Scripture, and with their unorthodox interpretations use these unclear passages to explain otherwise clear passages.[36] If one is to be led aright, therefore, "uncertain statements should be determined by certain ones [*incerta de certis*], and obscure ones by such as are clear and plain [*obscura de manifestis*]."[37]

The third principle of interpretation is the desire for the plain and simple meanings of texts, and is significant in light of heretics' tendencies to read the literal as allegory and the metaphorical as literal. For example, Hermogenes interprets "beginning" in Gen. 1 as a form of "substantial and embodied" matter itself, distorting the plain meaning of a text which is intended to be taken literally as "origin," in order to support his belief in preexistent matter.[38] At the same time Tertullian warns of passages that "must be understood in a sense different from the literal description" due to their use of figurative language.[39]

The most demanding and controversial hermeneutical principle is that believers are constrained to what is stated in Scripture. The silence of Scripture on a particular topic does not mean that believers have freedom in that respect. In this sense, Tertullian follows Irenaeus in proscribing a strict use of Scripture and the *regula*. Especially when it serves his polemical purposes, he allows nothing

---

[33] These principles are general in nature and neither form a system nor fit within a system. Tertullian's many and varying polemics and apologetics limit his ability to develop a systematic hermeneutic. J. H. Waszink, "Tertullian's Principles and Methods of Exegesis," in *Early Christian Literature and the Classical Intellectual Tradition*, ed. W. R. Schoedel and R. L. Wilken (Paris: Beauchesne, 1979), 17.

[34] Tertullian *De praes. haer.* 9, 17, 23; *Adv. Herm.* 20.4, 22.5; *Adv. Marc.*, 3.5.1, 4.2.2; *Adv. Prax.* 25.2; John F. Jansen, "Tertullian and the New Testament," *The Second Century* 2 (Winter 1982), 202; Timothy F. Merrill, "Tertullian: the Hermeneutical Vision of De praescriptione haereticorum and Pentateuchal Exegesis," *Patristic and Byzantine Review* 6 (1987), 155.

[35] Tertullian *Adv. Prax.* 20.

[36] Tertullian *De praes. haer.* 17.

[37] Tertullian *De resurrectione mortuorum* 21.2. See also Jansen, 203.

[38] Tertullian *Adv. Herm.* 19.

[39] Tertullian *Adv. Marc.* 3.5. See also Jansen, 204.

that is not derived from Scripture or the *regula*. Such is the case when he speaks against Hermogenes, saying that "if it is nowhere written [*Si non est scriptum*], then let it fear the woe which impends on all who add to or take away from the written word [*adicientibus aut detrahentibus destinatum*]."[40] He speaks similarly against Praxeas when he warns him to "be content with saying that Christ died, the Son of the Father; and let this suffice [*sufficiat*], because the Scriptures have told us so much [*et hoc quia ita scriptum est*]" and no more.[41] The most pointed statement along these lines is in a pastoral context and refers to the wearing of crowns, which Tertullian disdains on the basis of the principle that "what has not been freely allowed [*quod non ultro est permissum*] [in Scripture] is forbidden [*Immo prohibetur*]."[42] At least in principle, therefore, Tertullian demands full dependence on Scripture and rejects any arguments from silence.[43]

It is in this principle that the *regula* and the interpretation of Scripture come closest together. The *regula* is the primary means for ensuring that interpreters do not exceed the confines of Scripture by delving into allegorical interpretations of plain texts or by flitting off into speculative concerns that are otherwise unaddressed in Scripture. In a sizeable passage in *De praes. haer.* 8-14, the *regula* is clearly defined as the overall constraint on the seeking mind. In specific terms, the rule of reason asserts that the seeker is confined in the matter (*in re*), in the time (*in tempore*), and in the manner (*in modo*). One is encouraged to seek in order to discover what Christ taught. This is the matter, the substance of which is found in the *regula*. One should seek only *until* he has found the matter and no further, thus the temporal constraint. Finally, the manner consists of persistent seeking until the seeker finds the substance taught by Christ and believes.[44] This belief signals the discovery of truth and the end of its pursuit, for what reasonable man continues to seek for what he has already found? And if he has not found it, then why has he already believed? Once the individual finds and believes the *regula*, therefore, there is no reason to seek further, much like the woman who finds her lost piece of silver or the man who receives bread from his neighbor. Speculation beyond the confines of the *regula* will only lead one astray into the uncertain thinking of the heretics.[45]

---

[40] Tertullian *Adv. Herm.* 22.5.

[41] Tertullian *Adv. Prax.* 29. See also Tertullian *De spectaculis* 3.1; *Adv. Herm.* 21.3; *De idololatria* 24; Jansen, 206-7.

[42] Tertullian *De corona* 2.4.

[43] Tertullian does not evenly apply his principles to his own exegesis. His principles are "more shaped by the demands of doctrinal heresy" than by general hermeneutical standards. For the disparate relationship between his hermeneutical principles and his actual exegesis see Merrill, 162-4.

[44] Tertullian *De praes. haer.* 10; Merrill, 156-7, 160.

[45] For elaboration on legitimate curiosity and speculation within the bounds of the *regula* see Jean-Claude Fredouille, *Tertullien et la conversion de la culture antique* (Paris: Chateau-Gontier, 1972), 429-431. Cf. Jean Daniélou, *The Origins of Latin Christianity*, trans. David Smith and John Austin Baker (Philadelphia: The Westminster Press, 1977), 186-188.

Despite these admonitions, Tertullian does not apply these principles consistently, especially the prohibition against speculation. Sometimes he modifies his interpretive standards on account of changing contexts. Tertullian's polemical contexts in particular require him to modify his understanding of the *regula* and interpretation. At times he allows not only what is strictly within the *regula* and Scripture, but also what is compatible with them.

It might be said that where previously, for Irenaeus, to know the rule was to know all things, now "[t]o know nothing in opposition to the rule (of faith) [*adversus regulam nihil scire*], is to know all things [*omnia scire est*]."[46] While relatively subtle, the change opens inquiry and permits the inclusion of philosophical ideas where previously they might have been stifled. Again, despite the Latin father's strictness in disallowing the use of Scripture by heretics entirely, he permits the believer to seek after that "which can become an object of inquiry without impairing the rule of faith."[47]

Consequently, while Tertullian will forcefully demand that believers cease seeking entirely once they find the truth of the gospel in the *regula*, he does allow believers to seek, but only "in that which is our own, and from those who are our own, and concerning that which is our own."[48] The change is due to the polemical nature of the rhetoric involved. If forced to choose between the acknowledgment of a believer's freedom to seek and the denunciation of speculation on account of heretics, our author will clearly emphasize the latter, if for no other reason than the protection of simple believers.[49] It would be worse to let the simple be led astray than to restrict the freedom of other Christians. Regardless, Tertullian is not forced to choose one over the other and consequently allows some freedom to seek and speculate if such thought does not contradict the *regula*. Interestingly, his delineation of the *regula* itself in *Prescription Against Heretics* shows this flexibility as he "expand[s] the scope of this irreformable core, so that it would include as much as possible of what the various heresies denied."[50] The theological inquirer, therefore, need not constrain himself to strict obedience to the explicitly stated *regula* but may incorporate ideas compatible with the *regula*, especially when they provide additional ammunition against the heretics.

This limited openness in Tertullian's hermeneutic finds collaboration in his recognition of apostolic authority inherent in some customs and tradition. Even if such liturgical practices as the threefold immersion of baptism or the making of the sign on the forehead are not prescribed by Scripture they may still be confirmed by tradition and find their "(authorization in) the apostle's sanction."[51] So while Irenaeus' hermeneutical use of the *regula* might be compared to a train for which deviation from the rails means serious difficulty and potential destruction,

---

[46] Tertullian *De praes. haer.* 14.5.
[47] Ibid., 12.5. See also ibid., 15; Merrill, 154-7.
[48] Tertullian *De praes. haer.* 12.
[49] Tertullian *Adv. Prax.* 2-3, 9.
[50] Countryman, 213.
[51] Tertullian *De corona* 3-4.

Tertullian's use of the *regula* might be portrayed as a vehicle on a road where the curb or shoulder limits inquiry but nevertheless allows for variation within defined parameters.

Chapter 6

A Transitional Theology

In light of his more permissive use of the *regula*, Tertullian is more apt to speculate on theological matters than Irenaeus, a sometimes surprising conclusion considering the common perception that he denounces philosophy. He delves into the unknown especially when heretics advocate opinions contrary to the received faith, but he does so only to correct the deviant theology that confronts him. Tertullian is generally careful to remain within scriptural bounds even as his interpretation of the New Testament's Christology begins to incorporate more metaphysical vocabulary. His method is "to take an already existing idea, compare it with Scripture, and then modify or abandon it according to the biblical evidence," whether the existing idea belongs to theology or philosophy.[1] While he can be speculative, therefore, such inquiry is limited to the modification of previous thought or the solution of dilemmas posed by heretics and must at the very least complement Scripture and the *regula*. More often than not, he also provides biblical justification for his opinions incorporating speculative and ontological categories. As this high view of Scripture meets his relative dependence on other sources within his unique apologetical and polemical context, the result is a transitional theology characterized by a mixture of functional and ontological vocabulary.

Logos Endiathetos and *Prophorikos*

Tertullian and Irenaeus both emphatically assert monotheism, especially against Marcion and the Gnostics. Nevertheless, the advent of heretics unknown to Irenaeus such as Praxeas demands elaboration on God's ontological nature. While it is unnecessary for Irenaeus to address some subjects in detail, modalism forces Tertullian to explain the existence of the Son of God and the nature of his deity within a strict monotheism. The result is a modified form of the Apologists' Logos Christology.

---

[1] Gerald Bray, *Holiness and the Will of God: Perspectives on the Theology of Tertullian*, (Atlanta, GA: John Knox Press, 1979), 79.

Tertullian continues much of the early Apologists' teaching concerning the *Logos*, including the distinction between the *Logos endiathetos* and the *Logos prophorikos*, though he does not use the terms.[2] This distinction between the *Logos endiathetos*, the internal or unspoken Word, and the *Logos prophorikos*, the external or spoken Word, is an early attempt to justify christologically the recognition of both the Father and the Son as divine while maintaining a thorough monotheism. The oneness of God is evident in the *monarchia*, the single rule over creation held jointly by the Father and the Son. At the same time, Tertullian's nascent concept of the Trinity manifests itself in the *oikonomia* or dispensation of God according to the varying roles of the divine persons.

Prior to creation, the distinctive existence of the second person of the Trinity is limited to the presence of Reason (*rationalis*) and unspoken Word (*sermo*) within God. Unlike Irenaeus, Tertullian sees humanity's creation in the image and likeness of God as reason to apply the analogy of human thought to divine thought. Human beings have discourse with themselves and within themselves as their rationality instigates unspoken words and the words themselves bring additional thoughts. This word, both in the mind and potentially spoken, "is a second *person* within you [*ita secundus quodammodo in te*]" and "is itself a different thing from yourself [*ipse sermo alius est*]."[3] In a sense this word comes to have a distinct existence that is nonetheless dependent on the person it inhabits.

This interaction between reason and word is not identical in God, but it is analogous. The argument begins with the truth that "before all things God was alone," meaning that nothing existed external to him. While God was alone in this sense, his Reason and Word existed internally. Reason was prior to Word logically, but in practical terms Word is implied or embodied in Reason. In other words, Reason naturally leads to conceptualized Word in its functioning as Reason. At the same time, when God's rationality brings about Word within his mind the resultant internal dialogue instigates additional thought or Reason, making the two interdependent and unified.

Even more than human thought and word, God's Reason and Word constitute a distinct entity within God's being, enabling Tertullian to say as well that "before the creation of the universe [*Ante uniuersitatis constitutionem*] God was not alone [*solum non fuisse*], since He had within Himself both Reason [*habentem in semetipso proinde rationem*], and, inherent in Reason, His Word [*et in ratione sermonem*]."[4] The internal process of God's thought in both Reason and Word, therefore, defines Tertullian's understanding of the Apologists' *Logos endiathetos*. More importantly, this delineation of God's Reason and

---

[2] Cf. Justin Martyr, *Dialogue with Trypho the Jew*, 61; Tatian, *Discourse with the Greeks*, 5; Theophilus of Antioch, *Ad Autolycum*, 2.10, 22. Kearsley, 31-32, 56-58; Kelly, *Early Christian Doctrines*, 111-112; Simon Price, "Latin Christian Apologetics: Minucius Felix, Tertullian, and Cyprian," in *Apologetics in the Roman Empire: Pagans, Jews, and Christians*, ed. Mark Edwards, Martin Goodman, Simon Price, and Christopher Rowland (New York: Oxford University Press, 1999), 116.

[3] Tertullian *Adv. Prax.* 5.6.

[4] Ibid., 5.7.

Word explains how the second person of the Trinity can be eternal God even though he was generated temporally in the first act of creation.[5]

The explanation for this generation of the Son of God is based upon the Apologists' corollary idea, the concept of the *Logos prophorikos*, the spoken or manifested Word of God. In the time immediately preceding creation the second person of the Trinity is manifested in the beginning of the *oikonomia* as God's Wisdom. He is the Wisdom of God that is "generated in His own intelligence" according to Prov. 8:22. The generation of God's Wisdom, also called the speaking of the Word or the begetting of the Son by the Father, takes place in the divine command of Gen. 1:3, "Let there be light." As a human being has his own word within himself as part of his reason and speaks that word, in a fashion giving it distinct existence, so God speaks his Word. Yet, God's Word is more substantial than any human word. God's Wisdom, his spoken Word and begotten Son, constitutes a second *persona* distinct from God as Father but one with him in substance.[6]

This speaking of the Word is also the divine act that initiates the *oikonomia* and creation. Proverbs describes God's Wisdom as the means of creation following his generation, providing Tertullian with a scriptural tie to John 1 and additional scriptural support for his use of the *Logos prophorikos*. Furthermore, it is especially in the process of creation that Wisdom is manifested specifically as the second divine person. That is not to say that this divine person did not exist prior to Wisdom and creation, but his distinctiveness is less discernable. He exists eternally as the Reason and Word of God and was spoken as God's Wisdom.

---

[5] God had "within Himself, both in company with and included within His very Reason, as He silently planned and arranged within Himself everything which He was afterwards about to utter through His Word." Ibid.

[6] Tertullian *Adv. Marc.* 2.27; *Adv. Prax.* 7. "As He is Spirit of Spirit and God of God, He is made a second in manner of existence—in position, not in nature; and He did not withdraw from the original source, but went forth." Tertullian *Apol.* 21. See Moignt, 1039-1062; Karl Wölfl, *Das Heilswirken Gottes durch den Sohn nach Tertullian* (Rome: Libreria editrice del l'Universita Gregoriana, 1960), 134.

Besides *persona*, numerous other terms, including several discussed below, are significant for Tertullian. Several different views exist concerning Tertullian's role in the development of these theological terms. Each view generally considers Tertullian in a different context—juridical, philosophical, or otherwise—which is problematic when "we know almost nothing of Tertullian beyond the texts which he has left us." Bray, 31.

For the present work, the source of his vocabulary is much less significant than the context in which Tertullian utilizes it. Lexicography, therefore, is not as essential to understanding Tertullian's theology. The meanings of key terms are important to this understanding, especially in a close and detailed examination of particular concepts, but to assume with the *Sondersprache* school that there are fixed lexical meanings behind the key terms in patristic writers is unwarranted. Tertullian's polemical and catechetical contexts are more significant for the present discussion than the etymological or lexicographical data. The present study, therefore, follows Bray, 27-31. For a summary of the various viewpoints see Robert D. Sider, "Approaches to Tertullian," *The Second Century* 2 (Winter 1982): 251-252. See also Moignt and Braun, whose extensive works evaluate Tertullian's theology by means of his terminology.

It is in Wisdom's creative role in the *oikonomia* that humanity first sees the economic Trinity revealed. Consequently, the procession of the *Logos prophorikos* at creation is the procession of both the Word and the Son. In fact, the Word, Wisdom, and the Son are one and the same. Essentially, the prolation that takes place in the beginning of creation is the procession of the second person of the Trinity, the Word or Son who becomes incarnate as Jesus Christ.[7]

The Son also receives the names Mind, Power, Understanding, Spirit, and Might in addition to Reason, Word, and Wisdom.[8] These appellations are drawn from passages like Prov. 8:22, Jer. 10:12, Jer. 51:15, and Rom. 11:34, indicating Tertullian's strong dependence on Scripture. This also explains some of the confusion that arises in the use of these names. Varying scriptural contexts and interpretations, in addition to differing polemical contexts, can result in varying applications of certain names, but some general observations can be made. Word (*Sermo*) or *Logos* is the most general appellation and seems applicable to every stage of the Son's existence whether inherent within God's Reason or external as the spoken Word of God. Reason is attributable to the pre-creation mode of the Word's existence, and Wisdom is clearly correlative to the *Logos prophorikos* in accordance with the statement in Prov. 8 describing his beginning.[9] The remaining names are less clear. Particular contexts may dictate different uses of the same name or title, but the overarching theme remains the continuity of the Son's existence in various modes prior to, contemporaneous with, and subsequent to creation. The result is an explanation of the Son's ontology utilizing scriptural names and depictions based largely in functional language.

The significance of this functional language is best seen in Tertullian's interpretation of God as Father and Son. Prior to creation, while the *Logos* was still immanent within Reason, God did not exist as Father and Son. Father and Son are functional or relational titles as are Lord and Judge, pertinent only to the economic distinction between the *personae* in the Godhead.[10] Only after the procession of the Son from the Father when distinctions can be made in terms of the *oikonomia* can God be called by these relative names. Fortunately, Tertullian does not follow this line of thinking to some of its potential conclusions. This interpretation bears only a superficial resemblance to the Arian argument stating that there was a time when the Son was not. Yet, it does have difficulty explaining the Trinity in its eternal existence, or for that matter, addressing it in anything more than an economic context.

---

[7] Tertullian *Adv. Prax.* 7, 12; *Adv. Herm.* 18, 19, 45; *Adv. Marc.* 5.19; Rene Braun, *Deus Christianorum: Recherches sur le vocabulaire doctrinal de Tertullien*, Études Augustiniennes (Paris: Chateau-Gontier, 1962), 289-297; Raniero Cantalamessa, *La Cristologia di Tertulliano* (Freiburg: Edizioni universitarie, 1962), 18-27; Kearsley, 55; Wölfl, 155. Tertullian's statements in *Against Hermogenes* should be considered within their context. He aims to prove the beginning of everything (that is, matter) in contrast to the eternal nature of God. He does not intend to delineate the Word's origins in detail.

[8] Tertullian *Apol.* 21, 23; *Adv. Herm.* 45; *Carne Christi* 19; *De Poenitentia* 1; *Resurrectione Carne* 19.

[9] Tertullian *Adv. Herm.* 18-19.

[10] Ibid., 3.

Essentially, in Tertullian's understanding of the Trinity "the second and the third persons proceed from the *unitas substantiae* because they have a task to fulfill."[11] His christological concepts and vocabulary have expanded beyond those of the Apologists and others, but Tertullian is still bound to some of the same primitive principles such as the temporal procession of the Son. The Son's origins in the Godhead as Reason, Word, and Wisdom, therefore, while entailing ontological issues are primarily communicated in functional terms in this transitional perspective.

The *Monarchia* and *Personae*

One of the most productive theological subjects of inquiry for Tertullian is the relationship between the Father and the Son within the *oikonomia* after the Son's procession or generation. Like the previous subject, it portrays the manner in which Tertullian both relies upon the work of such predecessors as the Apologists and Irenaeus and departs from or adds to their theological constructions.[12]

The *oikonomia*, God's plan of creation, salvation, and final redemption in all of its dispensations, is the overarching means by which God reveals himself to humanity as a Trinity within unity.[13] Apart from God's movement toward humanity, we would know nothing of his nature beyond his existence. Consequently, understanding the relationship between the Father and the Son during Christ's earthly ministry and the rest of the *oikonomia* is essential to Tertullian's Christology and nascent Trinitarian theology.

The importance of this relationship is one of Tertullian's major points in the *regula* in *Adv. Prax.* 2 where he repeatedly cites the Father's relations with the Son: the Son was sent by the Father, raised by the Father, seated at the right hand of the Father, and he sent the Spirit by the Father's authority. In later arguments against Praxeas the existence of the Father and the Son as distinct subjects proves to be central. These activities naturally take place within the *oikonomia*, prior to which God is only known in his unity. All believers recognize that "there is one only God," but under the *oikonomia* the Son proceeds from the Father and God reveals himself in multiplicity.

Several analogies explain in part God's diversity within unity. The Son is a tree sprouting from the root, the Father; he is a river flowing from a fountain or spring; he is a ray shining from the sun. In all three analogies the Father is the source of deity and the Son is an outflow from the Father.[14] The analogies have the effect of communicating a common essence or substance in God while maintaining distinctions between the Father and the Son. The cost comes in the sub-

---

[11] Grillmeier, 120.
[12] See Kelly, *Early Christian Doctrines*, 110-111.
[13] See Daniélou, *The Origins of Latin Christianity*, 365; Moignt, 908-932.
[14] Tertullian *Adv. Prax.* 8. Justin and Tatian prefer fire kindled from fire as an analogy. Justin Martyr *Dialogue with Trypho* 61; Tatian *Discourses* 5.

ordination that results from the Father's existence as the source of deity.[15] Consistency would open the door to a deity for the Son derived from the Father and not necessarily innate or eternal, though Tertullian does not go this far. This emphasis on the Father as the font of deity also raises questions concerning the Son's procession and whether or not he was truly distinct prior to his procession as is maintained.

Difficulties aside, Tertullian works hard to maintain monotheism even as he seeks to explain Christ's inclusion within the unique divine identity. Two complementary terms, *substantia* and *monarchia*, are utilized to uphold the oneness of God. The first, *substantia*, is a claim for the ontological unity between the Father and the Son.[16] They are of the same substance as the analogies admit. While one can distinguish between parts of a tree or locations in a water system, distinguishing between the substances involved is impossible. A trunk or branch of a tree possesses "treeness" as much as its root. Similarly, the source of a river and its main stem both partake of "riverness." The same is true of the Trinity. While one can distinguish between activities and manifestations of the divine persons, their substance remains singular and indistinguishable. This indistinguishable substance explains the equally divine power of the Son, for it derives from his indissoluble unity with the Father.

The second term, *monarchia*, refers to the single divine rule and fills out the consubstantiality of the Father and Son in functional terms. Interestingly, *Against Praxeas*, especially chapters 3-4, contains the term's significant use. The term is not used to defend Christianity's monotheism from pagan attacks or to thwart Jewish charges of tritheism. Instead, it is used to delineate for modalists the manner in which orthodox Trinitarianism maintains its monotheistic roots. Tertullian's use of the *monarchia* rests in the assertion that single rule "does not, because it is the government of one, preclude him [God], either from having a son [*Filium non habere*], or from having made himself actually a son to himself [*ipsum se sibi filium fecisse*]."[17] In fact, it would be unheard of to claim that a monarchy ceased to be a monarchy based on the existence of a son. Instead, it would be assumed that the son would possess the dominion or authority of the crown, however differently it might be exercised. Only the removal of the monarch and the institution of a new government would constitute a change in that single rule.[18]

In addition to Ps. 110:1 and all of its New Testament quotations placing Christ at the right hand of the Father, 1 Cor. 15:27-28 supports the *monarchia*, clearly delineating the relationship between the Father and the Son and their shared authority. The single rule over creation "has been committed to Him [the

---

[15] Tertullian *Adv. Prax.* 9.

[16] Tertullian *Apol.*, 21; *Adv. Prax.* 2, 4, 12, 19, 25, 26. For analyses of *substantia* see Braun, 167-199; Moignt, 299-430; Cantalamessa, 100-107; Danielou, *The Origins of Latin Christianity*, 345-348; Kearsley, 121-132; Kelly, *Early Christian Doctrines*, 113; and Eric Osborn, *Tertullian, First Theologian of the West* (New York: Cambridge University Press, 1997), 131-133.

[17] Tertullian *Adv. Prax.* 3.2.

[18] Kearsley, 115-120.

Son] by the Father," presumably before creation at his procession, and after his return in glory and subsequent judgment it will "be again delivered up by Him to the Father."[19] That the rule of God is exercised by more than one person, therefore, does not deny monotheism, but reinforces it.

In addition to reasserting monotheism, this interpretation of the *monarchia* also supports a burgeoning Trinitarianism against those who deny multiplicity within the Godhead. Two agents are present in the handing of authority between the Father and the Son, not one as the modalists assert. The same person cannot both give and receive. At two different times there is a transfer of divine authority and sovereignty, at the beginning and the end of the *oikonomia*. Both transfers of power include a subject and an object, necessitating the differentiation of persons within God himself. Ps. 45:6-7 gives this concept scriptural weight when it "affirms that God is anointed by God" and likewise affirms "that Two are God [*hic duos deos*], by reason of the sceptre's royal power."[20] Tertullian's understanding of the *monarchia*, then, supports both singularity and multiplicity within God.

More significant for his defense of the threeness of God necessitated by Praxeas' modalism is Tertullian's articulation of the distinctions between *personae*. Here the fight against heresy requires the stability of doctrinal continuity within the apostolic tradition and ingenuity in explaining and communicating doctrinal truths. Tertullian may have been the first to apply *trinitas* to the distinctions within God, but *persona* was taken from the heretics. He is simply the first orthodox theologian to use *persona* in a precise theological sense.[21] Previously the word had been used in a rhetorical or exegetical sense, and it was the Gnostics who pioneered its use as a theological term. Tertullian, then, in addressing the monarchians is utilizing a fairly accessible term and standardizing it in an orthodox setting.[22] This development in vocabulary is another indication of the need to translate and reinterpret existing orthodox theologies whose previous articulations are inadequate for addressing the heresies of the day. It also shows the value of reclaiming theological vocabulary from the heretics for use in defending the apostolic tradition against their deviations.

Early in the argument against Praxeas, God is defined as three persons "not in condition [*statu*], but in degree [*gradu*]; not in substance [*substantia*], but in form [*forma*]; not in power [*potestate*], but in aspect [*specie*]."[23] Condition, substance, and power all describe God in his unity. He exists in one divine essence or substance and he possesses a single will and rule. At the same time he exists in three persons in degree, form, and aspect. These terms describe his differentiated ways of existing for humanity and the logical subordination that accompa-

---

[19] Tertullian *Adv. Prax.* 4.
[20] Ibid., 13.2. See also ibid., 4.
[21] Cf. Braun, 207-242; Cantalamessa, 150-176; Kearsley, 135-141; Moignt, 551-674; Osborn, 136-139; Johannes Quasten, *Patrology* (Westminster, MD: Newman Press, 1950), vol. 2, 325.
[22] Grillmeier, 126-127.
[23] Tertullian *Adv. Prax.* 2.4. Cf. Grillmeier, 125; Kearsley, 134-5; Moignt, 431-549.

nies this Trinitarian model. The terms are summed up in the concept of personality, which is differentiation by distinction, not division.[24]

The significance of the latter terms, form and aspect, are best seen in the myriad of scriptural examples cited that differentiate between the Father and the Son's economic manifestation for humanity. God initiated the *oikonomia* with the generation of his Son by speaking his Word and in the process manifested himself to humanity in his threeness. Creation presents us with this first manifestation of God's *personae*. In the creation account God clearly speaks in the first person plural with such statements as "Let us make man in our image, in our likeness" (Gen. 1:26). The Jewish argument for the inclusion of angels in the plural and the modalistic argument that sees the Father, Son, and Spirit as a single divine person are inadequate explanations according to Tertullian.

The presence of the Word in creation, a conclusion drawn from John's prologue and other New Testament passages, is the impetus for the plural pronoun. The dual reference to image in Gen. 1:27 supplements this argument. In other interpretations the fact that "God created man in his own image" is stated simply and clearly enough not to need the added phrase "in the image of God he created him." In truth, the latter phrase places the image of God in a locale distinct from God himself and indicates plurality within the divine substance. This image of God is the Son of God, his Word, who is described as God's image in the New Testament and is the perfect model for the creation of humanity (2 Cor. 4:4; Col. 1:15). The Son of God, therefore, is both the perfect image of God after whom Adam and the rest of humanity are modeled and a divine person, indicating distinctions within God.[25]

In addition to the creation account numerous other scriptural references affirm the distinctions between the divine *personae*. The Father and the Son are repeatedly placed in distinct positions as subject and object. The differentiated *personae* are shown by their interpersonal actions and communication—for example, the Son gives up his spirit to the Father, the Father raises the Son from the dead, and the Son commands the disciples "to baptize into the Father and the Son and the Holy Ghost, not into a unipersonal God."[26] The Father also sends the Son, loves the Son, commits judgment to the Son, and bears witness to the Son.

With respect to the last example, Christ would have little reason to cite the Father's witness to his person and ministry if he and the Father were not distinct. The Law requires the testimony of two people to verify truth, and modalism makes Christ's argument irrelevant if both Father and Son constitute only one person at a time. The Son's prayers to the Father, his obedience to a higher authority, his administration of the Father's word and work, the distinct existence of the Spirit, and many other scriptural examples prove the plurality of God in three distinct but undivided persons.[27]

---

[24] Tertullian *Adv. Prax.* 12, 25.
[25] Ibid., 12.
[26] Ibid., 26.
[27] Ibid., 21-26.

The most common designations for the first two persons of the Trinity in these examples are the relational titles Father and Son. They are titles applicable only to their existence within the *oikonomia* since they are distinguishable in this relational sense only after the Son's procession from the Father. Nevertheless, the attributions Father and Son reveal actual distinctions within the single *substantia* despite the fact that the relationship described is not eternal. Although difficult to explain, these distinctions are ontological and not purely economic, for "all things will be what their names represent them to be [*enim omnia quod uocantur, hoc erunt*]; and what they are and ever will be [*et quod erunt*], that will they be called [*hoc uocabuntur*]."[28] The Father and the Son are distinct persons, and their preexistent state both embodied and anticipated this economic distinction. Yet, explaining their distinctiveness in the preexistent state is difficult with a Logos Christology incorporating the *Logos endiathetos* and *Logos prophorikos*. The two states of the *Logos* define a distinction, but whether or not it substantiates full personhood prior to his spokenness is debatable.

Besides the difficulty defining the preexistent nature of the second person of the Trinity, the Logos Christology also presents a problem in its subordination of the Son to the Father. The three persons of the Trinity are differentiated not only in form and aspect, but also in degree. The Father is the Godhead, the source of deity, and the Son and the Spirit are prolations or emanations from the Father. This concept of *probolē* (*prolatio*) is very different from the Gnostic idea of emanation and indicates development rather than the material emanation that Valentinus and other heretics teach.[29] Nevertheless, the Son and the Spirit are subordinate to the Father. The Father is primary, the Son is secondary, and the Spirit is tertiary since "everything which proceeds from something else [*omne quod prodit ex aliquo*] must needs be second to that [*secundum sit eius necesse est*] from which it proceeds [*de quo prodit*]."[30]

This subordination flows naturally out of the analogies used for the Trinity, namely the tree, river, and sun. The root, spring, and sun are primary, and their secondary manifestations, the tree, river, and sunlight, would not exist except by the emission of the primary substance. The source, therefore, in one sense is more of the primary substance than its prolations while all entities exist entirely as the same substance. Jesus Christ himself substantiates this subordination in the Trinity with such statements as "My Father is greater than I" (John 14:28). In fact, Scripture verifies that "the Father is the entire substance [*toto substantia est*], but the Son is a derivation and portion of the whole [*deriuatio totius et portio*]."[31] At the same time, the substance of each secondary person is continuous with that of his source and cannot be separated from him. The consubstantiality of the Father, Son, and Spirit is maintained, but at the cost of a strong subordinationism that would later be softened by more precise language.

---

[28] Ibid., 9.4.
[29] ANF 3.602, footnote 15.
[30] Tertullian *Adv. Prax.* 8.7.
[31] Ibid., 9.2.

The Two-Natures Christology

In addition to his work on the unity and diversity within the Trinity, Tertullian also contributes to an early incarnational Christology. One of the basic presuppositions underlying his understanding of Jesus Christ's two natures is the immutability of God—that God "neither ceases to be what He was, nor can He be any other thing than what He is."[32] This basic tenet necessitates the distinctiveness of Christ's two natures within his one person. In God becoming human two possibilities exist, transfiguration and incarnation. In transfiguration the previous substance is destroyed by the new substance and the new substance itself is transformed. The transfiguration of the Son into human form, therefore, is impossible since the transformation of immutable deity is impossible. Incarnation, on the other hand, entails the clothing of the divine substance in flesh and remains a possibility.

Defining incarnation in this manner results in a person with two sharply differentiated natures. Jesus exists as both God and man, "inasmuch as the Word is nothing else but God [*quia neque sermo aliud quam Deus*], and the flesh nothing else but Man [*neque caro aliud quam homo*]."[33] Humanity and deity "co-exist" in Jesus Christ, but only in a limited sense in which "the property of each nature is so wholly preserved [*et adeo salua est utriusque proprietas substantiae*], that the Spirit on the one hand did all things in Jesus suitable to Itself, such as miracles, and mighty deeds, and wonders; and the Flesh, on the other hand, exhibited the affections which belong to it," including death.[34] Tertullian's use of the titles Son of God and Son of Man, indicating Christ's divine nature and human nature respectively, reflect this differentiation.[35]

Without this careful demarcation of the divine and human natures Jesus Christ would be a "*tertium quid*, some composite essence formed out of the two substances [*substantiae*]."[36] This third substance would retain none of the proper characteristics found in either deity or humanity and, instead, would develop its own distinctive properties. Such mixing would result in a being unable to identify with either God or humanity. Therefore, a Jesus Christ of mixed substance is incapable of mediating between the Creator and his creation. Furthermore, aside from mediatorial requirements, a mixing of natures eliminates the viability of a redemptive death in the crucifixion. One of two things would have happened in the confluence of properties, "either the Word underwent death, or the flesh did

---

[32] Ibid., 27.7. See also ibid., 29-30.

[33] Ibid., 27.10. Cf. Osborn, *Tertullian*, 140-141.

[34] Tertullian *Adv. Prax.* 27.11. Tertullian believes that only Christ's flesh died on the cross and that the Word, his spiritual and divine nature, returned to the Father. See also ibid., 29-30.

[35] Tertullian *Adv. Marc.* 4.10, 21, 35; *De Carne Christi* 5, 14; *Adv. Prax.* 23, 27, 28, 29.

[36] Tertullian *Adv. Prax.* 27.12.

not die ... because either the flesh was immortal, or the Word was mortal."[37] In light of the strong stance on God's immutability, in both cases the death of Jesus becomes problematic at best or impossible at worst. If the Word experienced death with the flesh then it ceased to be divine and immutable; whereas, if the flesh took on the immutable nature of the Word, Christ's death was only a farce. The two-natures doctrine, therefore, must be maintained in tension in order to retain Christ's place as mediator and to sustain the redemptive nature of his death.

Tertullian uses the Stoic concept of *krasis* or mixture to explain how the two natures are related to one another in the single person of Jesus Christ. The two-natures doctrine is reasonable if the relationship is understood as a mixture in which two substances are neither compounded, as in a chemical reaction, nor distinct, as with oil and water, but co-mingled. Both substances or natures completely interpenetrate each other without losing their distinctive qualities just as sand and water or soil and gravel might mix.[38] Within this relationship, both natures remain distinct but still interact. In fact, hints of the *communicatio idiomatum* within Christ are seen in the truth that God was born, cradled, circumcised, crucified, and buried.[39]

Yet, the solution to the question of the relationship between Christ's two natures in his one person remains a problem despite Tertullian's rare statements implying the *communicatio idiomatum* and his ardent defense of the coexistence of the two natures in Jesus Christ. The sometimes sharp distinction between his deity and humanity, displayed in such things as the titles Son of God and Son of Man or the death of Christ's flesh alone, could lead to conclusions that would later be deemed heretical. But this places a pre-Nicene theologian addressing very specific heresies within a post-Chalcedonian context. Despite his insistence upon Christ's deity and humanity "*in una persona*," Tertullian "has not yet considered what unity of person in Christ means."[40] The purpose of his speculative work is not to reason through all the christological issues that might arise but to deal with particular heretics, in this case monarchians, who threaten the apostolic faith.[41] In fact, Tertullian only anticipates in part the christological issues that will appear in the centuries to follow. Were he to follow through on his two-natures doctrine he would run into the problems of Nestorianism.[42] As it is, he ends his consideration of the subject before arriving at any such difficulties, having dispatched his immediate adversary with his understanding of Christ in two natures and the Trinity.

---

[37] Ibid., 27.13.
[38] Cf. Cantalamessa, 135-8; Grillmeier, 130.
[39] Tertullian *De Carne Christi* (CCSL) 5.1-4; Grillmeier, 122; Kelly, *Early Christian Doctrines*, 152.
[40] Grillmeier, 129.
[41] Modalistic monarchianism is the only reason Tertullian addresses the two natures of Christ in as much detail as he does. The problem arises from the modalists' attempt to make divinity all one spiritual being (Father, God, Christ) and the physical Jesus another being (man, flesh, Son). Tertullian *Adv. Prax.* 27; Grillmeier, 129.
[42] Grillmeier, 131.

The *Regula* and the Transition to Ontological Language

Tertullian's explicit use of *oikonomia*, the manifestation of the Trinity, and creation as the time of this manifestation reveal the continuation of many functional emphases, but he also reinterprets the Logos Christology and incorporates new concepts such as the *monarchia*, *substantia*, and *persona*. Consequently, Tertullian articulates Christ's inclusion in the unique divine identity with more precision than Irenaeus and the Apologists by utilizing a combination of functional and ontological language.

Tertullian's comparatively open hermeneutic enables concepts couched primarily in functional language to support increasing ontological inquiry. This hermeneutic also permits more vocabulary that is specifically ontological even when it is not scripturally derived. For example, the unity of God is explained more fully by means of the Father and Son's consubstantiality and the *monarchia*, and God's diversity is delineated by means of his *personae*. The exploration of the immanent relations within the Godhead prior to creation, the application of *persona*, and the developing doctrine of the two natures of Christ, therefore, reveal an openness to ontological speculation where Irenaeus often quotes Scripture and ceases inquiry. This hermeneutical adjustment is mandated in part by the heresies of the time. Modalism, as a functional explanation of the Son's deity, is only corrected by an ontological Trinity.

That is not to say that Tertullian embraces speculation wholeheartedly. Using a combination of functional and ontological terminology he fills in gaps in previous thinking, but he still runs into some roadblocks beyond which he is unwilling to pass. Included among these difficulties are the Son's generation, his subordination to the Father, and the relationship between Christ's divine and human natures. Although he is willing to speculate, he will only do so to a point and never simply for the purpose of speculating. The discussion ends, sometimes abruptly, on these questions when he has adequately answered the heterodox view before him. There is no value in exploratory theology when one possesses the apostles' teaching and has answered all challenges.

The *regula*'s place in Tertullian's theology is clearly revealed by its placement within polemical works. The two substantive versions of the *regula* in *Prescription Against Heretics* and *Against Praxeas* are central to the arguments of the respective works. They are used to limit the heretics' abuse of Scripture, to introduce the essential truths of the Christian faith, and to present most of the key concepts and terms upon which he later elaborates. In effect, the *regula* opens the door to speculation, but only wide enough for Tertullian to gain his polemical tools. The door is subsequently slammed shut. Above all, Tertullian is interested in refuting heretics and maintaining correct doctrine. His renditions of the *regula* allow him to do this with only the creativity required to service doctrinal integrity.

Part Four

Origen's Ontological Theology

Chapter 7

Theological Research Beyond the *Regula*

Origen was born in AD 185 or 186 in Alexandria to Christian parents. His father, Leonides, provided him with a thorough education in both Greek literature and the Scriptures. Much like Irenaeus, Origen personally experienced the effects of persecution early in life at the age of seventeen with the martyrdom of his father in AD 202. Eusebius shares the story that Origen's mother hid his clothes in order to incite his modesty and prevent him from joining his father in martyrdom. The bodily injuries he would suffer years later during the Decian persecution would contribute to his own death in AD 254.

Within a few months of his father's death, Origen turned to teaching literature to provide for himself and possibly his mother and younger siblings. He was also given leadership of the catechetical school in Alexandria where he began a lifelong labor of training others in the interpretation of Scripture. In this respect, Origen's perspective diverts from that of Irenaeus and Tertullian. While they certainly taught others doctrine, Origen does so predominantly in an academic environment. Although he is often pastoral, his pastoral concerns are derived from a well thought out theological perspective. Consequently, where Irenaeus and Tertullian are reticent to speculate on the philosophical and theological, often out of fears of heresy, Origen willingly indulges in speculation and encourages his readers to participate for the sake of the larger search for truth.[1]

Nevertheless, despite Origen's penchant for speculation, these three fathers have a common desire to dispel the false notions about Christians often held by pagans and to correct those teaching false doctrine. *Against Celsus* (*Contra Celsum*) is the most prominent example of the former, and interestingly, many of his commentaries on Scripture are at least in part written to address the latter. Ambrose, a former Valentinian Gnostic whose conversion was influenced by Origen, became a great benefactor to Origen, providing him with stenographers and copyists for the dissemination of his work. In light of Ambrose's experiences and support, it seemed necessary to Origen "that one who is able to intercede

---

[1] "Numerous are the instances where he propounds an interpretation while hoping that someone else might provide an improved resolution in future consideration. He urges his audience not to hesitate to adopt a better solution once they come across one." Panayiotis Tzamalikos, *Origen: Philosophy of History and Eschatology* (Boston: Brill, 2007), 19.

in a genuine manner on behalf of the teaching of the Church and reprove those who pursue the knowledge falsely so-called, must take a stand against the heretical fabrications by adducing in opposition the sublimity of the gospel message ...."[2] Essentially, his desire is for theological questioners to find true knowledge (*gnosis*) within the confines of the church's tradition by means of his commentaries rather than in heretical movements outside of the church.

Among his voluminous writings, the reader inevitably comes to Origen's *On First Principles* (*De principiis*), which is sometimes characterized as the church's first systematic theology. While not a systematic theology in the modern sense, it is arguably the first significant attempt by a Christian to articulate a complete system of belief incorporating biblical teaching and philosophical insight. Section four of the preface to *On First Principles* provides not only the fullest rendition of the *regula fidei* in Origen's extant works, but also the culmination of both form and content in the ante-Nicene *regula fidei*. His articulation of the *regula* is thorough, containing nearly all of the substance included in his predecessors' *regulae* and more. Its form is also the clearest. Three articles, the *regula* proper, address the Father, Son, and Spirit respectively, and subsequent articles discuss other important subjects as addenda.

Despite its clarity of form and thorough substance, Origen's *regula* presents some difficulties for the interpreter not only because of the often complex thought behind it, but also because of the textual difficulties involved. The text of the *regula* in *On First Principles* exists only in Rufinus' Latin translation. Rufinus' version of the work often departs from the original Greek through both the omission and addition of texts. Several references to "the rule of faith," "the rule of piety," and similar identifying phrases are suspect in the Latin since they do not occur in the extant Greek fragments, and Rufinus' tendency was to err on the side of orthodoxy. Nevertheless, the longer passages, including the preface, cannot be easily dismissed. Even Koetschau, one of Origen's most critical editors, accepts this pivotal preface as generally "an accurate representation of the Greek original, with interpolations and expansions by Rufinus which do not, however, seriously obscure the meaning."[3]

Yet, even with this general trust, the loss of the original Greek text can sometimes hinder analysis of Origen's *regula*. Specific words and phrases will have incomplete expositional value in and of themselves since oftentimes the significance of precise vocabulary will have diminished with the loss of the original. Therefore, the cumulative effect of multiple statements within the preface and corroboration from other texts is required to interpret meaningfully some of the

---

[2] Origen, *Commentaire sur saint Jean, Livres 1-5*, ed. and trans. Cécile Blanc, Sources chrétiennes, no. 120 (Paris: Éditions du Cerf, 1966); Origen, *Commentary on the Gospel according to John, Books 1-10*, trans. Ronald E. Heine, FOTC, vol. 80 (Washington, DC: Catholic University of America Press, 1989), 5.8. Two numbering systems are used for the *Commentary on John*. The numbering in SC and FOTC is used unless otherwise noted. All Greek quotations are taken from SC. All English quotations are taken from FOTC unless otherwise noted. ANF uses the other numbering system.

[3] Outler, 138. See also G. W. Butterworth, ed., *Origen on First Principles* (New York: Harper & Row, 1966), 48-52.

shorter passages and phrases. In light of these difficulties, Origen's statements of basic belief in his *Commentary on John* and similar texts will be valuable as confirmation of the *regula* in *On First Principles*.[4] In short, Rufinus' translation of *On First Principles* makes the interpreter's task more difficult, but the problem can be overcome in the present study by documenting multiple statements that verify the same beliefs. Origen's belief in Christ's divine sovereignty, for example, can be shown with several less direct statements that cumulatively suggest as significant a belief as is communicated by Tertullian's use of "at the right hand of the Father." This is easily done with Origen considering the extensiveness of this *regula*.

Of course Origen's *regula* does have the advantage of being presented in a systematic form designed most likely for a catechetical context. If *On First Principles* was not intended for Origen's classroom, it was surely available to his students. Furthermore, the manner in which the work builds on the preface gives the work corroborative value for the *regula* in its preface. Therefore, despite the difficulties with the text, Origen's *regula* remains invaluable for evaluating theological continuity in the early church.

The Christological Core in the *Regula*

Origen introduces this "definite line and unmistakable rule [*certam lineam manifestamque regulam*]" in order to accomplish two goals.[5] First, he wishes to dispatch conflicting opinion on the essentials of the Christian faith before moving to a more detailed theology. Second, the *regula* will provide the elementary principles from which more enlightened principles and truths can be logically derived. The form of the *regula* assists these goals by differentiating between the essentials of the faith and the subjects concerning which little consensus exists within the church.

The *regula* proper is broken into three distinct articles, each dealing with a person of the Trinity. Each of these articles enunciates the core christological theme, the continuity of the two covenants, though the theme dominates the first article. The second article on the Son naturally addresses Christ's inclusion in the unique divine identity.

Jesus Christ's divine sovereignty, the first criterion for his inclusion in the unique divine identity, is best seen in the fact that Christ "emptied himself [*se ipsum exinaniens*] and was made man [*homo factus est*] ... although he was God [*cum deus esset*]." The statement is a clear reference to Paul's description of the

---

[4] This passage is within a discussion of what it means to have all faith. The essential articles of faith provided are very concise statements of the Trinitarian articles of the *regula*. They are intended to serve only as examples for Origen, not as a complete delineation of the faith. Origen *Com. on John* 32.187-189.

[5] Origen *De princ.* pref., 4-9. All quotations from *De principiis* in Rufinus' Latin version or available Greek fragments are taken from SC. English quotations are taken from Butterworth, unless otherwise noted. See appendix for the complete text of the *regula*.

kenosis in Philippians and to his willing divestiture of the divine glory in his incarnation. While the Son gave up the external manifestation of this glory, he assuredly remains "what he was, namely, God [*mansit quod erat, deus*]," and retains his corresponding sovereignty.[6] According to the first article of the *regula* on the Father, prior to the incarnation Christ exercises this divine sovereignty by calling Israel. Subsequent to Israel's rejection of this call and the incarnation, Christ exercises his authority by calling the Gentiles into the kingdom of God.[7]

Unsurprisingly, Christ's sovereignty is closely related to his role in creation, the second criterion for inclusion in the unique divine identity. In being the instrumental cause for the existence of all things, Christ "ministered to the Father in the foundation of all things [*in omnium conditione patri ministrasset*]."[8] The common reference to the foundation of the world in this statement and a similar phrase in the first article is significant. That the one and only creator God is God "from the first creation [*deus a prima creatura*] and foundation of the world [*et conditione mundi*]" gives added credence to the assertion in the second article that Jesus Christ is God. Only the one God existed at the foundation of creation, and Jesus Christ ministered to the Father in this foundation.

The third criterion, the attribution of the divine name to Christ is more obvious in Origen's *regula* than in either Irenaeus' or Tertullian's versions. Jesus Christ is unequivocally named God twice in the second article on the Son, explicitly stating that he exists as God both before and after the incarnation. Furthermore, "Lord" is added to Jesus Christ both times that he is mentioned in the first article on the Father. The title is conspicuously absent in the other articles. Its presence in the first article seemingly lessens the subordination implied in his

---

[6] For Origen the *kenosis* refers only to Jesus Christ's preexistent human soul which always remained in perfect contemplation of the divine. In emptying himself, Christ's preexistent humanity descended to the physical fallen state of humanity and took on the form of sinful man without sin. See below. See also Henri Crouzel, *Origen*, trans. A. S. Worrall (San Francisco: Harper & Row, 1989), 192-194.

[7] More explicit statements of Christ's sovereignty are numerous. Origen plainly states in *De princ.* 1.2.10, in an extensive discussion on Wisdom's authority, that "the omnipotence of the Father and the Son is one and the same." See also Origen *De princ.* 3.5.7; Origen, *Contra Celsum*, in *The Ante-Nicene Fathers*, vol. 4, *Fathers of the Third Century*, ed. James Donaldson and Alexander Roberts (United States: Christian Literature Pub. Co., 1897; reprint, Peabody, MA: Hendrickson, 1994), 8.15. Origen also discusses the manner in which Christ is king in *Com. on John* 1.191-200. The discussion incorporates elements of his understanding of the two natures in Christ and their relationship.

[8] Wisdom, the second person of the Trinity, not only is the instrumental cause of creation, but also "contains within herself the species and causes of the entire creation," including both primary and secondary causes and beings. Origen *De princ.* 1.2.2-3. See also 1.2.10; 1.4.4-5; 1.7.1; 2.6.1-3; 2.9.4; 4.3.15; 4.4.3; *Com. on John* 1.110-111, 244; 2.102-104; 6.188; *Com. on Matt.* 12.2; *Con. Cels.* 6.69.

In *Com. on John* (ANF) 2.6, Origen addresses Christ's role in creation extensively, with a thorough explanation of why the Holy Spirit is the first creation of the Son. Although the Spirit is qualitatively different from the rest of creation, he is nonetheless created since the alternative is for the Spirit to be unbegotten, uncreated or *autotheos*, which for Origen describes only the Father.

obedience to the Father's command by expressing his dominion and authority as Lord.

The worship of Jesus Christ as God, the last criterion for his inclusion in the unique divine identity, is largely assumed in Origen's *regula*. The calling of Israel and the Gentiles by the Son implies his worthiness of worship. The presence of the disciples with Christ after his resurrection may also assume the worship of Christ, bringing recollection of the worship they proffered at his appearances. Finally, the honor attributed to the Holy Spirit in the third article is based on his worthiness held in common with the Father and the Son. The Son by implication, therefore, possesses the honor and dignity of God himself and is worthy of worship.[9]

Origen's *regula* does not always fulfill the criteria for Christ's inclusion in the unique divine identity as extensively as Irenaeus' and Tertullian's, but not because Origen's theology expresses christological monotheism any less than theirs. In some ways Origen is more concise than his predecessors, allowing him to address more specifics. For example, Christ's role in creation is stated only once in the preface to *On First Principles* while Irenaeus mentions it eight times in *Adv. haer.* 1.22.1.

Seldom repeating himself in the *regula*, Origen maintains a strong christological monotheism that is best seen in his simple assertion that Jesus Christ is God. Irenaeus and Tertullian call Christ "God" in their *regulae*, but Irenaeus includes it in a series of names and titles for Christ and Tertullian uses it as a synonym for deity by placing it in contrast to his humanity. Origen, on the other hand, in calling Jesus Christ God while referencing Phil. 2 communicates his deity with *erat* and *esset*, ontological terms with which he reaffirms the ever present deity of Christ. The christological monotheism within all three fathers does not change substantially, but the form in which it is articulated changes with the context.

While the language describing Christ's inclusion in the unique divine identity takes on a more ontological flavor in Origen's *regula*, the statements reinforcing the assertion that "Christ died for our sins, according to the Scriptures" remain concrete and functional. They even become more numerous as Origen repeatedly connects the old and new covenants, asserts the existence of one God, and relates him to believers in both testaments.

The first article of the *regula* is engrossed in stating and developing the continuity of the two covenants as a derivative of Christian monotheism. Once the foundational statement "God is one [*unus est deus*]" is given, a plethora of details explaining this one God is drawn from both testaments.[10] He is the one God "who created [out of nothing] and set in order all things [*qui omnia creauit atque composuit*]," who "caused the universe to be [*esse fecit uniuersa*]," and

---

[9] See Origen *Com. on Matt.* 11.7, 17; *De princ.* 4.1.1; *Con. Cels.* 1.40, 51; 3.43; 5.4; 8.9, 12-13. The worship of idols is contrasted sharply and repeatedly with the worship of the true God in *Contra Celsum*.

[10] Monotheism is foundational for Origen, as it is for Irenaeus and Tertullian. Origen *De princ.* 1.1.6.

who existed "from the first creation and foundation of the world [*a prima creatura et conditione mundi*]." After there is no doubt in the reader's mind that we speak of the Creator God, this same God is shown to be the one who "sent the Lord Jesus Christ." The Creator in the Old Testament and the Father spoken of in the New Testament are one and the same.

Extraordinary detail follows these basic statements. The one God is the God of all righteous men, including the antediluvian fathers from Adam to Noah, the patriarchs, Moses, and the prophets. Their God is not a vindictive Demiurge distinct from the true God; rather, he is the one who sent Christ in accordance with the announcements made through the prophets.[11] He promised salvation in the Old Testament and delivered it in the New Testament. He is the "just and good God [*deus iustus et bonus*]," who is holy and righteous while being gracious and full of mercy. There is not one God who is just and holy and a second God who is good and merciful; there is one God.[12]

The unification of themes bifurcated by the heretics continues with the declaration that "the Father of our Lord Jesus Christ, himself gave the law." He also gave the prophets and the gospels, two accumulations of divine words with a common theme and purpose distinguished only by anticipation and fulfillment.[13] In being the God of the patriarchs and the apostles he is nothing less than the God of both the Old and the New Testaments.

The second and third articles of Origen's *regula* reassert the continuity of the two covenants and, in doing so, tie the three articles together. The second article on Christ calls him "begotten of the Father before every created thing [*ante omnem creaturam natus ex patre est*]" and says that he "ministered to the Father in the foundation of all things [*in omnium conditione patri ministrasset*]." The Son of God, Jesus Christ, has a unique origin and an incomparable relationship with the Father.[14] But more than that, he himself was party to creation as the instrumental cause. Not only is Jesus Christ, the incarnate Savior, related to the Creator God as the Son of God, but he also *is* the Creator God. The righteousness of the law and the grace of the gospel meet and find their fulfillment in the re-creation enacted by the Creator himself.

The final confirmation of this unity of covenants is the common testimony of the Spirit in the saints. The same Spirit that inspired the apostles inspired the Old Testament prophets.[15] The heretics deceive when they teach that there "was one Spirit in the men of old and another in those who were inspired at the coming of Christ." The plan of God is uniform throughout, from its inception to its fulfillment, and to say otherwise is to deny the one true God.

At the center of this *oikonomia*, God's overarching plan, is Christ's participation in "our common death" and his subsequent resurrection. The Old Testament writers anticipated these events and the New Testament apostles testified to their

---

[11] Origen *Com. on John* 2.28.
[12] Origen *De princ.* 2.5.1-4.
[13] Ibid., 2.4.1-2; 2.7.1; *Com. on John* 32.190; *Com. on Matt.* 12.42.
[14] Origen *Com. on John* 32.191, 193.
[15] Origen *De princ.* 4.2.9; *Com. on Matt.* 11.61.

fulfillment. All of history looks to the incarnation of the God-man, creation anticipating its re-creation and the resurrection finding its initiation in Christ. Within this series of events God calls both Jew and Gentile to salvation. All humanity is given the opportunity to accept God's grace and forgiveness. This is the ultimate result and confirmation of the unity of the two testaments, the availability of salvation not for a few specially called but for all people.

Origen's Variations in the *Regula*

While Origen makes the continuity of the two testaments and Christ's inclusion within the unique divine identity abundantly clear, the form in which he presents the *regula* lacks some of the distinguishing marks of Irenaeus' and Tertullian's *regulae*. His predecessors frame the *regula* with very definite markers, distinguishing it from the context as a whole. Irenaeus, for example, begins the *regula* of *Adv. haer.* 1.22.1 with "[t]he rule of truth which we hold, is [*est*], ..." and marks the end of the *regula* with "[h]olding [*tenentes*], therefore, this rule," which is a definite indication of his transition to the *regula*'s ramifications. The remaining *regulae* are distinguished in similar fashion, making the essential statements obvious in the context.[16]

In contrast, Origen begins with the very definite statement that "the kind of doctrines which are believed in plain terms through the apostolic teaching are the following [*istae sunt*]," but he does not conclude with definitive clarity. Instead, the closing of the *regula* proper introduces questions concerning the Holy Spirit's beginning and the need to search Scripture to find answers. Where Irenaeus and Tertullian conclude with resounding authority, having laid down the apostolic tradition, Origen opens the field for inquiry and dialogue. Following the article on the Holy Spirit, he continues with a list of secondary doctrines varying in definitiveness and authority such as resurrection, free will, the devil, and Scripture. To conclude the preface he discusses the need to build on the foundational principles presented and to provide "a single body of doctrine" drawing from Scripture and reason.

The *regula*, therefore, does more than simply refute the work of heretics and guide the faithful in core beliefs. It also serves as the basis for inquiry into the deeper truths of the faith. The brief Trinitarian statement in the *Commentary on John* that bears characteristics of the *regula* mirrors this unique use of the *regula*. After three concise articles stating belief in the Father, Son, and Spirit, Origen gives several examples of incorrect doctrine that are refuted from the Trinitarian statement. The content of the refutations that follow elaborate upon the statement, providing details explaining the substance of the statement. For example, belief in Christ must include "all the truth about him in relation to his divinity and humanity." This statement is subsequently developed by dismissing

---

[16] Irenaeus *Adv. haer.* 1.10.1; 3.4.2; 5.20.1; Tertullian *De praes. haer.* 13.1; *Adv. Prax.* 2; *De virg vel.* 1.

the Docetists who deny his virginal conception and bodily existence and the Ebionites who deny his true humanity.[17]

Essentially, Origen advocates for a research theology that elaborates upon the core beliefs of the faith. The form of Origen's *regula*, therefore, supports his exegetical and theological methods which encourage allegorical interpretation developed upon literal understandings of texts. A literal interpretation of a text is essential, but "those who are gifted with the grace of the Holy Spirit in the word of wisdom and knowledge [*uerbo sapientiae ac scientiae*]" can build upon the literal interpretation through a spiritual understanding of the text in order to find "the inspired meaning."

Origen bases several variations in the *regula* upon ideas important to Irenaeus and Tertullian. He modifies and elaborates upon their ideas in a fashion analogous to his allegorical elaboration upon literal understandings of Scripture. Origen accepts most of his predecessors' views on the *oikonomia* and adds a more speculative view of Jesus Christ's human nature. The rendering may be Rufinus' words, but the sending of "the Lord Jesus Christ" for "the purpose of calling Israel" prior to his incarnation may anticipate belief in the preexistence of the man Jesus assumed by the Son of God. If the appellation correctly includes *Iesum*, Origen likely is looking towards his doctrine of Jesus' preexistence as a man since he would have been both Christ and Jesus prior to his physical manifestation on earth.

The fact that Jesus Christ calls both the Israelites and the Gentiles to repentance is also significant in that it implies not only Christ's sovereignty, but also human free will. The unbelief of Israel indicates the presence of free will as a decisive factor in the fall and redemption of humanity. All are called but not all accept since "we are not compelled by necessity to act either rightly or wrongly [*non tamen necessitate cogimur uel recte agere uel male*]." We are all called by God, but refusal remains a genuine possibility.

Christ's sovereignty and authority to call all the world to reconciliation with God comes from his ontological status as "begotten of the Father before every created thing [*ante omnem creaturam natus ex patre est*]." The statement anticipates the doctrine of the Son's eternal generation, a teaching resulting from the need to inquire "in regard to Christ and the Holy Spirit."[18] The eternal generation of the Son is the natural result of two important principles, the biblical assertion that the Son is begotten of the Father and that he exists eternally.[19] When Origen speaks of the Son being born *before* all other creatures, then, he is speaking to his logical priority not temporal priority. Essentially, that he was born

---

[17] Origen *Com. on John* 32.187-193.

[18] Ibid., (ANF) 1.32; *De princ.* 1.2.9.

[19] Jerome contends that the original Greek word used by Origen was *genēton* ("made") rather than *gennēton* ("begotten"). Nevertheless, in Origen's time the terms were not distinguished as clearly as they were for Jerome. Origen saw only two choices for the Son's beginning, either without beginning ("uncreated") or begotten ("created"). Since the Father is the only being without a beginning or source, the Son must be created, at least in this sense of the word. Butterworth, 3, footnotes 1, 3. See also Crouzel, *Origen*, 174.

before all creatures means that he is qualitatively different from and greater than the creation.

Origen also adds some noteworthy points in relation to the incarnation and the perpetuation of Jesus Christ's two natures. While he is not the first to address the *kenosis* of Phil. 2 in the *regula*, Origen's language is more ontological than Irenaeus'. Instead of "enduring the birth from a virgin" [*tēn ek tēs parthenou gennēsin hupomeinanta, quae esset ex Virgine generationem sustinuit*], Christ *emptied* himself [*se ipsum exinaniens homo factus est*].[20] In this case Origen's use of the New Testament language describes Christ's state of being more directly than Irenaeus' functional term. Both words display action, but *emptying* describes a change in Christ's state of being more effectively than condescending or enduring birth, which can be interpreted as merely a change in appearance.

The claim that having become a human being "he still remained what he was, namely, God [*mansit quod erat, deus*]," explains in more detail this change in his state of being. As a preexistent man he took on the sinful, bodily form of humanity without affecting substantially his divine nature. Therefore, while his ontological state did change, he lost nothing of who he was as God, a point with which both Irenaeus and Tertullian would agree but which neither found necessary to state explicitly in the *regula*. Tertullian comes the closest when he speaks of Christ "being both Man and God," but he speaks of Christ's incarnate state and does not relate it directly to the transition involved in Christ's *kenosis*.[21] In contrast, Origen intentionally includes the continuity of Christ's deity within the incarnational transition to explain further the *kenosis* that Christ experienced. The Son emptied himself in order to express deity in his nature as the perfect image of God. He is God in perfect detail unchanged except in his perceptibility. Christ became the image of God in bodily form in order to reveal God to humanity, just as a twenty foot replica of a statue filling the earth would reveal the work to people unable to comprehend the original.[22]

Several phrases unique to Origen's *regula* also address Christ's humanity. That Christ "took to himself a body like our body [*corpus assumsit nostro corpor simile*]" bears implications beyond the obvious. The statement not only testifies to Christ's genuine humanity, but it also anticipates Origen's doctrine of the incarnation in which the Son of God, united with a human soul prior to the incarnation, assumes human form.[23] Since Origen believes in human preexistence, Jesus Christ also preexists in his humanity and needs only to assume a body in the incarnation.

For a very different reason, refutation of heretics, Origen contributes several phrases that insist on Jesus' true humanity and corporeal existence. There is no possible way that he merely appeared to be human since "Jesus Christ was born and suffered in truth and not merely in appearance [*natus et passus est in uerita-*

---

[20] Irenaeus *Adv. haer.* 3.4.2.; Origen *De princ.* pref., 4; *Com. on John* 20.153-155.
[21] Tertullian *Adv. Prax.* 2.
[22] Origen *De princ.* 1.2.8.
[23] See Origen *Com. on John* 1.34; *Com. on Matt.* 14.17; Crouzel, *Origen*, 192-8.

te, et non per phantasiam], and truly died our common death." Furthermore, "he truly rose from the dead [uere enim et a mortuis resurrexit]" in a physical, corporeal sense. Finally, as confirmation of the last point, "after the resurrection [he] companied with his disciples." Therefore, in response to the Docetists especially, to believe faithfully in Jesus Christ is to accept his physical birth of a virgin, his passion and death, and his bodily resurrection.

These variations in Origen's *regula* are for the most part elaborations upon doctrines held by his predecessors. It is in one significant omission that Origen's *regula* deviates most from Irenaeus' and Tertullian's *regulae*, his failure to incorporate a christological eschatology. He never mentions within the *regula* the return of Christ, the manifestation of the Father's glory in Christ, or his role in the final judgment. Irenaeus and Tertullian pointedly name Jesus as judge of the living and the dead and the one with the authority to condemn to hell or save to everlasting life.

In contrast, Origen incorporates his own eschatology in what appears to be an addendum to the *regula*. The three articles on the Trinity carry unquestioned certainty and authority in their presentation, at least until Origen gets to the Holy Spirit where he begins to question the existence of consensus within the church. The implication is that these articles are the essentials of the *regula* that define the Christian faith univocally. The articles that follow, in which Origen outlines his eschatology, are the "Church's teaching [*ecclesiastica praedicatione*]," but they also include ideas that are "not very clearly defined in the teaching [*non satis manifesta praedicatione distinguitur*]." Origen is sure of the apostolic origin of his eschatology, but in light of the differing opinions in the church he relegates to it less authority than the *regula* proper. In lieu of a christological eschatology, therefore, he presents his views on resurrection, purgatorial fire, and the *apokatastasis* with measured restraint, though for him these views still maintain a relative amount of authority.

The *Regula* and Origen's Hermeneutic

While one might expect Origen's hermeneutical starting point to differ radically from that of Irenaeus and Tertullian, the truth is that he assumes the same foundational doctrine. All three church fathers require a basic faith that entails an elementary understanding of Scripture and the apostolic tradition, essentially the *regula*, and believers' trust in the one Creator God and his Son. Where Origen differs is in his belief in the availability of greater understandings of God and doctrine that can develop from this basic faith.

Origen is sometimes caricatured as a speculative philosopher interested only in finding the elusive deeper truth that is available to the spiritually advanced intellectual, even if it means sidestepping Scripture. Yet, however much he incorporates philosophical insights, his understanding of Scripture drives his use of philosophy, not vice versa.[24] Furthermore, in his reading of Scripture his exegesis begins with a literal interpretation of texts, not with an allegorical, spiritual *a priori*. What he considers literal is often more basic or literal than even modern exegetes consider practical. In the case of parables, anthropomorphisms, strict requirements of the law, and similar texts the literal interpretation considers the reality of the activity or description involved instead of the metaphorical meaning intended by the writer.

Among many examples, Origen cites the command to observe the Sabbath by remaining in one's place or home, a commandment that "is an impossible one to observe literally, for no living creature could sit for a whole day and not move from his seat."[25] Anthropomorphisms stating that God has hands or a face are similar and can only have meaning if they are interpreted in more than a literal sense. Certain aspects of parables, anthropomorphisms, and other literary devices, therefore, constitute impossible realities and prohibit the existence of literal interpretations. That is not to say that the passage as a whole does not admit to a literal interpretation. Adam and Eve's existence in the garden possesses literal meaning, but God walking in the garden can only be understood allegorically since God does not walk.[26]

When literal interpretations of texts are possible, they are essential not only for simple believers, but also for those who are more advanced in the faith. The benefit of the literal understanding of the text is seen first in "the multitudes of sincere and simple believers" who can comprehend no more than a ground level reading of Scripture.[27] From this literal reading, believers continue to grow in their understanding of the faith by delving into the higher meanings of texts.

The literal and higher interpretive levels correspond to the constituent parts of Origen's anthropology; the literal interpretation corresponds to the body, the moral interpretation to the soul, and the mystical interpretation to the spirit.[28] The moral and mystical interpretations always build upon the literal interpretation except when a literal interpretation is contradictory or meaningless. Reliance upon the literal interpretation keeps the higher understandings grounded and prohibits arbitrary interpretations.[29] Moral and mystical interpretations do

---

[24] Peter Widdicombe, *The Fatherhood of God from Origen to Athanasius*, rev. ed. (Oxford: Clarendon Press, 2000), 120.

[25] Origen *De princ.* 4.3.2.

[26] Cf. Ibid., 4.2.9, 4.3.1-5; *Com. on John* (ANF) 10.2-4, 24; Crouzel, *Origen*, 62; Butterworth, 296, fn. 3.

[27] Origen *De princ.* 4.2.6.

[28] Ibid., 4.2.4; Crouzel, *Origen*, 79.

[29] Crouzel, *Origen*, 61, 75; Karen Jo Torjesen, *Hermeneutical Procedure and Theological Structure in Origen's Exegesis* (New York: De Gruyter, 1986), 141-146. It should be noted that allegorical interpretations of texts do not indicate Origen's unbelief in the historicity of the story involved. Origen believes that even historical events have allegorical meanings, a belief that is substantiated by similar exegetical practices within the New Testament itself. For example, the raising of the bronze serpent by Moses is interpreted allegorically or typologically even though it is considered a historical event by Jesus (John 3:14). See also ibid., 63; Origen *De princ.* 4.3.4.

not depart from the literal meaning; rather they communicate greater truths through it. Interpretation is always *ex*egesis, never *iso*gesis. As with all the church fathers, Origen would have been deeply offended to be accused of rendering arbitrary interpretations unconnected to the text.[30]

This threefold classification is Origen's own system as described in *On First Principles*, but he does not abide by it consistently. Henri de Lubac attributes to Origen a fourfold interpretive scheme that is never explicitly acknowledged but seems more consistent with his hermeneutical practices.[31] In addition to its correlation with his actual exegesis, these four senses of a passage fit better with Origen's understanding of Scripture, the relationship between the two testaments, and his modified Platonist view of knowledge. Beyond the literal sense of a passage there potentially exist allegorical, moral/typological, and anagogical interpretations.

Allegorical interpretation brings Old Testament passages into a Christian context with the presupposition that "the Old Testament in its entirety is a prophecy of Christ."[32] In Platonic terms, the Old Testament is an image or copy of the temporal Gospel.[33] The Old Testament has great value and significance but only when it leads one to the New Testament. Left to itself the Old Testament becomes the letter that kills.

Lubac's moral or typological sense considers the application of Scripture to the believer living between the two advents of Christ. This level of interpretation incorporates Origen's understanding of the temporal Gospel, the Gospel codified within the New Testament. The temporal Gospel is the form or model for the Old Testament, but it is itself a copy or image of the eternal Gospel. Just as the Old Testament leads believers to the temporal Gospel, the temporal Gospel is intended to lead believers to the eternal Gospel. Yet this is where the parallelism ends, for the Old Testament and the Gospel exist independently of each other, but the Gospel remains one Gospel in temporal and eternal manifestations. The temporal Gospel indicates the manner in which believers truly know and participate in the words and life of Jesus Christ prior to his return, though it is as "in a glass darkly." The eternal Gospel, in contrast, is the believer's "face to face" eschatological experience of God and his Son.[34] So the moral or typological interpretation addresses application of the Gospel in this life while the anagogical interpretation is the eschatological significance of Scripture and is placed at the meeting point between the temporal Gospel and eternal Gospel.[35]

The threefold and fourfold hermeneutical models both have their disadvantages and advantages, the former being Origen's stated practice and the latter being more consistent with modern interpretations of Origen. Regardless, both models incorporate his distinction between the literal and spiritual meanings of

---

[30] Crouzel, *Origen*, 83-4.
[31] Henri de Lubac, *Exégèse Médiévale* (Paris, 1959), 198-219; Crouzel, *Origen*, 80.
[32] Crouzel, *Origen*, 64. See also ibid., 70-71; Origen *Com. on John* (ANF) 5.4.
[33] Origen *De princ.* 4.1.6; 4.3.12; *Com. on John* (ANF) 1.15.
[34] Origen *De princ.* 2.11.6-7; 3.6.8; 4.2.8; 4.3.13; *Com. on John* (ANF) 1.9-10.
[35] Crouzel, *Origen*, 76, 80.

texts. The differences between the second and third senses in Origen's stated method or between the three higher senses in Lubac's proposal are seldom easy to distinguish in Origen's vocabulary. What is clear is his "exemplarist vision of the world" seen in two sets of vocabulary. On the one hand, symbol, type, image, enigma, perceptible, corporeal, visible, and other terms engender the Platonist concept of copy and generally correspond to a literal interpretation. On the other hand, mystery, truth, realities, mystical, true, intelligible, spiritual, reasonable, and invisible bring into play Origen's equivalent to the Platonic forms, which correspond to the spiritual interpretations. Thus, the symbol, type, or image, being in some form perceptible, corporeal, or visible, is a shadow of the unintelligible, spiritual mystery, truth, or reality.[36]

This Platonic theory of knowledge modified to fit within a Christian worldview provides the basic framework for Origen's hermeneutic and explains the role of the *regula* in his theology. The *regula* delineates the foundational doctrines upon which believers build lives devoted to growing in the knowledge and understanding of God and Jesus Christ. Just as the spiritual understanding of a text never contradicts its literal interpretation, one's developing doctrine never gainsays the *regula*. Instead, one's theology becomes even more faithful to the *regula* as the believer more fully comprehends the mysteries of God.

Several principles and convictions explain the believer's ability to grow in this understanding of God while limiting arbitrary interpretations and doctrine.[37] First, the image of God in humanity, or Origen's preferred term 'the after-the-image,' is the reason human beings are able to comprehend the divine at all.[38] "Only like can know like," therefore humanity's reflection of the divine nature is what enables people to understand God and his message to them.[39] This image within humanity is something one develops through contemplation and prayer; it is not an innate ability. The more one is conformed willingly to the image of Christ, the more one is able to receive knowledge of God through the illumination of the Holy Spirit. Even as Jesus Christ opened the Scriptures to the disciples on the road to Emmaus, the Spirit opens the Scriptures by giving the mind

---

[36] Ibid., 79.

[37] Peter Martens considers Origen's ideal hermeneutical practices from the perspective of the committed Christian exegete. The Christian interpreter is not only to practice appropriate hermeneutical principles, but also to embody these principles in Christian living and the pursuit of salvation. "Ideal scriptural interpreters sought to *reverse* their original fall in an attempt to *reprise*, however fleetingly, their original state, the contemplation of God" and anticipate their restoration to God's presence. Peter W. Martens, *Origen and Scripture: The Contours of the Exegetical Life* (New York: Oxford University Press, 2012), 233.

[38] Origen *De princ.* 1.1.7; 4.4.9-10. For Origen only the Son of God himself is the image of God. A human being is an image of the image of God, or an after-the-image. Crouzel, *Origen*, 93. Cf. Origen *Com. on John* (ANF) 1.19; 2.3.

[39] Crouzel, *Origen*, 74, 96.

of Christ to those who are ready to receive it.[40] Thus, the Spirit has a significant role in individual interpretation.

Interpreters find balance for potentially individualistic interpretation in the context of the church. The apostolic tradition, which includes the *regula* and is given alongside of Scripture, articulates the essential doctrines of the faith as given by Jesus to the apostles. This tradition provides an external standard by which one can measure interpretations, for "that only is to be believed as the truth which in no way conflicts with the tradition of the Church and the apostles."[41] Interestingly, adherence to the *regula* sometimes even requires spiritual interpretation. Heretics often interpret Scripture "according to the bare letter" in direct contradiction to those "who keep to the rule ... through the succession from the apostles."[42] Heretics turn to literal interpretations of passages such as Amos 3:6 and Mic. 1:12 in order to substantiate their deviant portrayal of an evil and vindictive God, while adherents to the *regula* understand the spiritual meanings of the texts.[43]

The abundance of interpreters within the church serves as an extension of the *regula*'s authority. While Origen does not state it explicitly, exegetical humility on the part of the individual interpreter and consensus within the interpretive community in relation to dogmatic beliefs are important. Origen admits that there are mysteries that "fair-minded and humble men confess that they do not know," and when he does offer interpretations he often acknowledges that better ones may exist and should be sought.[44] As the consummate learner and educator his desire is to find the truth rather than to confirm his own perception of the truth.

For positively identifying this truth, especially the truth not explicitly given in the apostolic tradition, he puts great stock in the consensus of the church. In the addendum to the *regula*, especially in reference to eschatology, he identifies doctrines that are either clearly defined or not very clearly defined in the church's tradition. The former doctrines, having found unanimity within the church, are to be accepted since (to guard against heresy) the church is "the sole

---

[40] See Origen *De princ.* 1.1.2; 2.9.4; 4.3.15; *Com. on John* (ANF) 1.6; 5.4; 10.18; (FOTC) 10.286; *Com. on Matt.* 14.11; *Con. Cels.* 7.44-45; Crouzel, *Origen*, 73-4; Torjesen, 116-119. Origen speaks of "innumerable multitudes of believers" who recognize the need for the spiritual interpretation of many texts as a result of the Spirit's work. Some are able to understand more than others, but spiritual interpretation is not limited to a spiritual elite. Origen *De princ.* 2.7.2.

[41] "*Illa sola credenda est ueritas, quae in nullo ab ecclesiastica et apostolica traditione discordat.*" Origen *De princ.* pref., 2. Cf. ibid., 2.11.3; *Com. on Matt.* 13.1.

[42] Origen *De princ.* 4.2.2.

[43] See Ibid., 2.4.4; 2.5.2.

[44] Ibid., 4.2.2. See also ibid., 2.6.2, 7; 2.8.4-5; 4.2.3; 4.3.14; *Com. on John* (ANF) 10.17, 22; *Com. on Matt.* 14.24; Henry Chadwick, *Early Christian Thought and the Classical Tradition: Studies in Justin, Clement, and Origen* (New York: Oxford University Press, 1966), 97, 123.

authoritative interpreter of Scripture."[45] The latter are doctrines that warrant additional thought and contemplation.

It is in this admonition to search through the doctrines that are less clear that Origen most surpasses Irenaeus and Tertullian. The apostles remained silent on certain doctrines in order to supply those who "should prove to be lovers of wisdom, with an exercise on which to display the fruit of their ability."[46] Irenaeus, Tertullian, and Origen all trust the Scriptures as the words of God given to the church through the prophets and the apostles. They also find unanimity in their reliance upon the *regula* as an objective standard for interpreting the Scriptures. Where Origen departs from his predecessors is in relation to questions and the search for answers. Irenaeus and Tertullian often see the specters of heresy and deception in the same unanswered questions that bring to Origen the joy of discovering some new truth about God. While he recognizes the dangers of heresy and is prepared to answer them as did his predecessors, Origen will not let the threat of heresy deter him from striving toward a fuller knowledge of God.[47]

Essentially, Origen sees the *regula* as an opportunity to learn and grow. Just as a literal interpretation of a text can lead to a deeper, spiritual meaning, so the *regula* functions as a foundation for greater theological understanding and insight. Therefore, while the *regula* can be used to constrain inquiry or define theological parameters, it can also sustain a vigorous search for a greater knowledge of God.

---

[45] Origen *De princ.* pref., 4-10; R. P. C. Hanson, *Origen's Doctrine of Tradition* (London: S.P.C.K., 1954), 111. Origen considers the tradition of the church to be his guide in doctrine, even referring to it as "our doctrine, ... the faith of the Church." Origen *De princ.* 1.7.1. See also ibid., 2.4.1. For elaboration on the *regula* as a protection against heresy see Martens, *Origen and Scripture*, 113.

[46] "*Exercitium habere possent, in quo ingenii sui fructum ostenderent.*" Origen *De princ.* pref., 3.

[47] Cf. Chadwick, 81-82.

Chapter 8

An Ontological Theology

Well known and often disparaged for his theory of the preexistence of souls and his belief in an *apokatastasis*, Origen has more in common with the other church fathers than is often recognized. The theologies of Irenaeus, Tertullian, and Origen all rest on a strict monotheism in which God is immutable, incomprehensible, and distinct from his creation. While existing in one substance, God reveals himself as a Trinity, three distinguishable subjects, Father, Son, and Spirit.[1]

Likewise, the Son's role within this Trinity is consistent between all three fathers' theologies. The second person of the Trinity is the instrumental cause of creation, he maintains creation providentially, he reveals God to humanity, he becomes a man without diminishing his deity, he redeems humanity, and he subdues all enemies and brings all things into subjection before the Father. On the other hand, Origen's understanding of the Son's nature is characterized by both advancement beyond, and departure from, the norm, as is seen in the Son's eternal generation and his human preexistence respectively.

Interestingly, Origen's theories of the Son's eternal generation, the preexistence of souls, and the *apokatastasis* all find their origins in his understanding of God's nature. The latter theories derive in large part from God's nature as good and just. The fact that God is both just and good motivates Origen to emphasize free will more than either Irenaeus or Tertullian.[2] Consequently, it is on account of the creature's God-given free will in conjunction with God's goodness that Origen proffers the possibility of *apokatastasis*. Similarly, the preexistence of souls is Origen's attempt to resolve the tension between a good, just God and human beings' often pitiable beginnings. Unfortunately, readers do not always recognize the humility with which Origen usually offers these theories, especially in contrast to his vociferous assertion of the eternal generation of the Son, one of his greatest contributions to the church's Christology.

---

[1] Origen *De princ.* 1.3.2; *Com. on John* 10.21. The Spirit's origin and the manner of his existence in relation to the Father and the Son is not clear, but he undoubtedly exists in distinction from the creation since his name is "joined to that of the unbegotten God the Father and his only-begotten Son." Origen *De princ.* 1.3.2.

[2] Crouzel, *Origen*, 184; Jean Daniélou, *Origen*, trans. Walter Mitchell (New York: Sheed and Ward, 1955), 205-206.

109

The Eternal Generation of the Son

Origen's theology begins with a view of the transcendent, incomprehensible God, distinct from his creation. The Creator and creation are the original and image, or in light of Christ's mediation, the creation is the image of the image. God is inviolable substance, existing in and of himself. He alone is incorporeal while all of creation is material, whether in a solid earthly sense or in an ethereal celestial manner.[3] Even "with respect to time [he] is perceived not in terms of everlastingness or sempiternity (that is, being at *all* times), but in unambiguous terms of atemporality."[4] In contrast, every creature is created out of non-being and exists derivatively, its being subject to its relationship with true eternal being. The correlative Platonic scheme of the spiritual or intelligible world over against the physical or material world is sifted through this specifically Christian distinction between the Creator and the creation.[5]

The Father, being the source of divine being and "the beginning of the Son [*hoti archē huiou ho patēr*]," ontologically and not chronologically, is indivisible and *hautotheos*.[6] He is so transcendent that humanity cannot comprehend him apart from the Son even though he is the initiator of creation.[7] He exists solely in and of himself, independent of anything that he creates. God the Father, therefore, reveals himself through his Wisdom, the eternally generated Son of God.

Origen explains the Son's eternal generation in several ways. Besides the simple assertion that the Son is "without any beginning [*sine ullo tamen initio*]," the Son also exists as "an eternal and everlasting begetting [*aeterna ac sempiterna generatio*], as brightness is begotten from light."[8] This use of light to illustrate the divine relationship reminds one of Tertullian's illustration of the sun and its rays of light. Both fathers illustrate the truth that God can be both singular and multiple in different senses simultaneously, but Origen improves upon Tertullian's illustration by removing any implication of change or development

---

[3] Panayiotis Tzamalikos, *Origen: Cosmology and Ontology of Time* (Boston: Brill, 2006), 114.

[4] Ibid., 24.

[5] Crouzel, *Origen*, 181. "Any facet of his doctrine of creation, and certainly the notion of creation *ex nihilo*, has to do only with what God *did*.... Unlike Platonism, in Origen the creative act of God has nothing to do with the divine ontology." Tzamalikos, *Origen: Cosmology and Ontology of Time*, 148.

[6] Origen *Com. on John* 1.102.

[7] Origen *De princ.* 1.1.5. "God *is* being regardless of existence or non-existence of time. This comes to mean a conception of God in Himself, that is, God who is being in the absence of creation or even any *thought* of creation." Tzamalikos, *Origen: Cosmology and Ontology of Time*, 25.

[8] Origen *De princ.* 1.2.2; 1.2.4. See also Origen *Com. on John* 1.204. Not to believe in the eternality of the Son's generation would imply the intolerable conclusion that at some point God was either unable or unwilling to beget his Wisdom. Origen *De princ.* 1.4.4.

within God. God is light, everywhere at all times and outside of time, and similarly the Son is his brightness perpetually. That God is light, therefore, affirms that the Son is eternally begotten outside of time.[9]

Besides being perfect light, the Father is always a father and the Son is always a son. While Tertullian considers the fatherhood and sonship of God to be functional designations relative to the *oikonomia*, Origen recognizes them as ontological distinctions between the two subjects. This adjustment is the result of discarding the concept of the *Logos prophorikos* and the pretemporal change in God that comes with the speaking or procession of the Word. Since there is no time when the Word is spoken or *becomes* the Son, Origen also avoids the deficient conclusion later deemed heretical that "there was [a time] when he [the Son] was not." Instead, *ouk hestin hote ouk ēn*, there is no time when the Son does not exist, since "the statements we make about the Father and the Son and the Holy Spirit must be understood as transcending all time and all ages and all eternity."[10] On account of the Trinity's timelessness, the Father is always a father and the Son is always a son.[11]

The manner in which the Father generates the Son is also important. Since God is spirit, entirely incorporeal and immaterial, the Son is generated out of the Father's will.[12] Relying on John 4, every concept of God as corporeal, including the Stoic conception appropriated by Tertullian, is refuted in order to maintain the Creator-creation distinction and to disassociate the divine generation from human generation. However much the divine generation or begetting might evoke images of creaturely generation, they have nothing in common except the word itself.[13] In short, the divine generation of the Son is a matter of God's eternal and perpetual will.

The explicitly stated doctrine of the eternal generation of the Son opens many avenues of inquiry. It should be noted that the Son's generation from the will of the Father, who is *autotheos*, together with Christ's existence as the mediator can sometimes greatly subordinate the Son to the Father. So within Origen's thought there are strains of subordinationism alongside assertions of the Son's undiminished deity. The subordination of the Son to the Father finds support in the New Testament and throughout the early church, though it usually pertains to the Son's subordinate role and is not necessarily subordination in essence. It is not surprising, therefore, to see that Origen's portrayal of the eternal generation uses "all kinds of images, in forms that are dynamic rather than ontological, compel[ling] recognition that Origen is expressing the equivalent of

---

[9] Origen *De princ.* 1.2.11. See also ibid., 1.2.2; 4.4.1.

[10] Ibid., 1.2.9; 4.4.1; *Com. on Rom.* 1.5. "These are not, as has sometimes been thought, additions by the translator Rufinus, for the second text from the Treatise on First Principles is quoted in Greek by Athanasius and explicitly attributed by him to Origen with the formulation that we have reproduced." Crouzel, *Origen*, 187.

[11] Tzamalikos, *Origen: Cosmology and Ontology of Time*, 25.

[12] Origen *De princ.* 1.2.6; 4.4.1.

[13] Ibid., 1.2.4.

the Nicene *homoousios*."¹⁴ So Origen uses more ontological language than his predecessors, but his explication of the Son's origin remains relatively functional compared to Nicaea.

The *Epinoiai*

The eternal generation of the Son makes him the perfect image of the Father, who is himself absolute simplicity. Although the Son's being is one with the Father and one in himself, he is also multiplicity as manifested in his *epinoiai*. The *epinoiai*, which "represent the different functions or attributes that the Christ takes on in his role as Mediator in relation to us," exist both economically and ontologically in that the *epinoia* is "'title', 'expression', and at the same time objective reality."¹⁵ The Son's titles, addressed especially in the first book of his *Commentary on John*, not only express the Son's economic activity, but also reflect his being. The Son both *is* the Mediator and *functions* in a mediating role. Human beings, while the beneficiaries of the Son's work, can also participate actively in this mediation. The Son incorporates human beings and angels in his work by partaking of human nature and by means of the *epinoiai*, especially the *Logos*. Some *epinoiai*, particularly the *Logos* and Wisdom, are intrinsic to the Son's being, while others, such as the titles Shepherd or the Way, are relative to the *oikonomia*.¹⁶ Therefore, the articulation of the *epinoiai* will have functional or ontological emphases depending on each *epinoia*'s relationship to the Son's being and work.

Wisdom is first among the *epinoiai* that are eternal characteristics or roles of the Son, for only Wisdom "is the beginning [*sophia archē estin*]."¹⁷ The Son's existence as Wisdom provides a solution to a difficult and foundational problem.

---

¹⁴ Crouzel, *Origen*, 187. Cf. Daniélou, *Origen*, 254-255, 261; Mark Edwards, *Origen Against Plato* (Adlershot, England: Ashgate, 2002), 74-76; Rebecca J. Lyman, *Christology and Cosmology: Models of Divine Activity in Origen, Eusebius, and Athanasius* (New York: Oxford University Press, 1993), 69-70.

Russel Moroziuk proposes that Origen's condemnation years later was a result of a fundamental reorientation in theological thought due largely to Nicaea and *homoousios*. In pre-Nicene Christianity the divide between deity and humanity was epistemological. The divine and human spirits could still associate and by human contemplation and the work of the *Logos* the barrier could be removed. With Nicene theology the distinction between God and humanity became both epistemological and ontological. Russel P. Moroziuk, "Origen and the Nicene Orthodoxy," in *Origeniana Quinta: Historica, Text and Method, Biblica, Philosophica, Theologica, Origenism and Later Developments*, ed. Robert J. Daly (Leuven, Belgium: University Press, 1992), 489.

¹⁵ Crouzel, *Origen*, 189; Grillmeier, 141. Origen notes that one cannot find distinctions within the Savior's essence, only in his aspects or *epinoiai*. Origen *Com. on John* 1.200.

¹⁶ Origen speculates that only the *epinoiai* wisdom, word, life, and truth might have existed if there had been no fall. *Com. on John* 1.123.

¹⁷ Origen *Com. on John* 1.118, 222-223, 248; 2.90.

In order to maintain his immutability God cannot *become* the Creator; he must exist eternally as the Creator. But to be the eternal Creator he must always have a creation, that is, a coeternal creation.[18] Yet this eliminates a critical distinction between the Creator and the creation and is unacceptable, at least at first glance. The dilemma is resolved in the mediation of Wisdom, who "contains within herself both the beginnings and causes and species of the whole creation."[19] On the one hand, the creation is eternal since it exists nascent within God's eternal Wisdom in a fashion similar to the Platonic ideas or the Stoic reasons. In this sense "at no time whatever was God not Creator, nor Benefactor, nor Providence."[20] Yet, on the other hand, the creation is entirely distinct from the Creator in that it is created in Wisdom and is dependent upon God for its existence.[21]

This creator-creation distinction does not mean that God is entirely transcendent from his creation. Through his Wisdom, God "permeated all creation [*holēs tēs ktiseōs pephoitēken*]" in its making, and he continues to sustain the life that he made.[22] Wisdom, in her role as the giver of life, works in conjunction with the Son's role as the Word, the Son's second eternal *epinoia*. Where Wisdom *is* the beginning, the Word was *in* the beginning; consequently, the Word is in Wisdom.[23]

Being in Wisdom, the Word serves as the instrumental cause of creation and reveals the mysteries hidden within Wisdom to humanity and the rest of creation. He interprets Wisdom for the creation after destroying the irrational and dead within humanity. This spiritual surgery frees the *logos*, the rational nature or divine principle present in those created in the image of the Son.[24] Recalling the principle that only like can know like, created beings can only know the intelligible or spiritual if they possess something of that realm. Having been created in the "after-the-image," humanity is able to exercise the divine rationality once it is freed from irrationality and it receives the revelation of the divine from the Word. Thus, the Son as the Word is the means for creation, reveals the divine to humanity, and enables humanity to participate in the divine.[25]

---

[18] Origen *De princ.* 1.4.3. Origen makes the same argument in relation to God's nature as almighty in *De princ.* 1.2.10.

[19] "*Continens scilicet in semet ipsa uniuersae creaturae uel initia uel rationes uel species.*" Ibid., 1.2.2. See also ibid., 1.4.4-5; *Com. on John* 1.114.

[20] Origen *De princ.* 1.4.3. See also ibid., 1.2.10; *Com. on John* 6.188.

[21] Origen *De princ.* 1.4.4. God also places in Wisdom "objects of contemplation" (*theōrēmata*) by which seekers can come to understand the nature of the world and its creator. "They were formed and placed in the divine Wisdom out of an *act* of the Father. This is why at some points the Son is stated as 'creature' although it is also clearly enunciated that the Son is not a creature." Tzamalikos, *Origen: Cosmology and Ontology of Time*, 53.

[22] Origen *Com. on John* 6.189, 202.

[23] Ibid., 1.118, 289; 2.90.

[24] See ibid., 1.111, 268, 277; 2.108-9; *De princ.* 1.2.3.

[25] Crouzel, *Origen*, 190; Origen *De princ.* 2.6.3. "This conception of the Logos allows two notions to be correlated: first, God is timeless and radically transcendent to the world; secondly, God is the creator of this world, he communicates with it and indeed acts within it." Tzamalikos, *Origen: Cosmology and Ontology of Time*, 172.

Being God's Wisdom and Word, the Son is the ever present mediator between a transcendent singular God and a manifold creation. He is the model and means for the transcendent Father's creation, the revelation of God to humanity, and humanity's way of communication with God.[26] Communication can occur between rational beings and the divine rationality, the Word, but only when uninterrupted by sin and irrationality. The vast majority of Christ's *epinoiai* administer redemption for humanity, removing these obstacles and facilitating recognition of and participation in the divine. Origen himself lists a selection of Christ's names and titles identifying these *epinoiai* and then notes that it would be possible to collect ten thousand times as many from the Scriptures. Some of the more prominent include the light of the world, the resurrection, the door, the good shepherd, the true vine, the bread of life, the lamb of God, and the great high priest.[27] Many more could be listed, but these suffice to show the relative and functional nature of most of the *epinoiai*. Jesus Christ is not the door, the good shepherd, or the resurrection in an ontological sense; rather, these appellations define his mediating functions. But that is not to diminish the importance of Wisdom and Word, the first *epinoiai* and the most developed. Even in Christ's redemptive aspects, therefore, we find both ontological and functional language articulating his existence as Mediator and his mediating work.

Incarnation

Mediation is a persistent theme for Origen. Wisdom mediates the act of creation through the forms and causes within her, and Jesus Christ's *epinoiai* are his aspects most often revealed in mediation. Even Jesus Christ's own being requires mediation when it comes to the incarnation, the condescension of the divine to a fallen, sinful world. The immutable God cannot approach humanity in this very personal manner without something or someone interceding. This responsibility falls to the preexistent soul of Jesus, who is perfect, having persisted in the contemplation of the divine. His ability to mediate the two natures requires an understanding of Origen's anthropology.

According to Origen, human beings are preexistent both on account of the inadequacies of rival theories and in light of his view of free will.[28] The two

---

[26] Christ's perpetual role as revealer both prior to and in the incarnation is another demonstration of the continuity between the Old and New Testaments. "It was not only through his visible presence that the Logos communicated with the world and revealed the word of God, but he is also perpetually acting as a mediator between creatures and God. In all the instances of the Old Testament where God appeared to the patriarchs and prophets, this was God the Logos." Tzamalikos, *Origen: Philosophy of History and Eschatology*, 72.

[27] Origen *Com. on John* 1.126-150.

[28] Crouzel, *Origen*, 206-209. Origen notes in his *regula* in the preface to *On First Principles* that there is no consensus in the church on the origin of the human soul. Knowing the accuracy of this statement, his theory of preexistence is not heterodox according to the standards of the time and does not transgress the rule of faith.

competing theories for the origin of human souls, creationism and traducianism, contravene important principles within the *regula*. Creationism, the belief that God forms the human soul at conception, makes God unjust in light of the deplorable conditions into which many children are born. The theory also threatens God with responsibility for humanity's sinful condition. On the other hand, traducianism, the belief that the soul is passed from father to child at conception, is difficult to support scripturally and destroys the immortality of the soul, another belief stated in the *regula*. The preexistence of souls, in contrast to the rival theories, maintains the immortality of the soul and reconciles God's nature with humanity's destitute state by means of free will. If every human being receives his place in this life as a result of exercising his free will prior to this existence, then God is not responsible for our present conditions.[29]

A trichotomous constitution is also critical to Origen's anthropology.[30] Every created being possesses a body [*sōma*], even preexistent humans and angels, though their bodies are ethereal. Only God himself is incorporeal and entirely spirit.[31] Having been made in the image of Christ, every person also possesses a spirit [*pneuma*], the divine element granted as a gift from God. The spirit does not necessarily participate in the individual's decisions or personality, but it is an aspect of humanity. The more one is involved in good and righteousness, the more active one's spirit becomes, and vice versa.

The third constituent part of Origen's anthropology is the soul [*psychē*], the seat of decision and the substance of human preexistence. In its pristine state the soul exists as mind [*nous*], but when it falls from perfect contemplation of the divine it takes the nature of a soul.[32] The soul retains characteristics of mind, and when good decisions are made it is drawn to the spirit and experiences greater communion with the divine.[33] In its fall from the perfect, the soul also receives fleshly characteristics or a temptation to sin which will drag the soul down and alienate it from the spirit if permitted. This fleshly nature is not necessarily sin, but it is the persistent presence of temptation that results from failure to contemplate God. Naturally, the more the flesh is exercised the stronger it becomes and the greater successive temptations become. In the restoration of beings to perfect

---

[29] Origen *De princ.* 2.6.3; 2.9.3, 5-6; 3.1.21; 3.3.5; *Com. on Matt.* 13.23; Lyman, 60. Gerald Bostock argues that the preexistence of souls supports Christ's true humanity. Furthermore, Origen's source for the teaching is Philo and has roots in Jewish thought. It is not simply Greek philosophy as is often asserted. Gerald Bostock, "The Sources of Origen's Doctrine of Pre-existence," in *Origeniana Quarta*, ed. Lothar Lies (Tyrolia: Verlag, 1987), 260-261. Mark Edwards, on the other hand, rejects the attribution of the doctrine to Origen entirely. Edwards, *Origen Against Plato*, 89-93. Cf. Origen *Com. on John* (ANF) 2.31; 6.12.

[30] Origen *De princ.* 3.4.1; 4.1.11; *Com. on Matt.* 12.20; 13.2; 14.3; Crouzel, *Origen*, 87-92. For a thorough evaluation of Origen's anthropology see Jacques Dupuis, *L'esprit de l'homme: Étude sur l'anthropologie religieuse d'Origène* (Desclée de Brouwer, 1967).

[31] Origen is unwavering in his defense of the incorporeality of God throughout the first chapter of *On First Principles*. See also Origen *De princ.* 2.2.1-2; 2.3.2-3.

[32] Ibid., 2.8.3.

[33] Origen *Com. on John* 1.229; 6.66; *De prin.* 1.8.4; 2.8.2-3; 3.3.4; 3.4.2-4.

union with God the soul will be loosed from the fleshly nature and will once again exist as mind.[34]

Understanding Origen's anthropology, we can see how the Son of God can assume full humanity without diminishing his deity. The preincarnate human mind of Jesus is the mediator between the two natures.[35] He is a human mind like any other except that, because he has never ceased his contemplation of the divine, he has never fallen and remains in perfect communion with God. Consequently, in his preexistent state he is united with the Son and receives impeccability. The Christ-man, therefore, "exists in the pre-existence, long before the Incarnation."[36]

In the virginal conception, the power of God (an *epinoia* of Christ) takes the Son of God and the human mind of Jesus Christ, which are united in perfect communion, and clothes him in an earthly body. Since the mind of Christ has never fallen from union with God, the incarnation involves two major changes, the transformation of his mind into soul and the assumption of a body. The two actions constitute the *kenosis* spoken of in Phil. 2.[37] With this understanding of the *kenosis*, Jesus Christ possesses a fully human body, soul, and spirit, without denying, reducing, or impinging upon his divine nature in any way.[38] In fact, Christ's soul is entirely consistent with every other human soul in that he even possesses the fleshly characteristics of a fallen soul, though his will never exercises these characteristics. While remaining sinless and maintaining perfect communion with the Father, the Son experiences temptation, knows the weaknesses of the human state, and assumes the darkness of humanity's sinful condition for which he atones.[39]

Like his predecessors, Origen sometimes relegates Jesus Christ's experiences to either his deity or humanity in order to maintain divine impassibility. Even as Tertullian introduces a basic conception of the *communicatio idiomatum* but does not consider it consistently, Origen asserts it when the unity of Jesus Christ's person is important but qualifies it when the context demands otherwise. For example, to protect the divine nature from variability, Jesus' death on the cross pertains only to his human nature since "the Image of the invisible God

---

[34] Recognizing the difficulties and varying opinions on the nature of the soul, Origen offers his discussion on the various viewpoints in order for "the reader to choose which of them deserves the preference." Origen *De prin.* 3.4.4.

[35] Without the mediation of Christ's human *nous* one would be left with the two Christs of Paul of Samosata. The *Logos* would be an addition external to the human *psyche* of Jesus. Rowan Williams, "Origen on the Soul of Jesus," in *Origeniana tertia*, ed. Richard Hanson and Henri Crouzel (Rome: Edizioni dell'Ateneo, 1985), 134-135.

[36] Crouzel, *Origen*, 192. See also Origen *Com. on John* 1.236. The impeccability of Jesus' human soul comes from his unremitting contemplation of God, which "by the influence of long custom changed into nature." Origen *De princ.* 2.6.5. See also ibid., 2.6.3; *Con. Cels.* 2.9.

[37] Origen *De princ.* pref., 4; 1.2.8; 2.6.1; 3.5.6; 4.4.5; *Com. on John* 6.294; *Con. Cels.* 12.29.

[38] Origen *De princ.* 2.6.2; 4.4.3-4; Grillmeier, 146.

[39] Origen *Com. on John* 2.163-170.

... does not admit of death." Similarly, when the Pharisees' are unable to recognize the Father in the Son, Origen attributes it to their inability to recognize the Son's incarnated divine nature. "At one time the Savior is speaking of himself as of a man, but at another time he speaks of himself as of a nature that is divine and united with the uncreated nature of the Father," the latter being imperceptible to the Pharisees.[40] In a different context, his debate with Celsus, Origen consigns Jesus Christ's constituent parts to his human and divine natures.[41]

These departures from a nascent concept of the *communicatio idiomatum* can lead to the conclusion that Origen does not recognize a genuine unity between Jesus Christ's two natures.[42] Unfortunately, this conclusion neglects the common observation that Origen's voluminous output regularly invites discrepancies and contradictions. He is often credited with or accused of being the single source for opposing positions in the later trinitarian and christological debates. And like most of his predecessors and contemporaries, he often is caught between maintaining divine impassibility in the face of pagan and heretical accusations, (*e.g.* Celsus), and affirming the unity of Jesus Christ's person in light of Scripture and tradition. Other times it is simply a matter of emphasis or nuance. In a discussion on the soul of Christ, he makes statements affirming the unity of Jesus only a paragraph away from ideas interpreted as christologically dualistic. Shortly after saying that Jesus' human "soul that is 'sorrowful' and 'troubled' [in Gethsemane] must not be understood to be the Word of God" he affirms that "as the Son and the Father are one, so also the soul which the Son assumed and the Son himself are one."[43] The result is varying interpretations based on Origen's perceived emphasis and motivation. This instance of competing emphases may simply anticipate in a small way the christological controversy to come in the fifth century. Consequently, though he may be inconsistent at times, it is not surprising to find Origen following an established pattern of distinguishing Christ's two natures that avoids Tertullian's reviled *tertium quid* while adamantly maintaining the unity of Jesus Christ's person.

---

[40] Ibid. 28.159; 19.6.

[41] Origen *Con. Cels.* 2.9.

[42] "Even though he is committed to confessing the incarnation in some unitive sense for biblical and traditional reasons, Origen's main stance against Celsus, as it has been throughout his career, is to keep the divine and human elements of Christ neatly and safely distinct in their respective spheres." Christopher A. Beeley, *The Unity of Christ: Continuity and Conflict in Patristic Tradition* (New Haven: Yale University Press, 2012), 41.

[43] Origen *De princ.* 4.4.4. After noting Origen's statement concerning Jesus' troubled soul, Beeley says that "in passages such as these, Origen makes it clear that the *communicatio idiomatum* is merely a conventional practice of biblical language; it does not signify a real sharing of attributes, nor a singularity of subject to which both apply." Beeley, 37. While this appraisal may raise some legitimate concerns, the fact that Beeley completely overlooks the accompanying affirmation of Christ's unity of human soul and divine nature raises doubts about his overall assessment of Origen as a christological dualist. A nuanced understanding of Origen that considers particular contexts seems to explain the data more satisfactorily.

The affirmation of unity between Jesus' humanity and deity that comes from Origen's early conceptualization of the *communicatio idiomatum* is articulated best in *On First Principles*. Christ's communion with the Father is not an expression of his deity alone, nor is temptation or weakness pertinent only to his humanity. His human soul can be called the Son of God and Wisdom and Word, and the Son of God can be called Jesus, for in "scripture, while the divine nature is spoken of in human terms [*diuina natura humanis uocabulis appellatur*] the human nature is in its turn adorned with marks that belong to the divine prerogative [*quam humana natura diuinae nuncupationis insignibus decoratur*]." This communication of attributes is not only a transfer of functional appellations, but it is also recognition of the two natures' ontological union. Essentially, Jesus Christ so fully codifies the true union of God and humanity that it is indistinguishable whether his human soul "was wholly in the Son of God [*tota esset in filio dei*]" or "it received the Son of God wholly into itself [*totum in se caperet filium dei*]."[44]

Atonement

Considering the mediating roles of Wisdom, the Word, and the manifold *epinoiai*, as well as the union of the two natures in Christ, it is not surprising "that the central place in [Origen's theology] is held by the Christ in his divinity and in his humanity."[45] From the beginnings of creation embodied within Wisdom to the restoration of all things, the Son of God is the pivotal figure. Interestingly, the fact that much of this theological system stands outside the present world results in an equal emphasis on the subjective and objective results of the incarnation. Origen's concept of redemption takes on a more panoramic view than in Irenaeus' and Tertullian's theologies. Since the Son's mediation both precedes and extends beyond the incarnation, Christ's ministry on earth is not the only venue for his redemptive work.

Origen's understanding of the fall and redemption is summarized in his belief that "mind [*mens*] when it fell was made soul [*anima*], and soul [*anima*] in its turn when furnished with virtues will become mind [*mens*]."[46] The downfall of humanity to its present state resulted from the fall of preexistent minds from

---

[44] Origen *De princ.* 2.6.3. "But how this relates to him who has been destined the Son of God in power is something that constrains our comprehension; unless it be that because of the inseparable unity of the Word and flesh, everything that is of the flesh is attributed to the Word also, since also the things which belong to the Word are foretold in the flesh. For we often find the designations 'Jesus' and 'Christ' and 'Lord' referred to both natures." Origen, *Commentary on the Epistle to the Romans, Books 1-5*, trans. Thomas P. Scheck, FOTC, vol. 103 (Washington, DC: Catholic University of America Press, 2001), 1.6.2. See also *Con. Cels.* 6.47.

[45] Crouzel, *Origen*, 197.

[46] Origen *De princ.* 2.8.3. For an extensive discussion of the fall, redemption, restoration, and ascent of humanity see John Clark Smith, *The Ancient Wisdom of Origen* (Cranbury, NJ: Associated University Presses, 1992).

the perfect contemplation of the divine. The fall is a consequence of souls' *satietas*, boredom or apathy that develops after possessing perfection in contemplation.[47] The cooling of souls' affection for God in contrast to God's consuming or fiery being also describes this fall from perfection.[48] However it is described, a soul's fall from perfect mind is attributable only to the soul's free will, not to God or any determining principle.

In order to return to mind and union with God, then, the soul must freely choose to return to a life of obedience and submission to God. When a soul turns away from the flesh and unites with the spirit it takes steps to return to its original state of obedience. But the soul lacks motivation and the ability to return on account of its fallen state. Jesus Christ's work of redemption, therefore, motivates and educates souls in attaining virtue and obedience. Jesus Christ, whether before, during, or after the incarnation, teaches obedience, grants wisdom, and serves as the ultimate example of obedience, submission, and union with God.[49] This concept of redemption or deification is a continual process of conviction, purgatorial cleansing, enlightenment, and participation in Christ. Souls gradually progress toward God and regress away from him depending on their decisions, virtue, and reception of divine grace and wisdom. Ultimately, every soul is expected to regain its original place in perfect union with God through each soul's willing decisions. God has an indefinite time to teach, discipline, and persuade wayward souls and bring unity to his creation.[50]

While the Son's general responsibilities in this redemptive process are to teach and exemplify obedience and to bring humanity into union with the divine, humanity's sinful condition requires atonement in an objective sense in order to enable the spirit. Several redemptive models or schemes display this necessity, beginning with the mercantile scheme.[51] In this conception of the atonement Jesus Christ gives himself in exchange for human souls. The possessor of human souls is sometimes omitted from the metaphor and other times identified as the devil, who is willing to release them in exchange for Christ's humanity. In this trade the devil's inability to comprehend the divine plan of salvation blinds him to the strength of the Word joined with Christ's humanity. Jesus Christ therefore, after traveling to Hades, is able to free himself from Satan's grasp and gain victory over him and his cohorts.[52]

The warrior scheme has commonalities with the mercantile in that Jesus defeats sin and Satan in order to free his prisoners. This scheme omits any exchange, portraying Christ instead as the victor over sin, death, and all demonic powers. Jesus Christ's adversaries are either destroyed entirely or subjugated.[53]

---

[47] Origen *De princ.* 1.3.8; 1.4.1; Crouzel, *Origen*, 210.
[48] Origen *De princ.* 2.8.3-4.
[49] Ibid., 3.5.6; 4.4.4; *Com. on John* 2.107.
[50] Chadwick, 93-4.
[51] See Crouzel, *Origen*, 194-7; Daniélou, *Origen*, 270-273.
[52] Origen *Com. on Matt.* 12.28, 40; 13.8-9; *Com. on John* 1.250; 6.174-177, 274; Crouzel, *Origen*, 195.
[53] Origen *Com. on John* 1.233-4; 2.54-57; 6.285-289; *Com. on Matt.* 13.8-9.

The Old Testament and the book of Hebrews are the source of the sacrificial model in which Jesus Christ reconciles man to God as both priest and sacrifice. The lamb of God takes the sin of the world upon himself, and in so doing conquers his enemies, but not as one would expect. This sacrifice is a one time event with persisting benefits. Through his sacrifice Christ removes sin from individual souls and eventually every rational being is willingly brought to submission in the kingdom of God. Consequently, his adversaries are not destroyed but are instead freed from their sin and brought to obedience. In the sacrificial event Christ's humanity is the lamb and his deity is the priest, identifying him again as the mediator between God and humanity.[54]

Jesus' death and resurrection also bear the church through a mystical redemption in which believers die to sin and are resurrected to new life by participation in his passion. Christ's death contains the death of the church and his resurrection "contains the mystery of the resurrection of the whole body of Christ."[55] Thus, corporately we participate in the restoration of the preexistent church, the bride of Christ, but we also experience this participation individually when we identify with him by bearing about his death in our bodies in order that we might experience his life.[56]

Origen uses many additional metaphors and illustrations to articulate aspects of the atonement such as Jesus' willingness to bear our darkness and the replacement of our stone hearts with hearts of flesh.[57] All of these models, schemes, and metaphors draw upon biblical and traditional sources, and apart from the preexistence of souls, they depart little from the dominant soteriology contemporary to Origen. Deification is closely related to the New Testament concept of union with Christ, sacrifice is prominent in Hebrews and elsewhere, and Christ as victor, ransom, and redeemer are likewise solidly biblical. As with the other doctrinal areas, Origen's soteriology uses more ontological language than Irenaeus' and Tertullian's, especially in relation to humanity's fall and ascent. Nevertheless, Origen's language still retains all the traditional functional vocabulary which includes ransom, redeem, sacrifice, and reconcile, without which one could not construct an adequate theory of atonement.

Eschatology

While Origen's concept of atonement maintains the traditional language of Scripture and the early church, the eschatological statements, or lack of statements, in the preface to *On First Principles* anticipate his divergence from the teachings of his predecessors. His eschatological assertions in the *regula* include

---

[54] See Origen *Com. on John* 1.233-235, 255; 6.273-275, 285-286; 10.88-111; 19.119-120; 28.157-168; *De princ.* 2.3.5.
[55] Origen *Com. on John* 10.229.
[56] Ibid., 1.227.
[57] Ibid., 2.163; *De princ.* 3.1.15.

only the final resurrection, a fire of judgment and purgation, and the end of the world.[58]

In contrast to the literal millenarianism of Irenaeus and others, Origen utilizes spiritual interpretation to piece together an afterlife unfettered by thoughts of the present world.[59] The widespread belief in the church of an afterlife modeled after the present life only fuels the arguments of heretics and pagans. Questions such as the manner in which body parts are restored in the resurrection are nonsense, especially in light of Jesus' response to the Sadducees in Matt. 22:29-32. At the resurrection people "will be like the angels of heaven," having ethereal bodies that are distinct from their earthly bodies while continuous in identity. No soul, either in the intermediate state or following the resurrection is bodiless since only God himself does not possess a body of any kind.[60] In this life the body clothes the soul, but in the next life as "Christ is the clothing of the soul [*Christus Iesus indumentum sanctis esse dicatur*]," so the soul is "the clothing of the body [*indumentum corporis perfectam animam*]."[61] The soul will be the covering for the mortal body, clothing it with immortality and changing its quality to make it imperishable.

When God resurrects all people, both good and bad, they are divided according to their merits and clothed in bodies commensurate with their behavior. Judging on the basis of merit is just and righteous since God created every being with free will and every creature is responsible for his own actions. So it is no injustice when even the wicked are raised imperishable to possess immortal bodies that experience without dissolution all of the punishments for which they are destined.[62] They experience these punishments both before and after the resurrection in forms appropriate to their state, but the duration is not clear.

The destination of the wicked is variously called eternal fire, inextinguishable fire, Gehenna, and outer darkness even though Origen usually describes the experiences as remedial or purgatorial. The eternal or inextinguishable fire is explained two ways. First, Scripture calls God a consuming fire, burning out the chaff and removing all impurities.[63] Second, sinners kindle their own fires with sins, the wood, hay, and stubble in 2 Cor. 5:4 that must be burned away.[64] The widespread and dominant use of these passages by Origen's contemporaries suggests that his interpretation of a purifying or remedial fire is not uncommon.

---

[58] Origen *De princ.* pref., 5. For a full explanation and evaluation of Origen's eschatology see Tzamalikos, *Origen: Philosophy of History and Eschatology*, 237-356.

[59] For a thorough discussion see Charles Hill, *Regnum Caelorum: Patterns of Millennial Thought in Early Christianity* (Grand Rapids, MI: Eerdmans, 2001), 127-132.

[60] Origen *De princ.* 1.1; 2.2.2; 2.3.2-3; 2.10.1; 4.3.15.

[61] Ibid., 2.3.2. See also Origen *Con. Cels.* 5.18-19. Cf. 2 Cor. 5:4.

[62] Origen *De princ.* 2.10.3.

[63] Deut. 4:24; 9:3; See also Origen *Con. Cels.* 4.13; 6.70, 72; *De princ.* 1.1.1; 2.8.3.

[64] Origen *Con. Cels.* 4.13; 5.15-16; 6.25-26; *De princ.* 1.1.2; 2.9.8; 2.10.4; Crouzel, *Origen*, 245.

Furthermore, judgment for purification rather than damnation meshes well with Origen's theory of the ascent of souls to God.[65]

God never forces himself upon human beings, instead granting them free will to choose him in their own time. But too often souls choose poorly, turning to their own designs instead of to God himself. Consequently he will discipline, educate, reason, and exhort until his creation is restored to him, however long that takes.[66] In the end comes the *apokatastasis*, the restoration of all things under God's complete and unchallenged rule. All creation will willingly be subject to Jesus Christ and to God through Christ. All of humanity received the potential of perfection by being created in the Son's image, but the likeness of God comes only with the perfection found in union with God.[67] Likeness is the fulfillment of the image, the face to face knowledge of God that far exceeds the image. Humanity's reception of God's likeness, when everything is willingly subject to God as it was in the beginning, will indicate the end of the world and the beginning of the new, "for the end is always like the beginning [*semper enim similis est finis initiis*]."[68] This *apokatastasis* is not the innocence of Adam and Eve, rather it comes to pass when God "is also all things in each person in such a way that everything which the rational mind ... can feel or understand or think will be all God and that the mind will no longer be conscious of anything besides or other than God."[69]

This conclusion to God's cosmic plan explains Origen's most significant eschatological variations in the *regula*. The omission of the *parousia* from his version of the *regula* comes from a spiritual interpretation of the event rather than a literal interpretation. The *parousia* signifies "the manifestation of Christ and His divinity to all mankind" for the differentiation of the good and bad instead of a historical transition to a new world of similar order.[70] There is little reason for a decisive reappearance of Christ on earth since he has been working since the beginning and he continues to guide people in the pursuit of holiness until God's rule is consolidated.[71]

Essentially, the theory of the fall and ascent of souls together with the preexistence of souls and the final *apokatastasis* affect Origen's eschatology more than any other doctrinal area. Consequently, it is in relation to eschatology that Christology is most affected, though the variations generally remain isolated to Christ's return and his role as judge in a final judgment. These variations are significant reinterpretations of the tradition, but they do not nullify Origen's

---

[65] Cf. R. P. C. Hanson, *Allegory and Event: A Study of the Sources and Significance of Origen's Interpretation of Scripture* (London: SCM Press, 1959), 335-342.

[66] Origen *De princ.* 3.5.8; 3.6.6. Cf. Daniélou, *Origen*, 287.

[67] Origen *Con. Cels.* 4.30; *De princ.* 1.6.4; 2.11.3; 3.6.1; 4.4.9.

[68] Origen *De princ.* 1.6.2. See also ibid., 1.6.1; 2.1.3; 2.3.7; 3.5.3, 6; 3.6.8; *Com. on John* (ANF) 1.16; 2.7.

[69] Origen *De princ.* 3.6.3. Cf. Tzamalikos, *Origen: Philosophy of History and Eschatology*, 325-327.

[70] Kelly, *Early Christian Doctrines*, 473.

[71] Cf. Hanson, *Allegory and Event*, 342.

contributions in maintaining and advancing the church's understanding of Jesus Christ's person and work.[72]

The *Regula*, Ontological Language, and Speculation

Whatever the faults of his theology, Origen undoubtedly maintains the christological monotheism of the New Testament and his predecessors as well as the continuity of the two testaments. Jesus Christ is fully God and fully man, exercising sovereignty as Wisdom and Word, existing as the source of creation, receiving the names of God as his own, and rightly hearing the praise and adulation of his creation. Similarly, Origen never passes by an opportunity to tie the Old and New Testaments together in the person of Christ. Jesus Christ is the reason that the Old Testament has significance for Christians. The same Son of God works through all of history, from before this world to the patriarchal world to the apostolic period and on to the world to come. All of Scripture can be consistently read through the person of Christ by spiritual means.

Origen articulates this view of Jesus using categories and ideas that maintain the functional emphases of the early church while incorporating developments in ontological vocabulary. In relation to the Son's origins from eternity, the word "generation" is given new ontological meaning while related functional concepts are maintained. Being the eternal Son of God, Christ works as the instrumental cause of creation and reveals God to humanity. He accomplishes this through his *epinoiai*, which are both ontological and functional in nature, the vast majority being functional appellations while the dominant few are primarily ontological in nature.

Christ's incarnation is similarly described using more ontological terms, largely because of Origen's emphasis on the incorporeality of God and the corporeality of created beings, and also on account of his extensive anthropology complicated by the preexistence of souls. The greater utilization of the *communicatio idiomatum* is one manifestation of this tendency in which Origen uses developing ontological categories to explain rather than undermine or replace functional concepts. In this example Origen further develops the communication of attributes, a principle by which one can say that God was crucified without denying either his immutability, which was essential in the early church, or Christ's humanity. Thus the goal is not to discard the traditional Christology

---

[72] Hanson believes that Origen's eschatology leads to an understanding of God that is "all static rather than dynamic," thereby leaving all movement in reconciliation to humanity. Hanson, *Allegory and Event*, 355-356. This is true when considering the immutability and transcendence of the Father alone, but one must overlook Origen's Christology entirely in order to characterize Origen's overall theology this way. It is God himself who enables humanity's movement through his Son, the Wisdom and Word of God. God makes and cares for humanity in Wisdom, he reveals himself to humanity through his Word, he destroys death in the person of Jesus Christ, and he restores humanity in a practical sense through the mind of Christ given in the working of his Spirit.

embedded in functional terms and themes that he receives from his predecessors and replace it with an ontological Christology. Instead, Origen's aim is to maintain a biblical Christology with contemporary language in order to address contemporary issues and dilemmas.

This goal is evident most clearly in redemption and atonement where Origen repeats much of the New Testament's functional language, especially in Christ's mediating *epinoiai*. Humanity is saved, redeemed, and freed, by Jesus Christ, who is the way, the truth, the life, the door, the good shepherd, the lamb of God, the bread of life, and so forth. Christ is victorious over sin, death, and the devil, redeeming humanity with his own life and acting as both priest and sacrifice. This conception of atonement carries the dominant functional themes of the church's tradition, but to this Origen adds the ontology of the ascent of the soul. The latter does not replace the former; instead, it explains Jesus Christ's work from a cosmic, ontological perspective as it is applied to souls in individual and corporate settings.

Despite gains in such subjects as the eternal generation of the Son, it is this openness within Origen's hermeneutic to going beyond the tradition that later gets him in trouble. He offers speculation and inquiry outside of the norm, sometimes tentatively and other times more adamantly. His more unusual views are generally among the former. Nevertheless, when Origen is accused of teachings such as the inclusion of the devil and his demons in the universal salvation of the *apokatastasis*, he is usually condemned for it. But the dogmatism implied by his detractors is not Origen's intent. In his *Letter to Friends in Alexandria*, "Origen complains that a passage which ought only to be judged in the setting of a research theology ... has been hardened into a categorical statement."[73] His desire remains the search for and discovery of a greater knowledge of God.

Despite the sometimes significant latitude he takes with his theology, Origen is consistent with his intended use of the *regula*. With the exception of the *parousia*, he abides by the *regula*'s core christological statements, Jesus Christ's deity and humanity, his death and resurrection, his inclusion within the unique divine identity, and the continuity of the two testaments. But he also follows his intent to conduct research with the *regula* as the foundation, delving into the ontological nature of God, the Son's generation, his nature as Wisdom and Word, and his being as a preexistent man and incarnate human. While Irenaeus utilized only the New Testament's christological language, Tertullian and Origen, without discarding important concepts, incorporate increasingly more ontological language to explain the timeless truths of faith in Jesus Christ.

---

[73] Crouzel, *Origen*, 263.

Part V

Conclusion

The evaluation of the *regulae* in the works of Irenaeus, Tertullian, and Origen further substantiates the presence of a high Christology in the New Testament by showing the essential continuity of christological thought in the period between the New Testament and the first ecumenical council. Although Jesus Christ was not designated as *homoousios* with the Father until Nicaea, the devotion and worship given him by New Testament believers indicates their recognition of his unique divine status. The form and structure of christological statements in the early church changed over time, but Christians' devotion to Jesus and their fundamental beliefs about him that inspired such devotion did not change.

From the New Testament Church through the early centuries and down to the present, the church has always believed that in Jesus Christ God became a human being by means of his birth of a virgin. The church has taught that he lived and died as a man, he rose from the dead, conquering sin and death, and he ascended to heaven to sit at the right hand of the Father until his promised return. These events are the historical basis for the Christian faith maintained consistently throughout the *regulae*.[1]

These events, besides inspiring Christ devotion, also instigated the theological reflection that led to recognizing Jesus Christ's inclusion within the unique divine identity. Christ's sovereignty over creation, exercised especially in his providential care and his eschatological judgment, is an identifier of his uniquely divine status. This sovereignty derives in large part from his role as the instrumental cause of creation. Since the Son of God is the eternal preexisting agent of creation he has the ability and authority to care for it, judge it, and re-create it. Furthermore, his identity as Creator and Lord of everything entitles him to the divine name and the worship and obedience of his creation. Like the New Testament, the *regula* identifies these characteristics in Jesus Christ and acknowledges his inclusion within the unique divine identity.

As the Lord of creation and the author of its redemption, Jesus Christ embodies the unity of the two covenants. The Old and New Testaments together reveal the one true God who created all things, provided for their redemption, and will

---

[1] The lone exception to the inclusion of these events in the *regula* is Origen's allegorical interpretation of Christ's return. Yet, Origen's understanding still maintains the heart of the teaching, that believers will know and experience Jesus Christ face to face in his glory after their bodily resurrection. Origen is avoiding the chiliastic fervor of the period, not the return of Christ.

judge all of creation at the conclusion of the *oikonomia*. Christological monotheism is the only consistent explanation for integrating these truths. The *regulae*, irrespective of authors, stridently preach monotheism while acknowledging the deity of Christ both explicitly and implicitly.

This common substance within the *regula* does not preclude variations from author to author or between versions. Each author's context and purposes for reiterating the *regula* grants each version of the *regula* a distinctive character. Irenaeus' pastoral concerns make him an ardent defender of biblical truth, especially as he relates to those under his care. His desire to shepherd the believers under his care drives him to a strong dependence on the Bible, firmly asserting its concepts and departing little from its language. Tertullian's zeal for doctrinal integrity carries him a little further down the path. He uses the *regula* effectively as a tool for disarming heretics, demanding that only adherents to the faith of the *regula*, that is, members of the church, have the right to refer to Scripture. In addition, he has few qualms about sharpening his polemic with extra-biblical sources as long as they complement Scripture and the *regula*. Finally, Origen's context of discovery opens new vistas for theological discussion and insight. Not only does he retain the polemic against heretics, but he also often extends the attack when necessary. Yet, his primary interest is in theological inquiry and exploration. Considering all of the subjects on which the church possesses little consensus or certainty, Origen sees the need to indulge the seeking mind and discover the many theological truths that remain veiled. The foundational principles of the faith found in the *regula* remain unquestioned, and they provide a basis for exploration rather than a denial of inquiry.

These differences in the hermeneutical application of the *regula* explain many of the differences and variations among the three fathers' theologies. While they all integrate such common themes as monotheism, the *oikonomia*, the *Logos*, *creatio ex nihilo*, the two natures of Christ, and the Son's generation, their differing perspectives and hermeneutics result in adjusted emphases and extended or limited explanations. For example, the *oikonomia*, God's plan for his creation, is a theme utilized by all three fathers. In Irenaeus it takes a very concrete form with definite parameters physically and chronologically. Origen, on the other hand, sees the *oikonomia* as a supramundane plan stretching beyond the present world. Nevertheless, both fathers maintain the essential principles of the *oikonomia*, that God created, has a plan for his creation, is actively working in his creation, and intends to bring it to fulfillment.

Similarly, our writers respond very differently to the Son's generation from the Father. Irenaeus, in his defense of the faith, recognizes no need or value in searching out the nature of the Son's generation. Tertullian follows suit in part, but responds to heretics with basic explanations of the Son's divine origins, defending the church's nascent Trinitarian theology that asserts the threeness of God in continuity with monotheism. Origen goes beyond Tertullian's explanations, recognizing a need to reconcile some discrepancies while seeking a greater understanding of the divine. The contrast between Irenaeus and Origen on this subject is especially sharp considering Irenaeus' vehement rejection of inquiry leading to any explanation, while Origen, on the other hand, wholeheartedly embraces exploration into the Son's eternal generation. Nevertheless, both fathers draw on the same foundational principles to justify their positions. The transcendence and immutability of God explain Irenaeus' reluctance to delve into the subject at all. Yet Origen finds it necessary to articulate the eternal generation in order to avoid change or mutability in God. Thus, even when they are most dissonant, Irenaeus, Tertullian, and Origen hold far more substance in common than not, especially christologically. Origen's millennial position is the rare exception.

These differences between their perspectives appear dramatically in the language of the *regula* and in their theologies overall. Irenaeus overwhelmingly uses functional terminology derived largely from Scripture to maintain the New Testament's high Christology. Christ is ontologically divine because he does what only God himself can do. Tertullian and Origen use progressively more metaphysical language to communicate the same basic christological concepts. The result is not a later recognition or attribution of deity to Christ, but simply a translation of New Testament christological concepts into the theological language of the day. Not surprisingly, the work of the second and third century fathers, especially Tertullian and Origen, in coining and redefining theological terminology set the stage for the fourth and fifth century councils with much of the vocabulary needed for the continuing task.

This task of translating the New Testament's Christology into contemporary language remains no less significant today. The christological continuity of the *regula* within the transition of the early church remains a good model for the present work of translating the Christian faith into contemporary cultural, philosophical, and theological frameworks. Obviously we stand on the other side of a great deal of history and theological reflection and the councils that defined orthodoxy, and we must account for that in our theological efforts. Nevertheless, the present day church holds many things in common with the early church and its context. We live in a pluralistic society, dominated by an ethos of tolerance in which spirituality is on the rise and committed faith in Jesus Christ is too often plateaued or declining. Competing religious perspectives and various forms of heresy remain, sometimes claiming new adherents from the Christian faith just as the fathers saw occur in their day.

In essence the church's ministry needs and concerns have not changed. The first and most foundational concern is to maintain theological continuity with the New Testament and the early church. Doing so necessitates identifying essential doctrine and distinguishing it from *adiaphora*. Christologically this requires identification with the New Testament's teaching about Jesus, whether we do so conceptually, (e.g. by recognizing his inclusion in the unique divine identity), through explicit use of New Testament language, or by some combination of the two. The manner in which it is communicated then indicates at least in part the means by which we have received the apostolic message and how its continuity has been maintained. In the end, however it is communicated, when communicated well the result should be a growing devotion to Jesus Christ.

The second ministry concern, which is often intimated in the communication of the basic christological content, is the contextual application of the gospel.

Every believer, regardless of context, begins with the historical (and functional) foundation of Jesus' life, death, and resurrection, and for good and various reasons many are content and secure in that knowledge. Whether teaching children about Jesus or protecting vulnerable believers as in Irenaeus' circumstances, a functional emphasis on Jesus' person and work may be most appropriate. Whereas, in more complex polemical environments or in developing educational settings increasingly multifaceted and ontological concepts and vocabulary may be required to communicate christological content effectively and facilitate integration into larger theological frameworks.

However knowledge about Jesus is communicated, the implications of hermeneutical freedom and responsibility, a third general concern, will be apparent. While Origen exercises greater freedom in interpreting Scripture, he also demonstrates proportionately more involvement in the process of training leaders capable of engaging his type of interpretation and commentary. By contrast Irenaeus' and Tertullian's hermeneutical perspectives are comparatively narrow, placing more responsibility for proper interpretation on leaders who are often better prepared for the task. Consequently, in considering our hermeneutical approach to the foundational christological content of the New Testament we must consider the implications of such an approach. What interpretive parameters guide us, and what responsibility arises from these hermeneutical decisions?

Finally, healthy doctrine maintained in continuity with the New Testament requires regular revitalization. Whether in a personal or corporate context, a static theology will stagnate even as culture, vocabulary, and hermeneutical practices change. Irenaeus and Tertullian demonstrate this contextual revitalization in their multiple versions of the *regula* and their readiness to adjust to the issues at hand. More broadly we see the renewal that takes place as the fathers revisit past teachings to revise, update, and even dispose of various elements. Their varying approaches to the Logos Christology exemplify this need. Irenaeus' Logos Christology would have been quite insufficient in Origen's context.

The Trinitarian discussion and debate in the last century that continues today is an example of the theological revitalization and renewal that must regularly unfold if we are intent on understanding and applying the New Testament's abiding message contextually. Such revitalization follows in the footsteps of the fathers, and especially Origen, who himself affirmed the need for theological reevaluation and assessment. In fact, within the evangelical discussion of the Trinity the question of the Son's eternal generation, an important element in Origen's theology, is being revisited and debated.[2] The lasting significance of the debate remains to be seen, but even assuming that the traditional view of the Son's generation remains largely unchanged, the value of such revitalization is difficult to overestimate. Clarity and affirmation of biblical truth is worth the labor and engagement in dialogue that is required if we are to remain true to the one we worship.

---

[2] See Kevin Giles, *The Eternal Generation of the Son: Maintaining Orthodoxy in Trinitarian Theology* (Downers Grove, IL: IVP Academic, 2012).

"The apostolic confession that 'you are the Christ, the Son of the living God' (Matt. 16:16), meant that from the first, Jesus as 'Son of the Father', 'Son of God', would require articulation and definition in Christian experience."[3] Yet even as we revisit the significance of Peter's statement, the essential christological truths found within it that are restated in the rest of New Testament and later in the *regula*, continue to persist. Jesus Christ is God himself, the revelation of God to humanity, humanity's redemption, and its ultimate goal. We recognize this because of the historical events found in all of the *regulae*. That Christ was born of a virgin, lived a human life, died, rose again, and is returning to perfect his church and judge all creation identifies him as God, one included in the unique divine identity. Just as the early church fathers were faithful in articulating the gospel for the people of their day, so must we faithfully interpret, write, and proclaim the unchanging gospel of Jesus Christ.

---

[3] M. C. Steenberg, *Of God and Man*, 101.

Appendix: Texts of the *Regula Fidei*

Irenaeus

Against Heresies (ACW, SC) 1.10.1

The Church, indeed, though disseminated throughout the world, even to the ends of the earth, received from the apostles and their disciples the faith in one God the Father Almighty, the Creator of heaven and earth and the seas and all things that are in them; and in the one Jesus Christ, the Son of God who was enfleshed for our salvation; and in the Holy Spirit, who through the prophets preached the Economies, the coming, the birth from a Virgin, the passion, the resurrection from the dead, and the bodily ascension into heaven of the beloved Son, Christ Jesus our Lord, and His coming from heaven in the glory of the Father to recapitulate all things, and to raise up all flesh of the whole human race, in order that to Christ Jesus, our Lord and God, Savior and King, according to the invisible Father's good pleasure, *Every knee should bow [of those] in heaven and on earth and under the earth, and every tongue confess* Him, and that He would exercise just judgment toward all; and that, on the other hand, He would send into eternal fire the spiritual forces of wickedness, and the angels who transgressed and became rebels, and the godless, wicked, lawless, and blasphemous people; but, on the other hand, by bestowing life on the righteous and holy and those who

Hē men gar Ekklēsia, kaiper kath holēs tēs oikoumenēs heōs peratōn tēs gēs diesparmenē, para te tōn apostolōn kai tōn ekeinōn paralazousa tēn eis hena Theon Patera pantokratora ton pepoiēkota ton ouranon kai tēn gēn kai tēn thalassan kai panta ta en autois pistin, kai eis hena Kriston Iēsoun ton Huion tou Theou ton sarkōthenta huper tēs hēmeteras sōtērias, kai eis Pneuma hagion to dia tōn prophētōn kekēruchos tas oikonomias kai tēn eleusin kai tēn ek tēs Parthenou gennēsin kai to pathos kai tēn egersin ek nekrōn kai tēn ensarkon eis tous ouranous analēpsin tou ēgapēmenou Christou Iēsou tou Kuriou hēmōn kai tēn ek tōn ouranōn en tē doxē tou Patros parousian autou epi to anakephalaiōsasthai ta panta kai anastēsai pasan sarka pasēs anthrōpotētos, hina Christōi Iēsou tōi Kuriōi hēmōn kai Theōi kai Sōtēri kai Basilei kata tēn eudokian tou Patros tou aoratou tan gonu kampsē epouraniōn kai epigeiōn kai katachthoniōn kai pasa glōssa exomologēsētai autōi kai krisin dikaian en tois pasi poiēsētai, ta men pneumatika tēs ponērias kai angelous tous parazezēkotas kai en apostasia gegonotas kai tous asezeis kai adikous kai anomous kai blas-

kept His commandments and who have persevered in His love—both those who did so from the beginning and those who did so after repentance—He would bestow on them as a grace the gift of incorruption and clothe them with everlasting glory.

phēmous tōn anthrōpōn eis to aiōnion pur pempsē, tois de dikaiois kai hosiois kai tas entolas autou tetērēkosi kai en tē agapē autou diamemenēkosi, tois men ap archēs, tois de ek metanoias, zōēn charisamenos aphtharsian dōrēsētai kai doxan aiōnian peripoiēsē.

Against Heresies (ACW, SC) 1.22.1

The Rule of the Truth that we hold is this: There is one God Almighty, who created all things through His Word; He both prepared and made all things out of nothing, just as Scripture says: *For by the word of the Lord the heavens were made, and all their host by the breath of His mouth.* And again: *All things were made through Him and without Him was made not a thing.* From this *all* nothing is exempt. Now, it is the Father who made all things through Him, whether visible or invisible, whether sensible or intelligible, whether temporal for the sake of some dispensation or eternal. These He did not make through Angels or some Powers that were separated from His thought. For the God of all things needs nothing. No, He made all things by His Word and Spirit, disposing and governing them and giving all of them existence. This is the one who made the world, which indeed is made up of all things. This is the one who fashioned man. This is the God of Abraham and Isaac and Jacob, above whom there is no other God, nor a Beginning, nor a Power, nor a Fullness. This is the Father of our Lord Jesus Christ, as we shall demonstrate. If, therefore, we hold fast this Rule, we shall easily prove that they have strayed from the Truth, even though their statements are quite varied and numerous.

Cum teneamus autem nos regulam ueritatis, id est quia sit unus Deus omnipotens qui omnia condidit per Verbum suum et aptauit et fecit ex eo quod non erat ad hoc ut sint omnia, quemadmodum Scriptura dicit: *Verbo enim Domini caeli firmati sunt, et Spiritu oris eius omnis uirtus eorum, et* iterum: *Omnia per ipsum facta sunt, et sine ipso factum est nihil*—ex omnibus autem nihil subtractum est, sed omnia per ipsum fecit Pater, siue uisibilia siue inuisibilia, siue sensibilia siue intellegibilia, siue temporalia propter quandam dispositionem siue sempiterna et aeonia, non per Angelos neque per Virtutes aliquas abscissas ab eius sententia, nihil enim indiget omnium Deus, sed et per Verbum et Spiritum suum omnia faciens et disponens et gubernans et omnibus esse praestans; hic qui mundum fecit, etenim mundus ex omnibus; hic qui hominem plasmauit; hic Deus Abraham et Deus Isaac et Deus Iacob, super quem alius Deus non est neque Initium neque Virtus neque Pleroma; hic Pater Domini nostri Iesu Christi, quemadmodum ostendemus—, hanc ergo tenentes regulam, licet ualde uaria et multa dicant, facile eos deuiasse a ueritate arguimus.

Against Heresies (ANF, SC) 3.4.2

To which course many nations of those barbarians who believe in Christ do assent, having salvation written in their hearts by the Spirit, without paper or ink, and, carefully preserving the ancient tradition, believing in one God, the Creator of heaven and earth, and all things therein, by means of Christ Jesus, the Son of God; who, because of His surpassing love towards His creation, condescended to be born of the virgin, He Himself uniting man through Himself to God, and having suffered under Pontius Pilate, and rising again, and having been received up in splendor, shall come in glory, the Savior of those who are saved, and the Judge of those who are judged, and sending into eternal fire those who transform the truth, and despise His Father and His advent.

Ēi taxei peithontai polla ethnē barbarōn tōn eis Christon pepisteukotōn, aneu chartou kai melanos engegrammenēn echontōn dia tou Pneumatos en tais kardiais autōn tēn sōtērian kai tēn archaian paradosin epimelōs phulassontōn, eis hena Theon pisteuontōn, Poiētēn ouranou kai gēs kai pantōn tōn en autois, kai Christon Iēsoun, ton tou Theou Huion, ton dia tēn huperballousan pros to plasma autou agapēn tēn ek tēs parthenou gennēsin hupomeinanta, auton di heautou ton anthrōpon henōsanta tōi Theōi, kai pathonta epi Pontiou Pilatou kai egerthenta kai en doxē analēphthenta, erchomenon en doxē Sōtēra tōn sōzomenōn kai Kritēn tōn krinomenōn kai pemponta eis pur aiōnion tous paracharaktas tēs alētheias kai kataphronētas tou Patros autou kai tēs parousias autou.

Against Heresies (ANF, SC) 5.20.1

But the path of those belonging to the Church circumscribes the whole world, as possessing the sure tradition from the apostles, and gives unto us to see that the faith of all is one and the same, since all receive one and the same God the Father, and believe in the same dispensation regarding the incarnation of the Son of God, and are cognizant of the same gift of the Spirit, and are conversant with the same commandments, and preserve the same form of ecclesiastical constitution, and expect the same advent of the Lord, and await the same salvation of the complete man, that is, of the soul and body.

Tōn de apo tēs ekklēsias hē tribos holon ton kosmon emperierchomenē, ate bebaian echousa tēn apo tōn apostolōn paradosin, kai blepein hēmin charizomenē tōn pantōn mian kai tēn autēn pistin, pantōn heni kai tōi autōi Theōi Patri peithomenōn, kai tē autē oikonomia tēs sarkōseōs tou Huiou tou Theou pisteuontōn, kai to auto doma tou Pneumatos eidotōn, kai tas autas meletōntōn entolas, kai to auto schēma tēs peri tēn ekklēsian taxeōs diatērountōn, kai tēn autēn ekdechomenōn parousian tou Kuriou, kai tēn autēn sōtērian holou tou anthrōpou, toutesti psuchēs kai sōmatos, prosdokōntōn.

Tertullian

Prescription Against Heretics (ANF, CCSL) 13.1-6

Now, with regard to this rule of faith—that we may from this point acknowledge what it is which we defend—it is, you must know, that which prescribes the belief that 2. there is one only God, and that He is none other than the Creator of the world, who produced all things out of nothing through His own Word, first of all sent forth; 3. that this Word is called His Son, and, under the name of God, was seen "in diverse manners" by the patriarchs, heard at all times in the prophets, at last brought down by the Spirit and Power of the Father into the Virgin Mary, was made flesh in her womb, and, being born of her, went forth as Jesus Christ; 4. thenceforth He preached the new law and the new promise of the kingdom of heaven, worked miracles; having been crucified, He rose again the third day; (then) having ascended into the heavens, He sat at the right hand of the Father; 5. sent instead of Himself the Power of the Holy Ghost to lead such as believe; will come with glory to take the saints to the enjoyment of everlasting life and of the heavenly promises, and to condemn the wicked to everlasting fire, after the resurrection of both these classes shall have happened, together with the restoration of their flesh. 6. This rule, as it will be proved, was taught by Christ, and raises amongst ourselves no other questions than those which heresies introduce, and which make men heretics.

Regula est autem fidei ut iam hinc quid defendamus profiteamur, illa scilicet qua creditur. 2. Vnum omnino Deum esse nec alium praeter mundi conditorem qui uniuersa de nihilo produxerit per uerbum suum primo omnium emissum. 3. Id uerbum filium eius appellatum in nomine Dei uarie uisum a patriarchis, in prophetis semper auditum, postremo delatum ex spiritu patris Dei et uirtute in uirginem Mariam, carnem factum in utero eius et ex ea natum egisse Iesum Christum. 4. Exinde praedicasse nouam legem et nouam promissionem regni caelorum, uirtutes fecisse, crucifixum, tertia die resurrexisse, in caelos ereptum sedisse ad dexteram patris, 5. misisse uicariam uim spiritus sancti qui credentes agat, uenturum cum claritate ad sumendos sanctos in uitae aeternae et promissorum caelestium fructum et ad profanos iudicandos igni perpetuo, facta utriusque partis resuscitatione cum carnis restitutione. 6. Haec regula a Christo, ut probabitur, instituta nullas habet apud nos quaestiones nisi quas haereses inferunt et quae haereticos faciunt.

Against Praxeas (ANF, CCSL) 2.1

We, however, as we indeed always have done and more especially since we have been better instructed by the Paraclete, who leads men indeed into all truth, believe that there is one only God, but under the following dispensation, or oikonomia, as it is called, that this one only God has also a Son, His Word, who proceeded from Himself, by whom all things were made, and without whom nothing was made. Him *we believe* to have been sent by the Father into the Virgin, and to have been born of her — being both Man and God, the Son of Man and the Son of God, and to have been called by the name of Jesus Christ; *we believe* Him to have suffered, died, and been buried, according to the Scriptures, and, after He had been raised again by the Father and taken back to heaven, to be sitting at the right hand of the Father, *and* that He will come to judge the quick and the dead; who sent also from heaven from the Father, according to His own promise, the Holy Ghost, the Paraclete, the sanctifier of the faith of those who believe in the Father, and in the Son, and in the Holy Ghost.

Nos uero et semper et nunc magis, ut instructiores per Paracletum, deductorem scilicet omnis ueritatis, unicum quidem Deum credimus, sub hac tamen dispensatione quam oikonomiam dicimus, ut unici Dei sit et Filius, sermo ipsius qui ex ipso processerit, per quem omnia facta sunt et sine quo factum est nihil. Hunc missum a Patre in uirginem et ex ea natum, hominem et Deum, Filium hominis et Filium Dei et cognominatum Iesum Christum. Hunc passum, hunc mortuum et sepultum secundum scripturas et resuscitatum a Patre et in caelo resumptum sedere ad dexteram Patris, uenturum iudicare uiuos et mortuos. Qui exinde miserit secundum promissionem suam a Patre Spiritum sanctum, Paracletum, sanctificatorem fidei eorum qui credunt in Patrem et Filium et Spiritum sanctum.

On the Veiling of Virgins (ANF, CCSL) 1.3

The rule of faith, indeed, is altogether one, alone immovable and irreformable; the rule, to wit, of believing in one only God omnipotent, the Creator of the universe, and His Son Jesus Christ, born of the Virgin Mary, crucified under Pontius Pilate, raised again the third day from the dead, received in the heavens, sitting now at the right (hand) of the Father, destined to come to judge the quick and the dead through the resurrection of the flesh as well (as of the spirit).

Regula quidem fidei una omnino est, sola immobilis et irreformabilis, credendi scilicet in unicum Deum omnipotentem, mundi conditorem, et filium eius Iesum Christum, natum ex uirgine Maria, crucifixum sub Pontio Pilato, tertia die resuscitatum a mortuis, receptum in caelis, sedentem nunc ad dexteram Patris, uenturum iudicare uiuos et mortuos per carnis etiam resurrectionem.

Origen

On First Principles (Butterworth, SC) pref., 4

The kind of doctrines which are believed in plain terms through the apostolic teaching are the following:

First, that God is one, who created and set in order all things, and who, when nothing existed, caused the universe to be. He is God from the first creation and foundation of the world, the God of all righteous men, of Adam, Abel, Seth, Enos, Enoch, Noah, Shem, Abraham, Isaac, Jacob, of the twelve patriarchs, of Moses and the prophets. This God, in these last days, according to the previous announcements made through his prophets, sent the Lord Jesus Christ, first for the purpose of calling Israel, and secondly, after the unbelief of the people of Israel, of calling the Gentiles also. This just and good God, the Father of our Lord Jesus Christ, himself gave the law, the prophets and the gospels, and he is God both of the apostles and also of the Old and New Testaments.

Then again: Christ Jesus, he who came to earth, was begotten of the Father before every created thing. And after he had ministered to the Father in the foundation of all things, for 'all things were made through him', in these last times he emptied himself and was made man, was made flesh, although he was God; and being made man, he still remained what he was, namely, God. He took to himself a body like our body, differing in this alone, that it was born of a virgin and of the Holy Spirit. And this Jesus Christ was born and suffered in truth and not merely in appearance, and truly died our common death. Moreover he truly rose from the dead, and after the resurrection companied with his disciples and was

Species uero eorum, quae per praedicationem apostolicam manifeste traduntur, istae sunt.

Primo, quod unus est deus, qui omnia creauit atque composuit, quique, cum nihil esset, esse fecit uniuersa, deus a prima creatura et conditione mundi, omnium iustorum deus, Adam Abel Seth Enos Enoch Noe Sem Abraham Isaac Iacob duodecim patriarcharum Moysei et prophetarum; et quod hic deus in nouissimis diebus, sicut per prophetas suos ante promiserat, misit dominum Iesum Christum, primo quidem uocaturum Israhel, secundo uero etiam gentes post perfidiam populi Israhel. Hic deus iustus et bonus, pater domini nostri Iesu Christi, legem et prophetas et euangelia ipse dedit, qui et apostolorum deus est et ueteris ac noui testamenti.

Tum deinde quia Christus Iesus, ipse qui uenit, ante omnem creaturam natus ex patre est. Qui cum in omnium conditione patri ministrasset, *per ipsum* namque *omnia facta sunt*, nouissimis temporibus se ipsum exinaniens homo factus est, incarnatus est, cum deus esset, et homo factus mansit quod erat, deus. Corpus assumsit nostro corpori simile, eo solo differens, quod natum ex uirgine et spiritu sancto est. Et quoniam hic Iesus Christus natus et passus est in ueritate, et non per phantasiam, communem hanc mortem uere mortuus; uere enim et a mortuis resurrexit et post resurrectionem conuersatus cum discipulis

then taken up into heaven.

Then again, the apostles delivered this doctrine, that the Holy Spirit is united in honour and dignity with the Father and the Son. In regard to him it is not yet clearly known whether he is to be thought of as begotten or unbegotten, or as being himself also a Son of God or not; but these are matters which we must investigate to the best of our power from holy scripture, inquiring with wisdom and diligence. It is, however, certainly taught with the utmost clearness in the Church, that this Spirit inspired each one of the saints, both the prophets and the apostles, and that there was not one Spirit in the men of old and another in those who were inspired at the coming of Christ.

suis assumtus est.

Tum deinde honore ac dignitate patri ac filio sociatum tradiderunt spiritum sanctum. In hoc non iam manifeste discernitur, utrum natus aut innatus, uel filius etiam ipse dei habendus sit, necne; sed inquirenda iam ista pro uiribus sunt de sancta scriptura et sagaci perquisitione inuestiganda. Sane quod iste spiritus sanctus unumquemque sanctorum uel prophetarum uel apostolorum inspirauerit, et non alius spiritus in ueteribus, alius uero in his, qui in aduentu Christi inspirati sunt, fuerit, manifestissime in ecclesia praedicatur.

Bibliography

Primary Sources

Aland, Barbara, Kurt Aland, Johannes Karavidopoulos, Carlo M. Martini, and Bruce M. Metzger, eds. *UBS Greek New Testament*, 4th rev. ed. Stuttgart, Germany: Biblia-Druck, 1993.

Irenaeus. *Contre les hérésies, Livre 1*. Edited and translated by Adelin Rousseau and Lewis Doutreleau. 2 vols. Sources chrétiennes, nos. 263, 264. Paris: Éditions du Cerf, 1979.

———. *Contre les hérésies, Livre 2*. Edited and translated by Adelin Rousseau and Lewis Doutreleau. 2 vols. Sources chrétiennes, nos. 293, 294. Paris: Éditions du Cerf, 1982.

———. *Contre les hérésies, Livre 3*. Edited and translated by Adelin Rousseau and Lewis Doutreleau. 2 vols. Sources chrétiennes, nos. 210, 211. Paris: Éditions du Cerf, 1974.

———. *Contre les hérésies, Livre 4*. Edited and translated by Adelin Rousseau. 2 vols. Sources chrétiennes, nos. 100.1, 100.2. Paris: Éditions du Cerf, 1965.

———. *Contre les hérésies, Livre 5*. Edited and translated by Adelin Rousseau, Lewis Doutreleau, and C. Mercier. 2 vols. Sources chrétiennes, nos. 152, 153. Paris: Éditions du Cerf, 1969.

———. *Démonstration de la prédication apostolique*. Edited and translated by Adelin Rousseau. Sources chrétiennes, no. 406. Paris: Éditions du Cerf, 1995.

———. *Epideixis, Adversus haereses, Darlegung der Apostolischen Verkündigung, und Gegen die Häresien*. Translated by Norbert Brox. New York: Herder, 1993.

———. *Against the Heresies, Book I*. Translated by Dominic J. Unger with further revisions by J. J. Dillon. Ancient Christian Writers, no. 55. New York: Paulist Press, 1992.

———. *Against the Heresies, Book II*. Translated by Dominic J. Unger with further revisions by J. J. Dillon. Ancient Christian Writers, no. 65. New York: Paulist Press, 2012.

———. *Against the Heresies, Book III*. Translated by Matthew C. Steenberg and Dominic J. Unger. Ancient Christian Writers, no. 64. New York: Paulist Press, 2012.

———. *Against Heresies*. In *The Ante-Nicene Fathers*. Vol. 1, *The Apostolic Fathers, Justin Martyr, Irenaeus*. Edited by James Donaldson and Alexander Roberts. United States: Christian Literature Pub. Co., 1897; reprint, Peabody, MA: Hendrickson, 1994.

———. *On the Apostolic Preaching*. Translated by John Behr. Crestwood, NY: St. Vladimir's Seminary Press, 1997.

Origen. *Commentaire sur saint Jean, Livres 1-5*. Edited and translated by Cécile Blanc. Sources chrétiennes, no. 120. Paris: Éditions du Cerf, 1966.

———. *Commentaire sur saint Jean, Livres 6 & 10*. Edited and translated by Cécile Blanc. Sources chrétiennes, no. 157. Paris: Éditions du Cerf, 1970.

———. *Commentaire sur saint Jean, Livre 13*. Edited and translated by Cécile Blanc. Sources chrétiennes, no. 222. Paris: Éditions du Cerf, 1975.

———. *Commentaire sur saint Jean, Livres 19 & 20*. Edited and translated by Cécile Blanc. Sources chrétiennes, no. 290. Paris: Éditions du Cerf, 1982.

———. *Commentaire sur saint Jean, Livres 28 & 32*. Edited and translated by Cécile Blanc. Sources chrétiennes, no. 385. Paris: Éditions du Cerf, 1992.

———. *Commentaire sur l'Évangile selon Matthieu, Livres 10 & 11*. Edited and translated by Robert Girod. Sources chrétiennes, no. 162. Paris: Éditions du Cerf, 1970.

———. *Contre Celse, Livres 1 & 2*. Edited and translated by Marcel Borret. Sources chrétiennes, no. 132. Paris: Éditions du Cerf, 1967.

———. *Contre Celse, Livres 3 & 4*. Edited and translated by Marcel Borret. Sources chrétiennes, no. 136. Paris: Éditions du Cerf, 1968.

———. *Contre Celse, Livres 5 & 6*. Edited and translated by Marcel Borret. Sources chrétiennes, no. 147. Paris: Éditions du Cerf, 1969.

———. *Contre Celse, Livres 7 & 8*. Edited and translated by Marcel Borret. Sources chrétiennes, no. 150. Paris: Éditions du Cerf, 1969.

———. *Traité des principes, Livres 1 & 2*. Edited and translated by H. Crouzel and M. Simonetti. 2 vols. Sources chrétiennes, nos. 252, 253. Paris: Éditions du Cerf, 1978.

———. *Traité des principes, Livres 3 & 4*. Edited and translated by H. Crouzel and M. Simonetti. 2 vols. Sources chrétiennes, nos. 268, 269. Paris: Éditions du Cerf, 1980.

———. *Commentary on the Epistle to the Romans, Books 1-5*. Translated by Thomas P. Scheck. The Fathers of the Church, vol. 103. Washington, DC: Catholic University of America Press, 2001.

———. *Commentary on the Epistle to the Romans, Books 6-10*. Translated by Thomas P. Scheck. The Fathers of the Church, vol. 104. Washington, DC: Catholic University of America Press, 2012.

———. *Commentary on the Gospel According to John, Books 1-10*. Translated by Ronald E. Heine. The Fathers of the Church, vol. 80. Washington, DC: Catholic University of America Press, 1989.

———. *Commentary on the Gospel According to John, Books 13-32*. Translated by Ronald E. Heine. The Fathers of the Church, vol. 89. Washington, DC: Catholic University of America Press, 1993.

———. *Commentary on John, Books 1-10*. In *The Ante-Nicene Fathers*. Vol. 9. Edited by James Donaldson and Alexander Roberts. United States: Christian Literature Pub. Co., 1897; reprint, Peabody, MA: Hendrickson, 1994.

———. *Commentary on Matthew, Books 1, 2 and 10-14*. In *The Ante-Nicene Fathers*. Vol. 9. Edited by James Donaldson and Alexander Roberts. United States: Christian Literature Pub. Co., 1897; reprint, Peabody, MA: Hendrickson, 1994.

———. *Contra Celsum*. In *The Ante-Nicene Fathers*. Vol. 4, *Fathers of the Third Century*. Edited by James Donaldson and Alexander Roberts. United States: Christian Literature Pub. Co., 1897; reprint, Peabody, MA: Hendrickson, 1994.

———. *Contra Celsum*. Translated by Henry Chadwick. Cambridge: University Press, 1953.

———. *On First Principles*. In *The Ante-Nicene Fathers*. Vol. 4, *Fathers of the Third Century*. Edited by James Donaldson and Alexander Roberts. United States: Christian Literature Pub. Co., 1897; reprint, Peabody, MA: Hendrickson, 1994.

———. *Origen on First Principles*. Translated by G. W. Butterworth. New York: Harper & Row, 1966.

Tertullian. *Contre Hermogène*. Edited and translated by Frédéric Chapot. Paris: Ed. du CNRS, 1999.

———. *Tertulliani Opera*. Vol. 1, *Opera Catholica, Adversus Marcionem*. Corpus Christianorum: Series Latina. Turnhout: Brepols, 1954.

———. *Tertulliani Opera*. Vol. 2, *Opera Montanistica*. Corpus Christianorum: Series Latina. Turnhout: Brepols, 1954.

———. *The Ante-Nicene Fathers*. Vol. 3, *Latin Christianity: Its Founder, Tertullian*. Edited by James Donaldson and Alexander Roberts. United States: Christian Literature Pub. Co., 1897; reprint, Peabody, MA: Hendrickson, 1994.

———. "On the Veiling of Virgins." In *The Ante-Nicene Fathers*. Vol. 4, *Fathers of the Third Century*. Edited by James Donaldson and Alexander Roberts. United States: Christian Literature Pub. Co., 1897; reprint, Peabody, MA: Hendrickson, 1994.

———. "Prescription Against Heretics." In *The Library of Christian Classics*. Vol. 5, *Early Latin Theology: Selections from Tertullian, Cyprian, Ambrose, and Jerome*. Edited and translated by S. L. Greenslade. Philadelphia: The Westminster Press, 1956.

———. *Q. Septimii Florentis Tertulliani Adversus Praxean liber*. Translated by Ernest Evans. London: S.P.C.K., 1948.

Secondary Sources

Ayers, Robert H. *Language, Logic, and Reason in the Church Fathers: A Study of Tertullian, Augustine, and Aquinas*. New York: G. Olms, 1979.

Balas, David L. *Origen's View of Reality According to His "On First Principles" and "Commentary on John I-II" (From Metaphysics to Theology of Grace)*. Dallas, TX : University of Dallas, 1969.

Bardy, Gustave. *Origène*. Paris: J. Gabalda, 1931.

———. "La règle de foi d'Origène." *Recherches de science religieuse* 9 (1919): 162-196.

Barnes, Timothy David. *Tertullian: A Historical and Literary Study*. Oxford: Clarendon Press, 1971.

Bauckham, Richard. *God Crucified: Monotheism & Christology in the New Testament*. Grand Rapids, MI: Eerdmans, 1999.

———. "Devotion to Jesus Christ in Earliest Christianity: An Appraisal and Discussion of the Work of Larry Hurtado." In *Mark, Manuscripts, and Monotheism: Essays in Honor of Larry W. Hurtado*, edited by Chris Keith and Dieter T. Roth, 176-200. London: Bloomsbury, 2014.

Beeley, Christopher A. *The Unity of Christ: Continuity and Conflict in Patristic Tradition*. New Haven: Yale University Press, 2012.

Behr, John. *Asceticism and Anthropology in Irenaeus and Clement*. New York: Oxford University Press, 2000.

———. *Irenaeus of Lyons: Identifying Christianity*. New York: Oxford University Press, 2013.

Bender, Wolfgang. *Die Lehre über den heiligen Geist bei Tertullian*. Munich, Germany: Max Hueber, 1961.

Bengsch, Alfred. *Heilsgeschichte und Heilswissen: eine Untersuchung zur Struktur und Entfaltung des theologischen Denkens im Werk "Adversus haereses" des Hl. Irenäus von Lyon*. Leipzig: St. Benno-Verlag, 1957.

Benoit, André. *Saint Irénée: Introduction à l'étude de sa théologie*. Paris: Presses universitaires de France, 1960.

Bingham, D. Jeffrey. *Irenaeus' Use of Matthew's Gospel in Adversus Haereses*. Louvain: Peeters, 1998.

Birrer, Jakob. *Der Mensch als Medium und Adressat der Schöpfungsoffenbarung: eine dogmengeschichtliche Untersuchung zur Frage der Gotteserkenntnis bei Irenäus von Lyon*. Bern: Peter Lang, 1989.

Bissonnette, Leonard G. "Irenaeus' View of Salvation History." diss., University of Ottawa in cooperation with Saint Paul University, 1980.

Blosser, Benjamin P. *Become Like the Angels: Origen's Doctrine of the Soul*. Washington D.C.: The Catholic University of America Press, 2012.

Blowers, Paul M. *Drama of the Divine Economy: Creator and Creation in Early Christian Theology and Piety*. New York: Oxford University Press, 2012.

———. "The regula fidei and the Narrative Character of Early Christian Faith." *Pro Ecclesia* 6 (spring 1997): 199-228.

Bostock, Gerald. "The Sources of Origen's Doctrine of Pre-existence," In *Origeniana Quarta: Die Referate des 4. Internationalen Origeneskongresses (Innsbruck, 2.-6. September 1985)*, ed. Lothar Lies, 259-264. Tyrolia: Verlag, 1987.

Boulluec, Alain Le. "Controverses au sujet de la doctrine d'Origene sur l'ame du Christ." In *Origeniana Quarta: Die Referate des 4. Internationalen Origeneskongresses (Innsbruck, 2.-6. September 1985)*, ed. Lothar Lies, 223-237. Tyrolia: Verlag, 1987.

Bousset, Wilhelm. *Kyrios Christos: A History of the Belief in Christ from the Beginnings of Christianity to Irenaeus*. Translated by John E. Steely. Nashville, TN: Abingdon Press, 1970.

Braun, Rene. *Deus Christianorum: Recherches sur le vocabulaire doctrinal de Tertullien*. Études Augustiniennes. Paris: Chateau-Gontier, 1962.

Bray, Gerald. "Authority in the Early Church." *Churchman* 95 (1981): 43-53.

———. *Creeds, Councils, and Christ*. Downers Grove, IL: InterVarsity Press, 1984.

———. *Holiness and the Will of God: Perspectives on the Theology of Tertullian*. Atlanta, GA: John Knox Press, 1979.

Briggman, Anthony. *Irenaeus of Lyons and the Theology of the Holy Spirit*. New York: Oxford University Press, 2012.

Cadiou, René. *Introduction au système d'Origène*. Paris: Société d'édition "Les Belles lettres," 1932.

———. *Origen: His Life at Alexandria*. Translated by John A. Southwell. St. Louis, MO: Herder Book Co., 1944.

Cantalamessa, Raniero. *La Cristologia di Tertulliano*. Freiburg: Edizioni universitarie, 1962.

Chadwick, Henry. *Early Christian Thought and the Classical Tradition: Studies in Justin, Clement, and Origen*. New York: Oxford University Press, 1966.

Countryman, L. William. "Tertullian and the Regula Fidei." *The Second Century* 2 (Winter 1982): 208-227.

Crouzel, Henri. *Bibliographie Critique d'Origène et Supplément I et Supplèment II*. In *Instrumenta Patristica VIII*. The Hague: Abbaye de Steenbrugge, 1996.

———. *Le Christ Sauveur selon Origène*. In *Voies de salut dans le christianisme et les autres religions*, 63-88. Rome: Gregorian University Press, 1981.

———. *Origen*. Translated by A. S. Worrall. San Francisco: Harper & Row, 1989.

———. "Origène devant l'incarnation et devant l'histoire." *Bulletin de Littérature Ecclesiastique* (1960): 81-110.

———. *Origène et la philosophie*. Paris: Aubier, 1962.

———. *Théologie de l'Image de Dieu chez Origène*. Paris: Aubier, 1956.

d'Alès, Adhémar. *La théologie de Tertullien*. Paris: G. Beauchesne, 1905.

Daly, Robert J. "Sacrificial Soteriology: Origen's Commentary on John 1, 29." In *Origeniana secunda: Second colloque international des études origéniennes (Bari, 20-23 septembre 1977)*, ed. Henri Crouzel and Antonio Quacquarelli, 151-163. Edizioni Dell'Ateneo, 1980.

Daniélou, Jean. *Origen*. Translated by Walter Mitchell. New York: Sheed and Ward, 1955.

———. *The Origins of Latin Christianity*. Translated by David Smith and John Austin Baker. Philadelphia: The Westminster Press, 1977.

Drewery, Benjamin. *Origen and the Doctrine of Grace*. London: The Epworth Press, 1960.
Dufourcq, Albert. *Saint Irénée*. Paris: Librairie Bloud, 1905.
Dunn, James D. G. *Christology in the Making*, 2nd ed. London: SCM Press, 1989.
———. *Did the First Christians Worship Jesus?: The New Testament Evidence*. Louisville: Westminster John Knox Press, 2010.
Dupuis, Jacques. *L'esprit de l'homme: Étude sur l'anthropologie religieuse d'Origène*. Desclée de Brouwer, 1967.
Edwards, Mark. *Origen Against Plato*. Adlershot, England: Ashgate, 2002.
———. "Christ or Plato: Origen on Revelation and Anthropology." In *Christian Origins: Theology, Rhetoric and Community*, ed. Lewis Ayres and Gareth Jones, 11-25. London: Routledge, 1998.
Etcheverria, Ramon Trevijano. "Origenes y la 'regula fidei'." In *Origeniana: premier colloque international des études origéniennes (Montserrat, 18-21 Sept, 1973)*, ed. Henri Crouzel, et al., 327-338. Bari: Istituto di Letteratura Christiana Antica, 1975.
Farmer, William R. "Galatians and the Second Century Development of the Regula Fidei." *The Second Century* 4 (1984): 143-170.
Faye, Eugène de. *Origen and His Work*. Translated by Fred Rothwell. London: G. Allen & Unwin, 1926.
Fédou, Michel. *Christianisme et religions païennes dans le Contre Celse d'Origène*. Paris: Beauchesne, 1989.
———. *La Sagesse et le monde: essai sur la christologie d'Origène*. Paris: Desclée, 1995.
Fletcher-Louis, Crispin. *Jesus Monotheism, Vol. 1, Christological Origins: The Emerging Consensus and Beyond*. Eugene, OR: Cascade Books, 2015.
Fredouille, Jean-Claude. *Tertullien et la conversion de la culture antique*. Paris: Chateau-Gontier, 1972.
Grant, Robert M. *Irenaeus of Lyons*. New York: Routledge, 1997.
———. *Jesus after the Gospels: The Christ of the Second Century*. Louisville, KY: John Knox Press, 1990.
Gogler, Rolf. *Zur Theologie des biblischen Wortes bei Origenes*. Düsseldorf: Patmos-Verlag, 1963.
Grech, Prosper S. "The Regula Fidei as a Hermeneutical Principle in Patristic Exegesis." In *The Interpretation of the Bible: The International Symposium in Slovenia*, ed. Joze Krâsovec, 589-601. Sheffield: Sheffield Academic Press, 1998.
Grillmeier, Aloys. *Christ in Christian Tradition*. Vol. 1, *From the Apostolic Age to Chalcedon (451)*, 2nd rev. ed. Translated by John Bowden. Atlanta, GA: John Knox Press, 1975.
Gunton, Colin E. *Yesterday & Today: A Study of Continuities in Christology*. Grand Rapids, MI: Eerdmans, 1983.
Hägglund, Bengt. "Die Bedeutung der 'regula fidei' als Grundlage theologisher Aussagen." *Studia Theologia* 12 (1958): 1-44.
Hallonsten, Gösta. *Satisfactio bei Tertullian*. Lund: CWK Gleerup, 1984.

Hanson, R. P. C. *Allegory and Event: A Study of the Sources and Significance of Origen's Interpretation of Scripture*. London: SCM Press, 1959.
———. "The Church and Tradition in the Pre-Nicene Fathers." *Scottish Journal of Theology* 12 (March 1959): 21-31.
———. *The Continuity of Christian Doctrine*. New York: Seabury Press, 1981.
———. "Did Origen Teach that the Son is *ek tes ousias* of the Father?" In *Origeniana Quarta: Die Referate des 4. Internationalen Origeneskongresses (Innsbruck, 2.-6. September 1985)*, ed. Lothar Lies, 201-202. Tyrolia: Verlag, 1987.
———. *Origen's Doctrine of Tradition*. London: S.P.C.K., 1954.
———. *Tradition in the Early Church*. Philadelphia: Westminster Press, 1962.
Harl, Marguerite. "La préexistence des âmes dans l'oeuvre d'Origène." In *Origeniana Quarta: Die Referate des 4. Internationalen Origeneskongresses (Innsbruck, 2.-6. September 1985)*, ed. Lothar Lies, 238-258. Tyrolia: Verlag, 1987.
Hengel, Martin. *Studies in Early Christology*. Edinburgh: T & T Clark, 1995.
Heine, Ronald E. *Origen: Scholarship in the Service of the Church*. New York: Oxford University Press, 2010.
Hill, Charles E. *Regnum caelorum: Patterns of Millennial Thought in Early Christianity*. Grand Rapids, MI: Eerdmans, 2001.
Hitchcock, F. R. Montgomery. *Irenaeus of Lugdunum: A Study of His Teaching*. Cambridge: Cambridge University Press, 1914.
Holsinger-Friesen, Thomas. *Irenaeus and Genesis: A Study of Competition in Early Christian Hermeneutics*. Winona Lake, IN: Eisenbrauns, 2009.
Horbury, William. *Jewish Messianism and the Cult of Christ*. London: SCM Press, 1998.
Houssiau, Albert. *La christologie de Saint Irénée*. Louvain: Publications Universitaires de Louvain, 1955.
Hurtado, Larry W. *At the Origins of Christian Worship: The Context and Character of Earliest Christian Devotion*. Grand Rapids, MI: Eerdmans, 1999.
———. *How on Earth Did Jesus Become a God? Historical Questions about Earliest Devotion to Jesus*. Grand Rapids, MI: Eerdmans, 2005.
———. *Lord Jesus Christ: Devotion to Jesus in Earliest Christianity*. Grand Rapids, MI: Eerdmans, 2003.
———. "New Testament Christology: A Critique of Bousset's Influence." *Theological Studies* 40 (1979): 306-317.
———. *One God, One Lord: Early Christian Devotion and Ancient Jewish Monotheism*. Philadelphia: Fortress Press, 1988.
Inge, William Ralph. *Origen*. London: G. Cumberlege, 1946.
Jansen, John F. "Tertullian and the New Testament." *The Second Century* 2 (Winter 1982): 191-207.
Kannengiesser, Charles and William L. Petersen, eds. *Origen of Alexandria: His World and His Legacy*. Notre Dame, IN: University of Notre Dame Press, 1988.
Karpp, Heinrich. *Schrift und Geist bei Tertullian*. Gütersloh: C. Bertelsmann, 1955.

———. *Textbuch zur altkirchlichen Christologie. Theologia und Oikonomia.* Neukirchener Verlag, 1972.
Kearsley, Roy. *Tertullian's Theology of Divine Power.* Carlisle, UK: Paternoster Press, 1998.
Kelly, J. N. D. *Early Christian Creeds,* 3rd ed. Singapore: Longman, 1981.
———. *Early Christian Doctrines,* rev. ed. New York: Harper & Row, Publishers, 1978.
Kerr, Hugh Thomson. *The First Systematic Theologian: Origen of Alexandria.* Princeton: Princeton Theological Seminary, 1958.
Lashier, Jackson. *Irenaeus on the Trinity.* Boston: Brill, 2014.
Lawson, John. *The Biblical Theology of Saint Irenaeus.* London: The Epworth Press, 1948.
Lebreton, J. "La connaissance de Dieu chez S. Irénée." *Recherches des science religieuse* 16 (1926): 385-406.
Lies, Lothar. *Origenes' Peri Archon.* Darmstadt: Wissenschaftliche Buchgesellschaft, 1992.
Logan, A. H. B. "Origen and Alexandrian Wisdom Christology." In *Origeniana tertia : the Third International Colloquium for Origen Studies, University of Manchester September 7th-11th, 1981,* ed. Richard Hanson and Henri Crouzel, 123-129. Rome: Edizioni dell'Ateneo, 1985.
Lubac, Henri de. *Exégèse Médiévale.* Paris, 1959.
———. *Histoire et esprit: l'intelligence de l'Ecriture d'apres Origene.* Paris: Aubier, 1950.
———. *History and Spirit: The Understanding of Scripture According to Origen.* Translated by Anne Englund Nash. San Francisco: Ignatius Press, 2007.
Lührmann, Dieter. "Gal 2:9 und die katholischen Briefe: Bemerkungen zum Kanon und zur regula fidei." *Zeitschrift fur die Neutestamentliche Wissenschaft und die Kunde der Alteren Kirche* 72 (1981): 65-87.
Lyman, J. Rebecca. *Christology and Cosmology: Models of Divine Activity in Origen, Eusebius, and Athanasius.* New York: Oxford University Press, 1993.
Martens, Peter W. *Origen and Scripture: The Contours of the Exegetical Life.* New York: Oxford University Press, 2012.
Matera, Frank J. *New Testament Christology.* Louisville: Westminster John Knox Press, 1999.
McCready, Douglas. *He Came Down from Heaven: The Preexistence of Christ and the Christian Faith.* Downers Grove: InterVarsity Press, 2005.
McGrath, James F. *The Only True God: Early Christian Monotheism in Its Jewish Context.* Champaign: University of Illinois Press, 2009.
Meijering, E. P. *God Being History: Studies in Patristic Philosophy.* New York: American Elsevier Pub. Co., 1975.
Merrill, Timothy F. "Tertullian: The Hermeneutical Vision of De Praescriptione Haereticorum and Pentateuchal Exegesis." *Patristic and Byzantine Review* 6 (1987): 153-167.
Minns, Denis. *Irenaeus: An Introduction.* New York: T&T Clark, 2010.

Mitros, Joseph F. "The Norm of Faith in the Patristic Age." *Theological Studies* 29 (September 1968): 444-471.

Moholy, Noel F. "The doctrine of the recapitulation in Saint Irenaeus." D.S.T. diss., Universite Laval, 1947. Microform.

Moingt, Joseph. *Théologie trinitaire de Tertullien*, Vols. 1-4. Paris: Aubier, 1969.

Moroziuk, Russel P. "Origen and the Nicene Orthodoxy." In *Origeniana Quinta: Historica, Text and Method, Biblica, Philosophica, Theologica, Origenism and Later Developments*, ed. Robert J. Daly, 488-493. Leuven, Belgium: University Press, 1992.

Nagata, Takeshi. "Philippians 2:5-11: A Case Study in the Shaping of Early Christology." Ph.D. thesis, Princeton Theological Seminary, 1981. UMI.

Nautin, Pierre. *Origene: sa vie et son oeuvre*. Paris: Beauchesne, 1977.

Newman, C. C., J. A. Davila, and G. S. Lewis, eds. *The Jewish Roots of Christological Monotheism*. JSJ Supp 63. Leiden: Brill, 1999.

Nielsen, Jan Tjeerd. *Adam and Christ in the Theology of Irenaeus of Lyons: An Examination of the Function of the Adam-Christ Typology in the Adversus Haereses of Irenaeus, Against the Background of the Gnosticism of His Time*. Assen: Van Gorcum, 1968.

Norris, Richard A. *The Christological Controversy*. Philadelphia: Fortress Press, 1980.

———. *God and World in Early Christian Theology: A Study in Justin Martyr, Irenaeus, Tertullian and Origen*. London: Black, 1966.

O'Malley, Thomas P. *Tertullian and the Bible: Language, Imagery, Exegesis*. Nijmegen, Utrecht: Dekker & Van de Vegt, 1967.

Orbe, Antonio. *Teología de san Ireneo*. Madrid: Biblioteca de autores cristianos, 1985.

Osborn, Eric. *Irenaeus of Lyons*. Cambridge: Cambridge University Press, 2001.

———. *Reason and the Rule of Faith in the Second Century AD*. In *The Making of Orthodoxy*, 40-61. Cambridge: Cambridge University Press, 1989.

———. *Tertullian, First Theologian of the West*. New York: Cambridge University Press, 1997.

Outler, Albert C. "Origen and the *Regulae Fidei*." *The Second Century* 4 (1984): 133-141.

Pannenberg, Wolfhart. *Jesus, God and Man*. Translated by Lewis L. Wilkins and Duane A. Priebe. Philadelphia: The Westminster Press, 1968.

Price, Simon. "Latin Christian Apologetics: Minucius Felix, Tertullian, and Cyprian." In *Apologetics in the Roman Empire: Pagans, Jews, and Christians*, ed. Mark Edwards, Martin Goodman, Simon Price, and Christopher Rowland, 105-129. New York: Oxford University Press, 1999.

Purves, James G. M. "The Spirit and the Imago Dei: Reviewing the Anthropology of Irenaeus of Lyons." *Evangelical Quarterly* 68 (April 1996): 99-120.

Quasten, Johannes. *Patrology*. Westminster, MD: Newman Press, 1950.

Ramsay, Charles McKay. "The Concepts of God and of Salvation in the Writings of Irenaeus of Lugdunum." Ph.D. diss., Duke University, 1944. Microform.

Rankin, David. *Tertullian and the Church.* New York: Cambridge University Press, 1995.
Reijners, Gerardus Q. *Das Wort vom Kreuz: Kreuzes- und Erlosungssymbolik bei Origenes.* Koln: Bohlau, 1983.
Robeck, Cecil M. *Canon, Regulae Fidei, and Continuing Revelation in the Early Church.* In *Church, Word, and Spirit,* 65-91. Grand Rapids, MI: Eerdmans, 1987.
Roberts, Robert Edward. *The Theology of Tertullian.* London: The Epworth Press, 1924.
Rowe, J. N. "The Eventual Reconciling of Human Beings to the Father by Christ and His Consequent Subjugation to the Father." In *Origeniana tertia: The Third International Colloquium for Origen Studies, University of Manchester September 7th-11th, 1981,* ed. Richard Hanson and Henri Crouzel, 139-150. Rome: Edizioni dell'Ateneo, 1985.
———. *Origen's Doctrine of Subordination: A Study in Origen's Christology.* New York: Peter Lang, 1987.
Schmidt, Wolfgang Amadeus. "Die Kirche bei Irenäus: akademische Abhandlung." Thesis, Helsingfors, 1934.
Schoedel, W. R. "Philosophy and Rhetoric in the *Adversus Haereses* of Irenaeus." *Vigiliae Christianae* 13 (1959): 22-32.
———. "Theological Method in Irenaeus (*Adversus Haereses* 2.25-28)." *Journal of Theological Studies* 35 (1984): 31-49.
Sesboüé, Bernard. *Tout récapituler dans le Christ: Christologie et sotériologie d'Irénée de Lyon.* Paris: Desclée, 2000.
Sider, Robert D. "Approaches to Tertullian." *The Second Century* 2 (Winter 1982): 228-260.
Smith, John Clark. *The Ancient Wisdom of Origen.* Cranbury, NJ: Associated University Presses, 1992.
Steenberg, M. C. *Irenaeus on Creation: The Cosmic Christ and the Saga of Redemption.* Boston: Brill, 2008.
———. *Of God and Man: Theology as Anthropology from Irenaeus to Athanasius.* New York: T&T Clark, 2009.
Stuckenbruck, Loren T. and Wendy E. S. North, eds. Early *Jewish and Christian Monotheism.* Journal for the Study of the New Testament, Supplement Series, 263. London: T&T Clark, 2004.
Studer, Basil. *Trinity and Incarnation: The Faith of the Early Church.* Translated by Matthias Westerhoff. Collegeville, MN: The Liturgical Press, 1993.
Tiessen, Terrance L. *Irenaeus on the Salvation of the Unevangelized.* Metuchen, NJ: Scarecrow Press, 1993.
Timothy, Hamilton Baird. *The Early Christian Apologists and Greek Philosophy: Exemplified by Irenaeus, Tertullian and Clement of Alexandria.* Assen: Van Gorcum, 1973.
Torisu, Yoshifumi. *Gott und Welt: eine Untersuchung zur Gotteslehre des Irenäus von Lyon.* Nettetal: Steyler, 1991.
Torjesen, Karen Jo. *Hermeneutical Procedure and Theological Structure in Origen's Exegesis.* New York: De Gruyter, 1986.

Torrance, Thomas Forsyth. *Divine Meaning: Studies in Patristic Hermeneutics*. Edinburgh: T&T Clark, 1995.
Trigg, Joseph W. *Origen*. New York, Routledge, 1998.
———. *Origen: The Bible and Philosophy in the Third-Century Church*. Atlanta, GA: John Knox Press, 1983.
Tripolitis, Antonia. *Origen: A Critical Reading*. New York: Peter Lang, 1985.
Turmel, J. *Tertullien*. Paris: Bloud & Co. Library, 1904.
Tzamalikos, Panayiotis. *Origen: Cosmology and Ontology of Time*. Boston: Brill, 2006.
———. *Origen: Philosophy of History and Eschatology*. Boston: Brill, 2007.
Wanke, Daniel. *Das Kreuz Christi bei Irenaeus von Lyon*. New York: Walter de Gruyter, 2000.
Warfield, Benjamin Breckinridge. *Studies in Tertullian and Augustine*. New York: Oxford University Press, 1930.
Waszink, J.H. "Tertullian's Principles and Methods of Exegesis." In *Early Christian Literature and the Classical Intellectual Tradition*, ed. W. R. Schoedel and R. L. Wilken, 17-32. Paris: Beauchesne, 1979.
Widdicombe, Peter. *The Fatherhood of God from Origen to Athanasius*, rev. ed. Oxford: Clarendon Press, 2000.
Williams, Rowan. "Origen on the Soul of Jesus." In *Origeniana tertia: The Third International Colloquium for Origen Studies, University of Manchester September 7th-11th, 1981*, ed. Richard Hanson and Henri Crouzel, 131-137. Rome: Edizioni dell' Ateneo, 1985.
Wingren, Gustaf. *Man and the Incarnation: A Study in the Biblical Theology of Irenaeus*. Translated by Ross Mackenzie. Edinburgh: Oliver & Boyd, 1959.
Wölfl, Karl. *Das Heilswirken Gottes durch den Sohn nach Tertullian*. Rome: Libreria editrice del l'Universita Gregoriana, 1960.
Wood, Arthur Skevington. *The Principles of Biblical Interpretation as Enunciated by Irenaeus, Origen, Augustine, Luther, and Calvin*. Grand Rapids, MI: Zondervan, 1967.
Young, Frances M. *The Making of the Creeds*. Philadelphia: Trinity Press International, 1991.

Scripture Index

Genesis
1:3, *81*
1:26, *86*
1:27, *86*

Deuteronomy
4:24, *121*
9:3, *121*

Psalms
33:6, *38*
45:6-7, *85*
110:1, *7, 24, 84*

Proverbs
8:22, *81, 82*

Isaiah
11:10-12, *18*
45, *10, 14-15*
45:20-23, *18*
49:6, *18*
51:4-5, *18*
52:10, *18*
55:4-5, *18*
56:3-8, *18*
66:18-21, *18*

Jeremiah
10:12, *82*
51:15, *82*

Amos
3:6, *106*

Micah
1:12, *106*

Matthew
11:27, *7*
16:16, *131*
22:29-32, *121*
22:44, *7*
26:64, *7*
28:17, *8*

Mark
12:36, *7*
14:62, *7*
16:19, *7*

Luke
10:22, *7*
20:42-43, *7*
22:69, *7*

John
1:3, *38*
1:1-5, *8, 81*
3:35, *7*
4, *111*
5:21-23, *8*
13:3, *7*
14:28, *87*
16:15, *7*
20:28, *8*

Acts
2:34-35, *7*
10:36, *7*

Romans
8:34, *7*
11:34, *82*

1 Corinthians
8:6, *7, 10, 11, 25*
15:3, *17, 18, 20, 70*
15:14, *18*
15:24-28, *10, 11, 12*
15:25, *7*
15:27-28, *7, 84*

2 Corinthians
4:4, *86*
5:4, *121*

Ephesians
1:10, *7*
1:20, *7*
1:21-22, *7*

Philippians
2:5-11, *10, 14-15, 95-96, 97, 101, 116*
2:9, *8*
2:10-11, *25*
3:21, *7*

Colossians
1:15-17, *7, 86*
3:1, *7*

Hebrews
1:2-3, *8*

Hebrews, cont.
1:3, *7*
1:4, *8*
1:13, *7*

1:4-14, *7*
2:8, *7*
8:1, *7*
10:12-14, *7*

Revelation
3:14, *8*
5, *8*

Subject Index

Apologists, 49, 53, 79-81, 83
apostolic succession, 42, 46
atonement, 70, 119-120, 124

Bauckham, Richard, xi, 6-8, 9, 10, 11, 12, 15-17
binitarian theology, 15, 26, 42

christological monotheism, 6, 7, 18, 20, 26, 34, 35, 38, 39, 40, 50, 67, 69, 71, 97, 123
Christology
  Adam, 11-12, 15, 44, 49, 50, 55, 57
  continuity, xii, 4-5, 26-28, 67, 127, 129
Church
  authority for interpretation, 23, 46, 65, 74, 106, 128
  consensus, 102, 106, 114, 128
  councils, xi, 3, 4, 127, 129
  teaching, 3, 4, 41, 102
  unity, 42
communicatio idiomatum, 89, 116-118, 123
creation
  ex nihilo, 54, 68
  Wisdom mediating, 113
  without necessity, 54
Creator
  distinct from creation, 6, 10, 110, 111, 113
  and Father in the NT, 19, 27, 34, 38-40, 56, 70, 73, 98

deification, 58, 119
divine substance, 69, 71, 72, 81, 84-85, 86, 87-88
Dunn, James D. G., 9-13

emanation, 35, 41, 42, 54, 68, 87
eternal generation, 21, 53, 100, 109, 110-112, 129, 130
exalted beings, 6, 10

gnostic(s), 29, 38, 39, 41-42, 54, 56, 87
God
  communion with, 58, 60
  his hands, 35, 38, 50, 54
  immutability, 113, 129
  knowing God, 39, 51, 58
  monarchia, 66, 68-69, 72, 80, 84-85, 90
  personification of attributes, 6
  transcendence, 54, 110, 113-114

heresy, 33, 62, 65, 66, 85, 107
heretics, 18, 23, 33, 42, 61, 70, 79, 85, 87, 90, 98, 101,
  no right to Scripture, 65, 74-75, 77, 106, 128
Holy Spirit, 38, 72, 96, 99, 100, 102, 105-106
  anointing of, 56
human soul, origin of, 114-115
Hurtado, Larry, xi, 11, 13-16, 16-17

image of God, 15, 59, 110, see also *likeness of God*
   in humanity, 15, 80, 86, 105, 115, 122
   in Christ, 51, 54, 57, 86, 101, 105, 112, 113
incorruption, 35, 57-58
Irenaeus, 33
   monotheism, 34
   sufficiency of Scripture, 44-45

Jesus Christ
   deity of, xi, 20, 21, 25, 26, 36, 44, 56, 67, 69, 79, 84, 88-89, 90, 97, 101, 109, 112, 116, 118, 128, 129
   devotion to, 13-14, 16, 17, 127
   eternal, 21, 36, 56, 123, 127
   humanity of, 3, 12, 16, 25, 36, 44, 55-59, 88-89, 96, 99-101, 115, 116, 119, 120, 123, 124
   incarnation of, 9, 10, 19, 24, 27, 40, 42, 44, 51, 55, 57-60, 69, 70, 74, 88-89, 96, 100, 101, 114-116, 118, 123
   instrument of creation, 25, 38, 55, 68, 70, 96, 98
   judge, 24, 35, 37, 38, 60, 67, 69, 82, 102, 122
   return / *parousia*, 52, 59, 60, 69, 85, 122
   pre-existent humanity, 101, 114-116
   preincarnate, 27, 35, 37, 51, 53, 116
   priest, 120, 124
   ransom, 119
   resurrection, 11, 18, 19, 20, 21, 27, 29, 33, 38, 40, 42, 43, 57, 60, 71, 72, 73, 97, 98, 99, 102, 120, 121, 124, 130
   reveals God, 39, 51, 53, 109, 110, 113, 123
   sacrifice, 120, 124
   Savior, 24, 25, 34, 35, 36, 38, 52, 117
   sovereignty, 6-7, 24-25, 26, 34-35, 36, 37, 38, 40, 59, 60, 67-69, 71, 95-96, 100, 123, 127
   two-natures, 73, 88-89, 115-116
   temple, 9-10, 13
   victor, 59, 119
   virgin birth, 19, 20, 27, 35, 39, 42, 43, 69, 70, 72, 102, 127, 131
Jewish context, 5-8, 86, 115
judgment, 24, 34, 37, 43, 52, 59-60, 68, 70, 71, 85, 86, 102, 121, 122, 127
Justin Martyr, 49, 53, 80, 83

kenosis, 14, 96, 101, 116
krasis, 89

language
   functional, 4, 20, 21, 43, 61, 66, 69, 73-74, 82, 90, 112, 114, 120, 123-124, 129
   ontological, 4, 17, 21, 43, 69, 71-74, 90, 97, 111-112, 112-114, 120, 123-124
law (Mosaic), 37, 56, 58, 59, 66, 67, 73, 98, 103
likeness of God, 51, 57, 59, 80, 86, 122, see also *image of God*
Logos, see *Word*

modalism, 12-13, 61, 65, 71-72, 79, 85, 86, 90

oikonomia, 38, 39, 42-44, 49-52, 54, 57, 60, 61, 66, 70, 71-73, 74, 81, 82, 83, 86, 87, 100, 128
   dispensation of, 39
   trinitarian, 52
Origen, 93
   apokatastasis, 109, 122, 124
   available texts, 94-95
   contemplation of the divine, 105, 114-116, 119
   epinoiai, 112-114
   eschatology, 102, 120-123

Subject Index

Origen, cont.
   exegetical humility, 106, 109
   free will, 99, 100, 109, 114, 115, 119, 121, 122
   gospel, temporal and eternal, 104
   literal and allegorical interpretation, 100, 103-105

persecution, 13, 14, 93
persona, 66, 67, 68, 72, 81, 85, 89, 90
philosophy, 45, 79, 103, 115
Polycarp, 33, 46
Pontius Pilate, 73

Reason, 80, 81, 82, 83
recapitulation, 21, 34, 43, 49, 52, 55, 58, 59
Regula fidei
   christological commonalities in, 27
   as creed, 22, 28
   hermeneutical use of, 23-24, 61-62, 74, 76, 105, 107, 130
   as narrative, 30, 42
   performance, 29, 30
   as summary, 22-23, 28, 42
   textual relationship with NT, 22-23
   as tradition, 22, 23-24, 29-30, 47, 61, 74, 102, 106
   variability, 21-22, 28-30
religious experiences, 14
right hand, 7, 24, 35, 60, 67, 69, 71, 72, 83, 84, 95, 127

Satan, the devil, 59, 119, 124
   unable to comprehend Christ's deity, 119
Scripture
   and tradition, 20, 22, 23-24, 46-47, 61, 74
   relationship between OT and NT, 19, 38, 97-98, 123, 127
   continuity, 17, 27, 73, 95, 97, 98, 114, 123, 124

Son of God
   Creator, 56, 68, 70, 96, 127
   epinoiai, 21, 112-114, 118, 123, 124
   eternal, 52-53, 68, 100
   and the Father, 83-84, 98
   generation, 21, 36, 43, 45, 52-53, 81, 86, 100, 110-111, 128-129, 130, see also *Son of God, procession*
   mediator, 10, 11, 58, 89, 111, 112-114, 116, 120
   procession, 70, 71, 82-84, 111
   title, 17, 25, 35, 36
Son of Man, 25, 36, 69, 74, 88, 89
souls,
   preexistence of, 101, 109, 114-116
   redemption of, 118-119, 121
speculation
   to be avoided, 33, 43, 45, 53, 61, 76, 77
   to be encouraged, 69, 90, 93, 124
substantia, 84, 85, 87, 90

Tertullian, 65
   exegesis, 75-76
   monotheism, 66
   theological vocabulary, 81, 84, 85
theological development, 4, 9, 20, 29, 61, 71, 81, 85, 87, 110
theological reflection, 16-17, 127, 129
tradition, 20, 22, 23-24, 37, 42, 44, 45, 46, 61, 62, 74, 77, 85, 94, 106, 107, 124
Trinity, 50, 54, 71, 72, 84-87, 109, 130
   subordination within, 12, 83-84, 87, 90, 111
   timeless, 111

unique divine identity, 6-8
   creation, 7-8, 25, 35-36, 67-68, 96

unique divine identity, cont.
  criteria, 6-8
  divine name, 8, 25, 36, 68-69, 96
  divine sovereignty, 6-7, 24-25,
    34-35, 67, 95-96
  worship, 8, 25-26, 37-38, 69, 97
Wisdom, 6, 10, 11, 34, 35, 49, 50,
    81-82, 96, 112-114, 118, 124
  creator, 49, 50, 54, 96, 123
  the Holy Spirit, 50, 81, 52, 54
  and virginal conception, 56-57

  the Son, 81-82, 110
Word
  creator, instrument of creation,
    25, 27, 34, 35, 36, 38, 39, 41,
    49-50, 55-56, 68-69, 123
  eternal, 52, 56, 81
  as innate (*Logos endiathetos*), 53,
    70, 80
  as spoken (*Logos prophorikos*),
    52-53, 70, 81-82, 111

www.ingramcontent.com/pod-product-compliance
Lightning Source LLC
Chambersburg PA
CBHW052100230426
43662CB00036B/1713